CONTEMPORARY SOCIAL RESEARCH SERIES

General Editor: MARTIN BULMER

15

The Research Relationship

CONTEMPORARY SOCIAL RESEARCH SERIES

1 SOCIAL MEASUREMENT AND SOCIAL INDICATORS
Issues of Policy and Theory
by Michael Carley

2 MODELLING SOCIETY
An Introduction to Loglinear Analysis for Social Researchers
by G. Nigel Gilbert

3 THE USES OF SOCIAL RESEARCH
Social Investigation in Public Policy-Making
by Martin Bulmer

4 FIELD RESEARCH: A SOURCEBOOK AND FIELD MANUAL
by Robert G. Burgess

5 SECONDARY ANALYSIS IN SOCIAL RESEARCH
A Guide to Data Sources and Methods with Examples
by Catherine Hakim

6 THE SURVEY METHOD
The Contribution of Surveys to Sociological Explanation
by Catherine Marsh

7 DOCUMENTS OF LIFE
An Introduction to the Problems and Literature of a Humanistic Method
by Ken Plummer

8 IN THE FIELD
An Introduction to Field Research
by Robert G. Burgess

9 INTRODUCTION TO CAUSAL ANALYSIS
Exploring Survey Data by Crosstabulation
by Ottar Hellevik

10 DATA CONSTRUCTION IN SOCIAL SURVEYS
by Nicholas Bateson

11 SURVEYS IN SOCIAL RESEARCH
by D. A. de Vaus

12 SOCIAL SCIENCE AND SOCIAL POLICY
by Martin Bulmer et al.

13 RESEARCH DESIGN
Strategies and Choices in the Design of Social Research
by Catherine Hakim

14 RESEARCH METHODS FOR ELITE STUDIES
edited by George Moyser and Margaret Wagstaffe

15 THE RESEARCH RELATIONSHIP
Practice and Politics in Social Policy Research
edited by G. Clare Wenger

The Research Relationship

Practice and Politics in Social Policy Research

Edited by
G. Clare Wenger
University College of North Wales

London
ALLEN & UNWIN
Boston Sydney Wellington

Allen & Unwin, the academic imprint of

Unwin Hyman Ltd

PO Box 18, Park Lane, Hemel Hempstead, Herts HP2 4TE, UK
40 Museum Street, London WC1A 1LU, UK
37/39 Queen Elizabeth Street, London SE1 2QB

Allen & Unwin Inc.,
8 Winchester Place, Winchester, Mass. 01890, USA

Allen & Unwin (Australia) Ltd,
8 Napier Street, North Sydney, NSW 2060, Australia

Allen & Unwin (New Zealand) Ltd in association with the
Port Nicholson Press Ltd, Private Bag, Wellington, New Zealand

First published in 1987

British Library Cataloguing in Publication Data

The Research relationship: practice and politics in social policy research. – (Contemporary social research series; 15)
1. Social sciences – Research – Great Britain
2. Policy sciences – Research – Great Britain
3. Great Britain – Social policy
I. Wenger, G. Clare II. Series
361.6′1′0941 HN390
ISBN 0-04-312037-7
ISBN 0-04-312038-5 Pbk

Library of Congress Cataloging in Publication Data

The Research relationship.
(Contemporary social research series; 15)
"Several of the chapters were initially prepared as papers for presentation in a symposium entitled 'Contract Research and the Problem of Customer Interest' which took place at the XIIth International Congress of Anthropological and Ethnological Sciences, held in Québec in August 1983"—P.
Includes index.
1. Social sciences – Research – Methodology. 2. Social policy – Research – Methodology.
I. Wenger, G. Clare.
II. International Congress of Anthropological and Ethnological Sciences (11th : 1983 : Québec, Québec)
III. Series.
H61.R466 1987 300′.72 86-17236
ISBN 0-04-312037-7 (alk. paper)
ISBN 0-04-312038-5 (pbk. : alk. paper)

Set in 10 on 12 point Times by Fotographics (Bedford) Limited
and printed in Great Britain by
Billings and Sons Ltd, London and Worcester

For R.D.H.

Contents

Acknowledgements

Discussions with colleagues, including many who have written chapters for this book, helped to contribute to its final form, and I appreciate the help of all those whose interest has helped to sustain my own. Martin Bulmer, as series editor, played an important role in suggesting additional contributors and in clarifying the direction the book should take. Both he and Roger Hadley read the final manuscript and made several helpful suggestions. My special thanks go to them both.

My biggest debt of gratitude, however, is to Angela Fortune, who struggled with my own manuscript contributions, retyped papers and handled a multitude of revisions, corrections and addenda with unfailing cheerfulness, speed and efficiency.

Notes on Contributors

Anil K. Gupta is associate professor at the Indian Institute of Management, Ahmedabad, India. His major areas of interest are in natural resource management and rural development, particularly in less-favoured ecological regions. He has served as a consultant to a wide range of development bodies and projects including the Development Studies Division of UNESCO, the Bangladesh Agriculture Research Council and the Ministry of Economic Co-operation of the FDR (West Germany). During the academic year 1985–6 he acted as consultant in farming systems research at the Bangladesh Agriculture Research Institute. Among his recent papers are: 'Social effects of rural projects: monitoring through people's participation', in the *International Review of Administrative Sciences* (1981), vol. XLVII, no. 3, pp. 241-51; and (with Kuldeep Mathur) 'Action-research for micro level planning: a self-appraisal' (1984), *International Review of Administrative Sciences*, vol. XLX, no. 1, pp. 60–8.

Roger Hadley is professor of social administration at the University of Lancaster, England. Before becoming a university teacher he was a researcher and consultant in the field of industrial democracy, which was also the subject of his doctorate. He was a lecturer in social administration at the London School of Economics from 1966 to 1974, when he became professor at Lancaster. He has served on two national committees of inquiry, the Wolfenden Committee on Voluntary Organisations (1974–6) and the Barclay Committee on the role and tasks of social workers (1980–2). He has published extensively in the fields of work with the elderly, voluntary action and the decentralization of social services. His most recent books are *Going Local: Neighbourhood Social Services* (with Morag McGrath, eds.) (1980), National Council for Voluntary Organisations, Occasional Paper No. 1, London, Bedford Square Press; *When Social Services Are Local: The Normanton Experience* (with Morag McGrath) (1984), London, Allen & Unwin; *Decentralizing Social Services: A Model for Change* (with Peter Dale and Patrick Sills) (1984), London, Bedford Square Press.

Josephine Jaeger is an assumed name. The author felt unable to use her real name because she did not want it to be possible for the authority with whom she worked to be identified. She felt that the animosity which existed at the end of her research could conceivably lead to serious repercussions for her should she be identified. Previously, she worked as a teacher for thirty-four years and was a deputy headteacher when she took up her research appointment. She is not currently working.

Richard Jenkins is a lecturer in sociology at University College, Swansea, Wales. After completing his doctorate in social anthropology, he spent 1980–3 involved in research on ethnic relations at the Social Science Research Council's Research Unit at the University of Aston, Birmingham, England. He is the author of *Racism and Recruitment: Managers, Organizations and Equal Opportunity on the Labour Market* (1986), Cambridge, Cambridge University Press; and the editor, with John Solomoss, of *Equal Opportunity and the Limits of the Law: Racism, Regulation and Employment* (1987), Cambridge, Cambridge University Press.

Kathleen McDermott is a research fellow at the Centre for Social Policy Research and Development at University College of North Wales, Bangor. She took her doctorate at the University of California, Berkeley, in anthropology, and has done fieldwork in Hong Kong and Wales. From 1981 to 1983 she was involved in research on government-sponsored youth opportunities programmes in rural Wales funded by the Manpower Services Commission. She is the author with Sally Dench of *Youth Opportunities in a Rural Area: A Study of Youth Opportunities in Mid-Wales* (1983), London, Manpower Services Commission; and of 'Impact of YOP on a rural labour market', in *Employment Gazette* (July 1983), vol. 91, no. 7, pp. 290–4. She is also co-editor of a special issue of *Urban Anthropology* on 'De-industrialization, downward mobility and unemployment' (1986).

John Kent McNamara describes himself as an applied researcher at the Human Resources Laboratory, Chamber of Mines of South Africa, Johannesburg. He has a doctorate in social anthropology and wrote his dissertation on 'Black worker conflicts in South African gold mines: 1973–1982'. He has worked for the Chamber of Mines since 1975 undertaking research focused on labour relations, the quality of life of employees and the origins of conflict. He is the author of 'Brothers and workmates: home-friend networks in the social life of black migrant workers in a gold mine hostel', in P. Mayer (ed.), *Black Villagers in an Industrial Society* (1980), Cape Town, Oxford University Press.

P. J. M. Nas is senior lecturer in applied sociology and anthropology at the Institute of Cultural and Social Studies, University of Leiden, the Netherlands. His doctorate is in the anthropology and sociology of non-Western countries from the University of Nijmegen. He has done fieldwork in Spain (1968) and Indonesia (1977–8). He was previously lecturer at the University of Nijmegen and Universitas Indonesia. He is secretary of the International Commission on Urban Anthropology of the International Union of Anthropological and Ethnological Sciences. He is co-editor with G. Ausari of *Town-Talk: The Dynamics of Urban Anthropology* (1983), Leiden, E. J. Brill.

W. J. M. Prins is lecturer in non-Western sociology at the Institute of Cultural and Social Studies and the Leiden Institute of Development Studies and Consultancy Services, both at the University of Leiden, the Netherlands. He has a master's degree in social anthropology and specializes in urban and applied sociology and anthropology. He is the author of 'The struggle for the Third World city' and 'Past, present and future of Dutch urban anthropology', both in G. Ausari and P. J. M. Nas (eds.), *Town Talk: The Dynamics of Urban Anthropology* (1983), Leiden, E. J. Brill; and co-author of 'Access and participation: a theoretical approach', in B. Galjart and D. Buys (eds.), *Participation of the Poor in Development* (1982), Leiden, Leiden Development Studies, No. 2.

Wasif A. Shadid is senior lecturer in social methodology at the Institute of Social and Cultural Studies of the University of Leiden, the Netherlands. His doctorate is in the anthropology and sociology of non-Western societies. He has conducted a number of studies on inter-ethnic relations in the Netherlands. His publications in English include: *Moroccan Workers in the Netherlands* (1979), Leiden, University of Leiden Press; 'Integration of minorities in the Netherlands', in the *European Demographic Information Bulletin* (1981); and 'Moroccans in the Netherlands: integration, conflict and discrimination,' in *New Community* (1981).

Diana de Treville is a senior researcher at the Institute for Development Anthropology at Binghamton, New York, USA. She has a doctorate in social anthropology from the University of California, Berkeley. She has undertaken extensive fieldwork and administered and implemented rural development projects in Egypt. She has done design and evaluation work in Egypt, Sudan, Zimbabwe and Lesotho for an exhaustive list of organizations including the Ford Foundation,

Save the Children Federation, Agricultural Co-operative Development International and the US Agency for International Development. In 1983 she conducted the first major evaluation of USAID/WID overseas programming. Relevant publications include 'A medical survey of the Bishari and Ababdi in the Red Sea Governorate, Egypt', in *Journal of Egyptian Public Health* (1982) (co-author), vol. 57, nos. 1–2, pp. 60–9; and *Nomads in the Southern Part of the Red Sea Governorate of Egypt* (1980) (co-author), Cairo, United States Agency for International Development.

Donald P. Warwick is an Institute Fellow of the Harvard Institute for International Development and senior lecturer in sociology at Harvard University, Boston, Mass., USA. He holds a doctorate in social psychology. From 1973 to 1981 he was project manager on the Project on Cultural Values and Population Policy. From 1979 to 1984 he was co-organizer of a development programme implementation study, jointly sponsored by Harvard and the government of Indonesia, which involved a study of four major development projects including the national family planning programme. He has done extensive research abroad including work in Peru, Mexico, Singapore and Indonesia. He was visiting professor in the Department of Political Science at the National University of Singapore, 1985–6. He has published extensively, including *Bitter Pills: Population Policies and their Implementation in Eight Development Countries* (1982), Cambridge, Cambridge University Press; *Handbook of Cross-Cultural Psychology*, Vol. I (1980); 'The politics and ethics of cross-cultural research', in H. C. Triandis, W. W. Lambert and J. W. Berry (eds.), *Handbook of Cross Cultural Psychology; Vol. I* (1980), Boston, USA, Allyn & Bacon, pp. 319–71; he edited *Social Research in Developing Countries: Surveys and Censuses in the Third World* (1983) with Martin Bulmer.

G. Clare Wenger is senior research fellow at the Centre for Social Policy Research and Development, University College of North Wales, Bangor. She has a doctorate in social anthropology from the University of California, Berkeley, USA. She has conducted field research in several social-policy-relevant fields including rural development and social gerontology. She is a member of the executive committee of the International Commission on Ageing and the Aged of the International Union of Anthropological and Ethnological Sciences. Relevant publications include *Mid-Wales: Deprivation or Development* (1980), Board of Celtic Studies Monographs, No. 5,

Cardiff, University of Wales Press; 'The problem of perspective in development policy' in *Sociologia Ruralis* (1982), vol. xxii, no. 1, pp. 5–16; and *The Supportive Network: Coping with Old Age* (1984), London, Allen & Unwin.

1

Introduction: the Problematic Relationship

G. CLARE WENGER

The 1980s are proving to be a difficult decade for research. In Britain, a worsening economic situation coupled with and related to cuts in the existing levels of university funding through the University Grants Committee have meant that fewer resources to support research programmes have been available. All research has been affected, but the cuts have made the greatest impact on the social sciences. The 1981 letter to universities from the University Grants Committee urged that cuts be applied unevenly, protecting the hard and technological sciences and cutting back most extensively in the social sciences.

Government is now the main source of support for social research in all European countries (Houghton, 1985). Not only has this increased competition for funds but it has resulted in a greater proportion of researchers engaging in applied or policy-related research sponsored by a wide range of government, private and commercial agencies. This has come about partly because of the shrinkage in grant money available for pure or theoretical research, partly from the heightened interest of university administrations in contracts which provide overheads that help to offset cuts, and partly also from the need to provide research training for young postgraduates. In Britain, much of the money for pure or theoretical research has also come from the government through the research councils, but by 1980 the Social Science Research Council (now the Economic and Social Research Council) had shifted its emphasis towards policy areas (Bell, 1984), and the same shift is observed in other countries (Kallen *et al.*, 1982). Under frequently overt pressure from administrators and more subtle moral pressure from colleagues anxious about departmental survival, academics who previously might have eschewed applied or contract research in favour of grant-funded research have been forced to consider this option in order to ensure the continuance of their disciplines through postgraduate research training. At the same time, social scientists have become more interested in social change as output and have returned to an earlier interest in prescription (Sharpe, 1978). It is probably not an exaggeration to suggest that, if trends continue, by the end of the decade the majority of social research could be conducted under contract for government and other agencies who seek policy-relevant investigations. This shift towards commissioned and contracted research throws into heightened relief, amongst other considerations, the importance of greater understanding of the relationships with contracting agencies and with other bodies whose policy areas become the object of research investigation.

This book concentrates primarily on the relationship between researchers on the one hand and funding agencies and other involved policy-making bodies on the other hand. Several of the chapters were initially prepared as papers for presentation in a symposium entitled 'Contract Research and the Problem of Customer Interest', which took place at the XIth International Congress of Anthropological and Ethnological Sciences, held in Quebec in August 1983. This was a small symposium, reflecting perhaps the lack of status enjoyed by contract research within the ivory tower. However, the size of the gathering made it possible for the proceedings to be conducted in the manner of a seminar, and the interest of those present ensured that the meeting went on long beyond the end of the scheduled period. The need for a publication which explored the relationship between social researchers and involved sponsors was raised at this meeting, and two additional papers were volunteered. These papers form the core of the book. Some additional contributions were later solicited.

The original topic of the symposium has been extended to the relationship between policy researchers and policy-makers. Not all the research on which chapters are based was commissioned by the agencies with which researchers subsequently had involvement, but all the research related to critical policy areas. The book concentrates on the problems experienced by researchers, and the contents are written by academics who have been involved in the policy field. It could be argued that a more balanced view would also present the views of policy research sponsors. That book may yet be written. The present volume concentrates on looking at the question in terms of the role and perspective of the researcher, although the contributors also demonstrate some appreciation of the problems faced by administrators.

The often problematic relationship between policy-makers and researchers has been long recognized. While some researchers manage to establish a good working relationship with the contracting agency (Mamak, 1978; Stretton, 1978) this is usually achieved only as the result of careful negotiation and cannot be taken for granted. Orlans (1967), writing twenty years ago, commented that 'givers and recipients of social research funds are often troubled by misunderstandings and a sense of unfulfilled expectations that may lead readily enough to moral recriminations', and noted that 'money does not come free' (pp. 3–5).

During the last ten years, increasing sociological interest has been shown in the research context itself in contrast to the subjects of research (Platt, 1976; Bell and Newby, 1977; Bell and Encel, 1978; Roberts, 1981; Bell and Roberts, 1984). These more recent publications have echoed the concerns of earlier authors (e.g. Hammond, 1964; Sjoberg, 1967) in terms of the discontinuities between the experiences of fieldwork or other data collection and the published report of the work; the ethical dilemmas of researchers *vis-à-vis* relations with the study populations and with granting agencies; the personal, strategic and organizational problems which influenced the conduct of the research; and, not least, the political contexts, at all levels, in which research was conducted. As Bell and Roberts (1984) have pointed out, 'Sociologists are going to have to take much more seriously than they have hitherto the political and economic context of their research activity' (p. 14). In many contexts, the political aspect of the research is not overt. However, it is probably safe to say that social research is rarely without policy implications. When research is commissioned in the social policy arena, the political nature of the endeavour is implicit and often explicit.

Despite the increased interest in the research process, most of what has been written with a few notable exceptions has been personal and introspective. Authors have explored and analysed their own research experiences, seeking to understand the implications of the process for outcomes and objectivity; grappling with ethical dilemmas and, as Bell and Encel (1978) comment, 'complaining against the ways in which social research normally is written up, published and taught' (p. 4). Essentially they all tell stories about doing research, but so far there have been few serious empirical attempts to subject the research process to the same sort of scrutiny that has been brought to bear on other areas of human or social behaviour. This is understandable, in as much as during their academic careers most researchers can be involved in only a limited number of research projects. The experience of the individual is, therefore, too limited to enable generalizations to be made. However, if we consider the stories told about doing research to be the foundations of an ethnography of the research process, attempts to perceive patterns and to make generalizations about doing research mark the early development of an ethnology or sociology of social research – moving from description to theory.

Those comparative studies which have been conducted have been dependent on the published accounts available and have, therefore, concentrated on patterns which relate to the research process. These studies have come predominantly from sociology. For instance, O'Toole (1971) made a systematic study of the organization and management of research, while Baldamus (1972) reanalysed the accounts of doing research in Hammond's (1964) *Sociologists at Work*, looking at sociological practice. Both these authors worked with material from the United States. In the United Kingdom, Platt (1976) conducted what is, so far as I know, the only empirical study of a sample of research projects. Her study was limited to research using social survey methodology but is an important building-block in the move towards what she describes as the 'sociology of the social research process'. While her study concentrated on the conduct of the research and the behaviour and experience of the involved researchers, she was also able to draw some conclusions about the wider social environment within which research is conducted, the external constraints which operate on the work and the relationship of researchers with their sponsors.

Amongst her conclusions, Platt proposes two hypotheses: (1) 'If the interests of sponsors and researchers in a project do not coincide, or cannot be pursued jointly, trouble is likely to ensue' (pp. 178–9); and (2) 'If sponsors have contractual control over the form to be taken by data collection or publication they are likely to exercise it in ways that do not serve the interests of sociology' (p. 179). Cox, Hausfeld and Wills (1978), writing about experience working for government agencies in Australia, although not expressing it in the same way, appear to support Platt's first hypothesis. They claim that a positive relationship exists between the degree of explicitness of role definition, on the one hand, and the number of work-based problems and difficulties, on the other. Orlans (1967) also stressed the need for clarity, lack of which he felt led to 'persistent ethical dilemmas'. In other words, if there is not clear agreement between sponsors and researchers about the nature of the research venture, then trouble can be predicted. Payne *et al.* (1980), however, consider that 'In those studies in which the problem is clearly defined by the sponsor, the sociologist becomes little more than a technician, which is intellectually unrewarding' (p. 152).

McNaul (1972) suggests that there are at least six areas where conflict may be expected between researchers and policy-makers: (1) the evaluation of knowledge; (2) methods of communication; (3) time frame; (4) uniqueness vs patterns; (5) the degree of finality of knowledge; and (6) the use of environmental controls. These areas of conflict result from the different intellectual and social frameworks within which researchers and policy-makers work. As Cox, Hausfeld and Wills (1978) suggest, both are subject to a range of pressures which are at variance with one another. The desirable explicitness of role and objectives, referred to above, is frequently difficult to achieve, not necessarily because of any lack of goodwill or intent on the part of the contracting parties. In their experience, the agency was itself unclear as to whether the researcher had been hired as a specialist in the subject or as an expert in the techniques of data collection and analysis. Each side, they suggest, operates with 'hidden agendas' which are implicit to their respective roles but not seen as relevant to the research in progress.

Hidden agendas include the relationship of the policy body's representative to the agency in both personal, professional and public terms. S/he seeks to perform within institutional constraints and criteria for promotion and with agency expectations of outcomes. Research questions may be defined or perceived differently by the researcher and the policy body. In some instances the difference may be overt, in which case discussions of definition may occur early in the research relationship. Researchers have on occasion withdrawn where no agreement can be reached. In other instances compromises may be reached where both sides feel that they can achieve what they want from the study. However, in other cases the different understanding of the research problem may remain unrecognized, thus almost guaranteeing the 'moral recriminations' that Orlans (1967) predicted. The criteria for doing the policy job well may be in conflict with the researcher's need to conduct the research well. The researcher's reference group is usually the academic community and within that other members of the discipline. This is particularly marked in terms of time scale and outcomes, as McNaul (1972) has indicated.

But if problems for the researcher can be minimized only by explicit expectations on the part of the policy body, as Cox, Hausfeld and Wills (1978) suggest, where does this leave the committed social scientist? Bulmer (1978) suggests that few social scientists can mechanistically 'do what the customers want'. In the United Kingdom as elsewhere, a considerable body of social scientists have eschewed policy research and limited themselves to, as Bulmer categorizes it, 'basic social science research', which concentrates solely on advancing knowledge without any declared usefulness – or to 'strategic social science', which is grounded in an academic discipline but is problem-oriented. Such research is generally more theoretical than descriptive and is not commonly supported by policy-making agencies, which are more concerned with what Bulmer calls 'specific problem-orientated research' or 'intelligence and monitoring' research. Bulmer's influence, though not acknowledged, is evident in a similar categorization arrived at by Payne *et al.* (1980), who identify a 'gulch' between policy and academic research. In this they disagree with Bulmer, who sees the different types of research as forming a continuum. Payne *et al.* go on to say that 'we would argue that sociologists should undertake policy research, including commissioned work, as long as they are aware that *they are not likely to be doing sociology*' (p. 152; italics added).

This perception of policy or applied research as non-scientific is hardly unique. As Bulmer (1978) has commented, in the United Kingdom there has been a 'blanket scepticism about policy research particularly among British sociologists on the grounds of disciplinary purism or moral distaste' (p. 23), and British scholars have not been alone in maintaining an arm's-length attitude (Lambiri-Dimaki, 1985). Such scepticism is based on fears that, by defining the nature of questions for research, sponsors control outcomes in such a way that the interests of those with power are served in maintaining the *status quo* by supporting research on only those problems which do not question the basic structures of society or the values of the funding agency (e.g. Hanmer and Leonard, 1984).

The present funding famine faced by social research has made it more difficult for purists to limit their research and that of their students to basic social scientific questions funded from dwindling non-policy sources. As a growing proportion of funded social research falls in the policy area, ethical problems increase. Orlans (1967) urges, 'if you disagree with the objectives of an agency don't decry the morality of its staff, try to change it from within and in the interim don't take their money' (p. 5). This stance, however, raises ethical dilemmas for researchers in the current economic context. These recently received some notice in the national press as a result of the Health Education Council putting pressure on researchers to reject money offered by the tobacco industry's Health Promotion Research Trust (Ferriman, 1986). Professor Hilary Rose, commenting on her rejection of money from this source for two studentships to conduct research on women and alcoholism, states, 'Both my search for funds for this work and my eventual decision not to accept the HPRT funding when offered must be set against the chronic underfunding of health research in Britain' (Rose, 1985). This statement, it seems to me, sums up the difficult choice facing social scientists in any context where research funding is limited.

There is, of course, another side to the debate about involvement in policy research. More than a quarter of a century ago, Mills (1959) in *The Sociological Imagination* argued that social scientists had a moral responsibility to engage in research and in the dissemination of findings which were specifically policy relevant and which sought to affect policy decisions. While basic research may have relevance for policy, it is less likely to influence policy-makers than research findings from sponsored, commissioned, or specifically problem-oriented work which is brought to their attention. Those social scientists who work in the policy field can be seen, in Mills's terms, as acting more responsibly than those who do not. Some have seen this as the best way to represent the powerless by presenting their views. In fact, tensions between researchers and policy-makers frequently stem from the need of the researcher both to retain professional integrity and to represent the interests of those who are the subject of study. As Bulmer (1978) has commented, 'Conducting policy research is not incompatible with moral commitment' (p. 25); and, as many of the chapters in this collection will illustrate, social scientists can and do criticize policy and can make an impact. Speaking for anthropology, Hinshaw (1980) has urged greater involvement in the communication of policy-relevant knowledge. More recently, Lambiri-Dimaki has identified what she calls 'a non-traditional role' for the social scientist in examining values underlying policy and identifying alternatives (1985).

The research process and the social context in which it takes place exert influences upon one another. As various authors have pointed out, doing the research is a social act and is itself of sociological/anthropological interest (Bell and Encel, 1978; Roberts, 1981). To ignore the intervening variables of external events and their effect on the findings would be unscientific. It follows from this that in most instances the researcher learns a lot about interactions with the funding agency or other involved or interested policy bodies. Payne *et al.* (1980), while suggesting the treatment of the research project as part of the subject of study, raise anxieties about the ethics of such a procedure unless the sponsors are aware of this intention. Without pursuing that ethical argument, it is clear that any policy-relevant research will inevitably produce a large body of formal and informal data relating to existing policy and to the researcher's dealings with those agencies making policy decisions in that subject area. This fact is well documented in all the accounts of research endeavours which have been published (e.g. Hammond, 1964; Sjoberg, 1967; Platt, 1976; Bell & Newby, 1977; Bell and Encel, 1978; Roberts, 1981; Bell and Roberts, 1984). Perhaps because such data are in many ways a by-product of the research process and as a result are primarily qualitative rather than quantitative both researchers and sponsors, clients or policy-makers seem uneasy about them. As Payne *et al.* (1980) comment, 'The researcher who publishes critical findings is likely to find that both he and his institution are prevented from undertaking further investigations in the particular site' (p. 154). They, of course, refer to findings directly or indirectly critical of policy or the policy agency.

Not surprisingly much conflict between researchers and policy-making groups stems from such criticism or fear of criticism leading to restrictions on data collection or dissemination. Researchers for their part are cautious about the publication of adverse findings because of the need for continued financial support. As Bell and Encel (1978, p. 6) state:

> There is, as we have suggested, a great personal (and very understandable) reluctance to give accounts that might prejudice future research projects. Yet that reluctance means that potentially misleading accounts of social research are given – not only by commission . . . but also by omission. Accounts of the behaviour of sponsors, both public and private, are necessarily circumspect or even totally absent. (p. 6).

This collection concentrates on the behaviour of sponsors and other policy-making bodies affected by the research discussed. Some of the accounts are more outspoken than others, ranging from the highly critical and detailed to the more restrained and cautious. My own assessment is that the authors have been as forthcoming as the security of their professional position allowed. Their frankness or conversely their guardedness reflects the power relationships of their particular situation, and readers are invited to consider the accounts with this observation in mind.

In the introduction to each of the three accounts of the research process that Bell has co-edited (Bell and Newby, 1977; Bell and Encel, 1978; Bell and Roberts, 1984), he and his respective co-editors have commented on chapters or parts of chapters which they had hoped to include but which for one reason or another they were unable to publish. The reasons included: concern about libel laws; reluctance on the part of in-house researchers to jeopardize their future prospects; contravention of the Official Secrets Act; threats from senior social scientists where junior researchers had revealed censorship of research; and the fears of young (female) authors concerned about the repercussions of exposing high-handed treatment by a (male) superior. All of these reasons further emphasize the importance of power relationships in the research endeavour. Other chapters failed to materialize due to 'pressure of work', which may have been a gloss for any of the above reasons for second thoughts.

This collection of accounts of relationships with policy-makers has faced similar problems. In one case, the offer of a chapter which was to have discussed the problems of working as a consultant for a foreign government was withdrawn because the potential author, on thinking things over, felt that it would not be possible to write the intended chapter without jeopardizing further consultancy work. I have, however, been able to include a chapter by an in-house researcher (McNamara) and one dealing with gender discrimination (Jaeger). The chapter by Jaeger, however, despite the fact that the author no longer works for the education authority by whom she feels she was badly treated, is included under an assumed name. Jaeger felt that she might risk a libel case and that animosity towards her might still threaten her professionally if her contribution was published under her real name. The chapter was co-authored because of Jaeger's subsequent ill-health. Her chapter on gender discrimination, those by Jenkins and McNamara, which deal with race, and Warwick's paper on birth control are perhaps the most consciously self-edited as well as dealing with more sensitive social issues.

While the previous books in this genre have concentrated on the sociological research process in the United States (Hammond, 1964; Sjoberg, 1967), the United Kingdom (Bell and Newby, 1977; Roberts, 1981; Bell and Roberts, 1984) or Australia (Bell and Encel, 1978), this book looks at the researcher/policy-maker relationship in an international context. Similarities in the problems experienced supersede national boundaries (Nowotny and Lambiri-Dimaki, 1985). It includes chapters from the United Kingdom, the United States, the Netherlands, South Africa and India, but the research discussed covers a broader geographic range and includes one multinational comparative study. It is also multi-disciplinary within the social sciences. The authors' disciplines include social anthropology, sociology, social administration, social psychology, agricultural management and education. With the exception of Jaeger, all authors have had wide experience in social policy research.

The chapters are presented in five parts which relate to different problem areas, although as the reader will quickly realize there is considerable overlap between the chapters themselves. Part One deals with studying the research context and presents one chapter by Nas, Prins and Shadid, which urges the development of a new area of study that would include the research process and bridge the divide between pure and applied research. The second chapter by Wenger, makes a similar plea for closing the divide in the form of a case study which illustrates the interrelationship between the research and the research context. Part Two looks at the advocacy role in which researchers frequently find themselves. De Treville's chapter describes her role in the implementation of development policy in Egypt, while McNamara discusses his changing role working for the Chamber of Mines in South Africa. In Part Three, Hadley and Gupta discuss the frustrations and difficulties which attach to the desire to influence policy-makers to take research findings into account; while in Part Four, McDermott and Jenkins discuss the problems of hidden agendas. Part Five, in chapters by Jaeger and Warwick, considers what happens when things do not work out as anticipated. Each part is introduced by a brief discussion of the topic in general terms.

References

Baldamus, W. (1972), 'The role of discoveries in Social Science', in T. Shanin (ed.), *The Rules of the Game* (London: Tavistock), pp. 276–302.

Bell, C. (1984), 'The SSRC: restructured and defended', in C. Bell and H. Roberts (eds.), *Social Researching: Politics, Problems, Practice* (London: Routledge & Kegan Paul), pp. 14–31.

Bell, C., and Encel, S. (eds.) (1978), *Inside the Whale: Ten Personal Accounts of Social Research* (Sydney: Pergamon).

Bell, C., and Newby, H. (1977), 'Introduction: the rise of methodological pluralism', in C. Bell and H. Newby (eds.), *Doing Sociological Research* (London: Allen & Unwin), pp. 9–29.

Bell, C., and Roberts, H. (1984), 'Introduction', in C. Bell and H. Roberts (eds.), *Social Researching*, pp. 1–13.

Bulmer, Martin (1978), 'Social science research and policy-making in Britain', in Martin Bulmer (ed.), *Social Policy Research* (London: Macmillan), pp. 3–43.

Cox, E., Hausfeld, F., and Wills, S. (1978), 'Taking the queen's shilling: accepting social research consultancies in the 1970s', in C. Bell and S. Encel, op. cit., pp. 121–41.

Ferriman, A. (1986), 'Tobacco industry snubbed over cash', *Observer*, 29 January.

Hammond, P. (1964), *Sociologists at Work* (New York: Basic Books).

Hanmer, J., and Leonard, D. (1984), 'Negotiating the problem: the DHSS and research on violence in marriage', in C. Bell and H. Roberts (eds.), *Social Researching: Politics, Problems, Practice* (London: Routledge & Kegan Paul).

Hinshaw, R. E. (1980), 'Anthropology, administration and public policy', *Annual Review of Anthropology*, vol. 9, pp. 497–522.

Houghton, H. (1985), 'Summary and conclusions', Nowotny and Lambiri-Dimaki, op. cit., pp. 111–34.
Kallen, D. B. P. *et al.* (1982), *Social Science Research and Public Policy-Making: A Reappraisal* (Slough, England: NFER/Nelson).
Lambiri-Dimaki, J. (1985), 'The difficult dialogue between producers and users of social science research: some comments on the theme', in Nowotny and Lambiri-Dimaki, op. cit., pp. 15–25.
Mamak, A. (1978), 'Nationalism, race–class consciousness and social research on Bouganville Island, Papua New Guinea', in Bell and Encel, op. cit., pp. 164–81.
McNaul, J. P. (1972), 'Relations between researchers and practitioners', in S. Z. Nagi and R. G. Corwin (eds.), *The Social Contexts of Research* (New York: Wiley-Interscience).
Mills, C. W. (1959), *The Sociological Imagination* (London, Oxford University Press).
Nowotny, H., and Lambiri-Dimaki, J. (eds.) (1985), *The Difficult Dialogue between Producers and Users of Social Science Research* (Vienna: European Centre for Social Welfare Training and Research).
Orlans, H. (1967), 'Ethnical problems in the relations of research sponsors and investigators', in Sjoberg, op. cit., pp. 3–24.
O'Toole, R. (1971), *The Organization, Management and Tactics of Social Research* (Cambridge, Mass.: Schenckman).
Payne, G., Dingwall, R., Payne, J., and Carter, M. (1980), 'Sociology and policy research', in G. Payne, *et al.*, *Sociology and Social Research* (London: Routledge & Kegan Paul), pp. 142–59.
Platt, J. (1976), *Realities of Social Research: An Empirical Study of British Sociologists* (London: Sussex University Press).
Roberts, H. (1981), *Doing Feminist Research* (London: Routledge & Kegan Paul).
Rose, H. (1985), Letter to the editor under headline 'Why tobacco funds tempt the women's health researchers', *Guardian*, 7 November.
Sharpe, L. J. (1978), 'Government as clients for social science research', in M. Bulmer (ed.) *Social Policy Research* (London: Macmillan).
Sjoberg, G. (ed.) (1967), *Ethics, Politics and Social Research* (London: Routledge & Kegan Paul).
Stretton, H. (1978), 'Capital mistakes', in Bell and Encel, op. cit., pp. 67–92.

I

Studying the Research Context

Introduction to Part One

Sociologists have noted the distance between pure and applied research. These two aspects of social research have been described as being completely separate (Payne *et al.*, 1980) or at least forming the two ends of a continuum (Bulmer, 1978). While acknowledging the historical reasons for this divide in the United Kingdom, opinion has moved towards the bridging of this division. One of the problems related to policy research, which has accentuated the dichotomy, has been the tendency for much commissioned or contracted applied research to be atheoretical. Both the chapters in Part One emphasize the need for an integration of pure and applied social research. It is perhaps not surprising that both have been written by anthropologists, for – as Nas, Prins and Shadid point out – anthropology, having a different history, combined science and practice from its beginnings. Both Nas *et al.* and Wenger urge that attention be paid to the development of a theoretical applied social science, what Nas, Prins and Shadid call 'praxeology', or the science of application.

Renewed interest in applied social science was preceded by the growing recognition of the validity of the research process as a subject of research (Cicourel, 1964; Hammond, 1964; Roth, 1966). The need for a sociology of the social research process has been acknowledged (Platt, 1976). Subsequently, more attention has been paid to the social and political context of research (Bell, 1984; Bell and Roberts, 1984). The theoretical approach to applied social science suggested both by Nas, Prins and Shadid and by Wenger includes study of the research process and context as integral parts of the research endeavour.

In making a plea for the development of praxeology, Nas, Prins and Shadid seek to move towards a theory of intervention which acknowledges the role of the social scientist as an agent of change. They claim that policy-makers might take applied researchers more seriously if their approach was more theoretical. Certainly, policy-relevant sociological research in the United States, which has tended to be more theoretically based, has had more impact on policy than the more descriptive policy research conducted in Britain (Bulmer, 1978;

Sharpe, 1978; Payne *et al.*, 1980) – although whether this correlation is the effect of research perspectives or historical accident is not clear. However, Nas, Prins and Shadid go further to suggest that policy research by its nature implies intervention and that besides defining problems it should also involve a science of intervention based on findings. They call for the development of a science that would integrate theories of social change with theories of intervention strategy, including the influence of the research process and the implementation of policy.

Wenger's chapter suggests similar objectives, but here the emphasis is on a case study of the research process, which illustrates the interrelationships posited by Nas, Prins and Shadid. This chapter demonstrates the type of relationship which develops between the researcher and the research on the one hand and the social, political and economic context on the other, the way the context influences the research, and that both the fact that the research is being conducted and the interim findings feed back into and change the context in a reflexive way.

It is interesting that, in Wenger's study, tensions developed not with the funding body although its original conception in the research was overtly political, but with the rural development board which was working in the research region. Wenger was able to develop a relationship which Sjoberg (1967) has described as a 'negotiation model' with the funding agency to achieve far-reaching changes in the originally proposed research. These changes brought the research interest squarely into the domain of development policy. The development board, not having commissioned the research, had no control over its conduct and initially reacted by questioning the authority of the university to conduct research or disseminate findings without its agreement! This 'fear of scrutiny', particularly at the middle-management level, has been noted by Payne *et al.* (1980).

Wenger's chapter illustrates the social and professional contingencies which affect the progress and outcomes of research (Platt, 1976), the complications of status differences (Platt, 1976; Bell and Roberts, 1984) and the complications which may attend the dissemination of findings. In this case, Wenger disseminated findings to the subject population and the academic community during the research period, thus reinforcing public reaction to policy.

It is interesting to speculate what might have been the outcome of Wenger's work had a praxeological approach, as urged by Nas, Prins and Shadid, been adopted. This perspective would presumably have been able to predict what the reactions of both policy-makers and subject population might have been and might have led to a different proposal. This raises some important questions about whether such an approach might make social science research less saleable. Bulmer (1978, p. 42) has commented:

> If the purpose of research is to bring political controversy closer to realities, it is likely to involve an examination of the goals of policy, the values implicit in policy and the consequences for different groups of the pursuit of particular lines of action. To raise such questions is to steer perilously close to the preserves of politicians and administrators.

Elsewhere Bulmer has suggested that 'British social policy research will only fructify if academic social scientists and policy-makers can adjust to each other' (p. 21); while Payne *et al.* (1980) feel that 'Sociologists . . . have perhaps to master two sociologies: the sociology of the academic and the more applied sociology of the administrator' (p. 158). Writing in 1967, Sjoberg made a comparable suggestion that social researchers need to work out compromises with non-scientists to attain their objectives. In 1985 Nowotny urged team-work between users and producers of social research. The two chapters in Part One present arguments for putting such an implied partnership on a theoretical foundation.

References

Bell, C. (1984), 'The SSRC: restructured and defended', in Bell and Roberts, op. cit., pp. 14–31.

Bell, C., and Roberts, H. (eds.) (1984), *Social Researching: Politics, Problems, Practice* (London: Routledge & Kegan Paul).

Bulmer, M. (1978), 'Social science research and policy-making in Britain', in M. Bulmer (ed.), *Social Policy Research* (London: Macmillan), pp. 3–43.

Cicourel, A. V. (1964), *Method and Measurement in Sociology* (New York: Free Press).

Hammond, P. (1964), *Sociologists at Work* (New York: Basic Books).

Nowotny, H. (1985), 'Social science research in a changing policy context', in H. Nowotny and J. Lambiri-Dimakis (eds.), *The Difficult Dialogue between Producers and Users of Social Science Research* (Vienna: European Centre for Social Welfare Training and Research), pp. 7–14.

Payne, G., Dingwall, R., Payne, J., and Carter, M. (1980), 'Sociology and policy research', in G. Payne *et al.* (eds), *Sociology and Social Research* (London: Routledge & Kegan Paul), pp. 142–59.

Platt, J. (1976), *Realities of Social Research: An Empirical Study of British Sociologists* (London: Sussex University Press).

Roth, J. A. (1966), 'Hired hand research', *American Sociologist*, vol. 1, no. 4.

Sharpe, L. J. (1978), 'Government as clients for social science research', in M. Bulmer (ed.), *Social Policy Research* (London: Macmillan).

Sjoberg, G. (ed.) (1967), *Ethics, Politics and Social Research* (London: Routledge & Kegan Paul).

2

A Plea for Praxeology

P. J. M. NAS, W. J. M. PRINS and W. A. SHADID,
Institute of Cultural and Social Studies, University of Leiden, the Netherlands

Abstract
The application of sociology and anthropology is one of three important orientations of social research and has never been properly developed. The authors make a plea for the formalization of existing knowledge to stimulate theoretical questions preliminary to intervention. They present an outline for a praxeological approach, which is situated between basic and applied research. It includes theoretical, methodological and action branches. It is directed towards (1) the thematic application of theory, (2) the study of intervention strategies and (3) the study of the research process in relation to the use of results. Within this praxeological approach applied research is emphasized. In this context, the authors present short characterizations of four types of research: thematic-, policy-, action- and evaluation-oriented. They defend the point of view that the dichotomy between basic research and applied research is inadequate to cover the whole range of social scientific methodology.

Introduction

In undertaking social scientific research one can concentrate on various goals. Some researchers may concentrate mainly on theoretical questions, while others are more engaged in the study of social problems and their solutions. According to Wippler (1973) these orientations include three scientific approaches, which also offer standards for the evaluation of research. First, there is the empirical-theoretical approach, which aims at the formulation of theories with a high level of information. This type of research is carried out to promote the increase of reliable theoretical knowledge concerning a restricted part of reality. Secondly, there is the philosophical-critical approach, which is primarily directed towards the evaluation of knowledge and not so much towards an increase of knowledge. In the third place, Wippler mentions the praxeological approach, which arrives at a science of application by use of the results of the other approaches. Based on certain goals and the available scientific knowledge, guidelines for action have to be developed.

This chapter concentrates on the last mentioned approach, which unfortunately has never been properly developed. In 1979 Van Lier stressed the necessity to develop a science of application: 'One of the most urgent needs however for the application of the social sciences is a systematic development of an art of intervention: in this respect there is much know-how that needs to be formalized. Applied social science is in need of theoretical thinking in questions preliminary to intervention and the modalities of interventions' (p. 9). He has also pointed out the poor state of the theoretical basis of applied social research. According to him, this is the reason that policy-makers do not bother much about researchers (1980a).

Inspired by these critical considerations, we have asked ourselves basic questions about the character of applied social science and how applied sociological and anthropological research is related to the other branches of social research. At this point we can also formulate a number of specific questions which will be discussed in the following pages. First there is a series of questions with regard to the place of applied sociology and anthropology, including: Is it useful to make a distinction between basic and applied research? If so, can we point out different types of applied research? How did applied sociology and anthropology develop? What are the other main types of research and how do they relate to each other and to applied research? Second, there are questions dealing with the application of the results of applied research. To what degree are the results of applied research used for policy formulation and planning? What relations and mutual role-expectations exist between policy-makers and researchers? Is there a need for the development of a theoretical science of application?

By answering these questions we hope to respond to the strongly felt need to shed more light on the nature of applied social research. Also we intend to formulate a proposal for the codification of the large number of related concepts.

Theoretical and Social Relevance

Divergent views exist about social scientific research and its significance for the solution of social problems. According to some scholars, scientific research and the application of its results are two entirely separate activities. Others reject this strict separation and consider application part of research.

De Groot (1961) expresses the view that problems can be selected because of their theoretical as well as their social relevance. Moreover, scientific questions can have social relevance and, vice versa, the study of social problems can contribute to the formulation of theories. Research, however, is in the first place directed towards the increase of scientific knowledge and follows the empirical cycle, passing through the phases of observation, induction, deduction, testing and evaluation. Van de Braak (1975), on the other hand, opposes the firm separation between science and application. He views social scientific research as the sum of the cyclic reciprocal processes between researcher and researched (the so-called empirical cycle) with the aim of exchanging information and influencing the situation. According to him, research is to be understood as a social process in which application in various degrees is part of the research process. Therefore 'to address oneself to' fluently passes into 'intervention'.

To obtain a clear view on the position of theoretical and social relevance of research we will trace the historic development of applied sociology and anthropology. With regard to the theoretical and social orientation, several stages can be distinguished in the development of sociological and anthropological research. These stages, however, are only roughly placed in a time perspective.

The development of the social sciences from philosophy took place in times of rapid change and increasing complexity, associated with the Industrial Revolution, the rise of nationalism and democracy and the formation of the modern state. The social sciences formed a reaction to the problems caused by these processes, and sociological research was directed towards the betterment of society. The concentration on the study of concrete social problems was considered self-evident. In the second stage, beginning in the 1920s, the creation of an autonomous sociology was attempted, an elevated, pure science which did not deal with common, day-to-day problems and did not aim at the formulation of directives for intervention. Sociology became independent of any concrete social goal. In that way sociologists tried to gain status and influence (Lazarsfeld and Reitz, 1975; Van Lier, 1979).

Until the Second World War, anthropology showed a somewhat different development. Quite early a distinction appeared between researchers with a more theoretical and those with a more practical orientation. There was, however, an early acceptance of the fact that anthropology could be useful in attempts to dominate the indigenous people of the colonies and to change their life-style, culture and social structure. Missionaries applied anthropological knowledge for their conversion activities, and civil servants used or gathered anthropological knowledge for colonial government. From the beginning of the twentieth century a course in anthropology was part of their training (Foster, 1969). In contrast to sociology, anthropology did not develop in reaction to concrete social problems. The anthropologist in the first place aimed at the description and understanding of the culture and social structure of hitherto unknown societies. Because this information proved to be useful in practice (especially for the colonial administration) there existed a unity between science and practice.

After the Second World War, both sociology and anthropology changed. Within sociology attempts were made to re-establish the ties between sociological knowledge and practical work. In this stage of reorientation, which is still going on, attempts have been made to arrive at a synthesis that in our view can best be realized by the development of a praxeology in which the process of the use of sociological knowledge is analysed. A second development within sociology is its extension to developing countries. Attention is especially directed towards the rapid social change resulting from the increasing integration in national and international political, economical and cultural systems. In the Netherlands a sociology of non-Western peoples developed out of Indology, partly under the influence of anthropologists who were seeking alignment with sociology.

The processes of emancipation and decolonization in the developing countries and neo-colonial relations confronted anthropologists and non-Western sociologists with ethical problems. In the last part of the colonial era anthropologists could decreasingly associate themselves with the goals of the colonial governments, which aimed at retarding the decolonization process. Anthropologists were in many cases confronted with the choice of taking the side of those in power or supporting the powerless. Many anthropologists chose initially to be neutral but eventually became conscious of criticism when the interests of the population concerned were harmed. This resulted in a divergence between science and practice. The role of anthropologists in development programmes became smaller instead of larger (Foster, 1969). The increasing importance of development co-operation in the 1970s, however, renewed the ties between science and practice. In the Netherlands the linkage between anthropology and sociology was also brought about by the development of non-Western sociology in the 1950s.

When we compare the development of applied sociology and

anthropology, it is evident that both go through a number of comparable stages, the developments in anthropology taking place in time somewhat later than in sociology. This can be explained by the different factors affecting these transitions in the following stages.

From our classification it will become clear that we make a distinction between theoretically and socially oriented research. However, we do not want to deny the direct contribution of general theoretical research to concrete social problems or the role which the study of these concrete problems can play in the development of theory. Moreover, it is our view that the development of general theory is of fundamental importance for research directed towards application.

Codification

When studying the literature on applied sociology and anthropology, readers are soon in grave danger of losing their way. This is because the various authors use a wide range of concepts, which in some cases have not even been properly defined, and because sometimes one concept is given several divergent meanings. In the literature one has to be aware of stumbling over the following concepts: theoretical research, basic research, autonomous research, pure research, discipline-induced research, praxeology, applied research, application-oriented research, operational research, policy research, action research, science-application, field-induced research, input research, throughput research, output research, counterput research, etc.!

'Applied research' is a good example of a concept which has various connotations. Van de Braak (1975) for example holds the view that applied research is directed towards policy formulation and therefore is not concerned with theoretical questions. Bastide (1973), on the other hand, states that applied anthropology aims at theory formulation. It is obvious that conceptual clarity is lacking when there is no agreement on such a central concept.

'Action research' is also defined in several ways. Bastide regards action research and evaluation research as two parts of operational research, which is directed at concrete problems. Action research, then, is to gather data and to design an action programme. In contrast, Van de Vall (1980) places action research, as a type of throughput research, in the category of applied research, which is directed towards policy formulation and implementation. Van de Braak situates action research between fundamental and applied research because it ought to contribute to both policy development and theory development. It is clear that no consensus exists with regard to action research.

The definition of 'science-application' given by Albinski (1978) is a very broad one. He described it as the use of scientific knowledge for the realization of human goals, and contrasts it to application-oriented research.

Some authors lose their confidence when confronted with this confusing host of concepts. Lazarsfeld and Reitz state: 'No wonder that we enter this arena with trepidation. We certainly do not wish to add further definitions' (1975, p. 35). We agree with these authors that it is not much use to introduce further definitions. Nevertheless we should not avoid a discussion of terminology. We would like to take up the challenge to wipe out obsolete ideas and to arrive at a better categorization of concepts. In this chapter we will formulate a proposal for such a codification.

At the basis of this codification lies the discussion on the existence of two paradigms, namely, of basic and applied research. Some authors simply reject this distinction, while others support it partially or completely. Lazarsfeld and Reitz take this pair of concepts as of little value although they realize that it is generally used. They see it as 'the little man who is not there and does not want to go away' (1975, p. 33). Albinski (1978) calls it a false dichotomy, which is not based on one, but on several, dimensions. He argues that the distinction between basic and applied research is based on the following questions: Does the research problem originate from the field? Does the research contribute to the existing body of sociological knowledge? And are the collected data of direct importance to intervention? Based on these three dimensions he constructs a classification consisting of eight, unfortunately unnamed types of research. From a theoretical point of view such a classification can be made, but in practice it is of less value because the types cannot be properly distinguished. Albinski therefore seeks a solution by using the term 'application-oriented research', which does not pretend to give a comprehensive characterization but merely indicates the directedness of research. We will make use of this concept in our codification.

The anthropologist Foster (1969) does make use of the distinction between basic and applied research. According to him, the main difference lies in neither the approach nor the research methods nor the nature of the phenomenon that is studied, but in the way the problem is selected, in the management and the organization of research and in the short-term goals. According to Foster in both types the researcher has the same education and preparation. He or she uses the same concepts, methodology and research methods, and works with the same standards of precision, neutrality and objectivity.

Both Foster and Albinski indicate a number of differences which lie at the root of the distinction between basic and applied research. We will continue this approach and systematize the differences which are mentioned in the literature. We will first discuss the study of Van de Vall (1980) in which he pleads strongly in favour of two paradigms, one for basic and the other for applied social research, which he calls policy research. Van de Vall is to be distinguished from the other authors, because he has made an empirical analysis of 120 research projects and should therefore be considered an exception amongst authors who do not base their views on empirical research.

According to Van de Vall two paradigms exist, based on differences in strategy, approach, framework, theory, research methods and reports. To be effective, policy research should, besides a diagnosis of the problem, also imply intervention. Moreover it is more directed towards a dynamic or a combined static and dynamic approach. Also it should not be limited to a socio-psychological frame of reference but should additionally offer a social-structural basis for intervention. In relation to theory, it should be more effective to make use of grounded concepts, rather than formal concepts, and of greater diversity of methodologies, and to place less emphasis on epistemological rules of pure science. Concise reports are also of importance, while in general other techniques are used for communication, such as diffusion techniques and feedback strategies to promote the application of research results. In Table 2.1 we present the differences between basic and applied research in a systematic way. We hope to support convincingly our decision to treat basic and applied research as two separate paradigms of social research.

One has to realize, however, that the concept of applied research has been given a new meaning which runs counter to its popular use. Up to now it was described as the application of theories and methods of pure science to the diagnosis and solution of concrete social problems; or, according to Foster (1969), as the application of data and theory of basic social science to practical goals. We reject this conception of applied research: first, because the social sciences are not characterized by rigid laws that allow prediction (if they were, the applied sociologist or anthropologist could indeed act as a social engineer or a technician); second, because the contributions of social science to practical problems are in most cases based on general concepts and less on a methodology with rigid epistemological requirements.

In our view, applied anthropology and sociology have their own paradigm. Contrary to Van de Vall (1980), we do not consider it useful to substitute the concept applied by another one, because in spite of important differences basic and applied research cannot be totally

Table 2.1 *Differences between basic and applied research*

Differences	*Basic*	*Applied*
(1) Initiator	Researcher	Employer, customer, or researcher
(2) Selection of problems	Discipline-oriented	Oriented to society
(3) Goal	Extension of scientific knowledge	Exploration of themes and change of human behaviour
(4) Strategy	Diagnostic	Both diagnostic and intervention-oriented
(5) Approach	Static or dynamic	Both static and dynamic
(6) Framework	Social-structural or socio-psychological	Social-structural basis for intervention
(7) Theory	Formal concepts	Grounded concepts
(8) Methods	Epistemological validity	Less concern for epistemological validity
(9) Groups of reference	Scientists	Policy-makers, clients and scientists
(10) Communicative characteristics	Scientific publication	Use of several communicative techniques
(11) Management and organization	Oriented at the researcher	Oriented at the employer

separated. There exists much resemblance in research design, theory, methodology and methods and therefore there is much mutual influence. Applied research is to be considered research for practical use within a certain field of problems, not the application of basic science. The increasing importance of applied research related to certain problems corresponds to a process in society in which science and practice develop separately. Van de Vall calls this the process of professionalization, which can be observed in other sciences. In the field of health care, for instance, both positivistic-oriented branches such as biochemistry and physiology exist beside the diagnostic practice of medical science. Also in the natural sciences theoretical physics exists next to architecture.

We believe that we have given sufficient argument for a distinction between basic and applied research. One problem, which has already been mentioned, remains unresolved, however. How is it possible that some authors characterize applied research as directed towards theory formulation, while others take the viewpoint that applied research contributes to both theory formulation and policy development? Then the question arises whether a dichotomy between basic and applied research is adequate. In our opinion this is certainly not the case. In addition to basic research, theoretical research on application has to be distinguished, which implies a science of practice called 'praxeology' by Wippler (1973) and Van Lier (1979). As a branch of scientific-oriented research, praxeology is dedicated towards the theoretical comprehension of social change, intervention strategies and the nature and influence of the research process. Contrary to basic research it is application-oriented. Our classification of social research is presented in Figure 2.1.

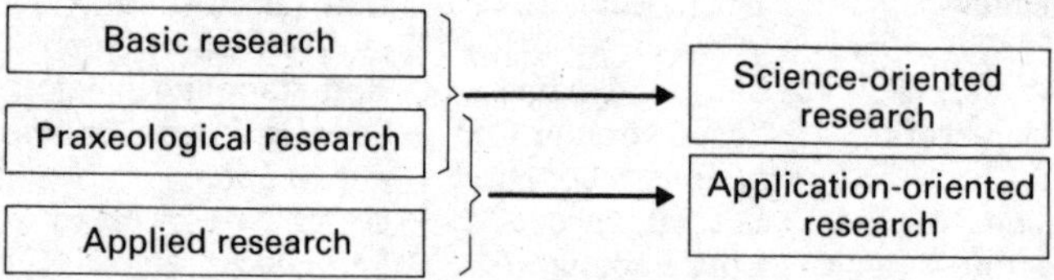

Figure 2.1 *General types of social research*

From our study of the relevant literature, we conclude that there are three main types of social research: basic, praxeological and applied research. Basic social research is not meant to contribute directly to the solution of social problems, although it nevertheless sometimes does. It is directed towards the development of general knowledge for the understanding of human behaviour. Praxeological research is directed towards the development of a science of practice. It includes the study of social change and intervention strategies as well as the methodology of the research process in relation to the process of use of social scientific knowledge. Both basic and praxeological research are to be considered science-oriented research because they operate at a theoretical level and are not directed towards concrete social solutions. But praxeological research, just like applied research, is application-oriented, because both are dealing with research on application and social change. Applied research is not in the first place directed towards theorizing about application but analyses concrete social problems in actual life. It is research aimed at application in specific fields. Within applied research a number of thematic specializations have been developed. These include the sociology and anthropology of medicine, education, urbanization and race relations. Applied research consists of three types: thematic research, policy research and action research. A dynamic aspect is brought into all three types by means of evaluation research. Concerning application-oriented research we now present the schema in Figure 2.2.

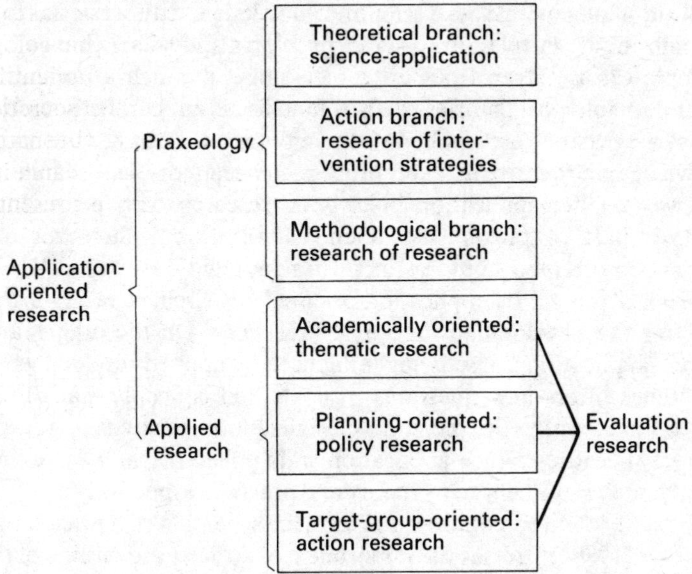

Figure 2.2 *Types of application-oriented research*

In the following pages this classification of praxeology and applied research will be discussed in more detail.

Praxeology

Praxeology has been described as the science of application, which is directed towards

(1) the thematic application of theory;
(2) the study of intervention strategies;
(3) the study of the research process in relation to the use of results.

Successively they represent the theoretical, action and methodological dimensions of praxeology. Van Lier was quite right when he stated: 'What is missing is a praxeology . . . An applied sociology on a theoretical base is the necessary final piece in the construction of a mature social science' (1979, p. 9). We agree with his opinion and will therefore attempt to present the outlines of praxeology to stimulate its development.

The first and theoretical dimension of praxeology we have named science-application. Contrary to Albinski (1978) we define this as the application of general social scientific knowledge, within the thematic specializations, in relation to social problems and social change. An example can be given from urban sociology in which a number of general sociological theories, such as functionalism, conflict sociology and system theory are applied to the city to gather basic theoretical knowledge on the urbanization process and related social change. In this way science-application links basic research with praxeology. Being a part of praxeology, science-application is however also application-oriented, but distinct from applied research. As the theoretical branch of application-oriented research, it offers a firm basis for the development of applied research. On the other hand, science-application is also being influenced by applied research which sometimes offers new questions, insights and concepts that can be incorporated within the thematic specializations. Partly they go their own way because science-application and applied research have their own dynamics, influenced by theory and practice respectively.

The study of intervention strategies is the second part of praxeology. Van Lier (1980a) stresses the importance of an accurate outline of this field in which the intervention process with its starting-points and effects lies. According to Wippler (1973), the praxeological approach attempts to design action strategies based on projected goals and the scientific knowledge available from the empirical-theoretical and the philosophical-critical approach. The central issue is to understand theoretically the introduction of change in cultures and societies. According to Bastide (1973), action and planning should be studied, in the same way as an anthropologist analyses kinship systems. Making use of the experimental method, it should be directed towards gaining more insight into the rules of consciously introduced social change and cultural mutation. It is not action and planning themselves but the analysis of action and planning which is of importance here. Research on evaluation methods plays a significant part in this. We consider it important that theory formation concerning intervention is developed. The stages of intervention, from awareness to implementation, related to different types of intervention, such as action and policy, should take a central place.

An important part of this is the study of projects – development projects, for example – which were meant to effect change. The project, or perhaps the programme as an aggregate of projects, is the most important means of intervention. Therefore the study of the structure and management of projects, the dynamics of social relations in projects, and multi-disciplinary and other project characteristics has to be part of the action-oriented branch of praxeological research.

Additionally, attention has to be paid to the context in which projects are carried out. The social structure and the cultural and political situation have to be taken into account. The analysis of action, as part of praxeology, is to be separated from action research which is part of applied research. However, mutual influence exists between them.

The third, methodological branch of praxeology deals with the research process and research techniques especially in relation to the use of research results. This can be viewed as research of research. On the one hand, it is directed towards the relations between the social scientist, the employer and the target group, towards the role of the sociologist or anthropologist and the use of research data. On the other hand, it includes the development of research techniques which are of importance for the study of change. Evaluation techniques and techniques which offer quick results – which we call 'thunderbolt research' – such as the mini-survey, are of great importance. This third branch of praxeology can be presented as in Figure 2.3.

Many authors deal extensively with the relationship between the social scientist and the employer. They all focus on the communication process which takes place between them. The sociologist or anthropologist can make use of a number of sources like theories, concepts, results of previous research, data pools and research techniques. These have to be translated in the terms of the client, the policy-maker, who formulates a problem in his or her own way based on experience in the past, future plans and the existing tensions and conflicts. The translation process forms a cognitive circle, in which the gap towards recommendations has to be narrowed. The social aspects of interaction are of great importance here. The social scientist can play a number of roles ranging from therapist, evaluator and teacher to employee and researcher.

Based on empirical research Archibald (1970) distinguishes between three types of role for the sociologist. These are the client-oriented clinical sociologist, the problem- or decision-oriented strategic

Figure 2.3 *Methodological dimension of praxeology*

sociologist and the discipline-oriented academic sociologist. The clinical sociologist deals with a direct social problem and makes a diagnosis. In harmonious interaction with the client he or she offers help for an exact formulation of the problem. The strategic sociologist on the other hand tries to influence the client, and does not so much try to help. He or she stresses the conflict in the relation between the sociologist and the employer. Discipline-oriented sociologists direct their research results in the first place to their colleagues. They do not concentrate on the specific problems of their employer, and the possible implications for policy from their research are directed in a separate second stage. Gouldner (1975), however, makes a distinction between social engineers, who carry out their research in terms of their employer, and clinical sociologists, who do not take their client's views for granted, because the client may have a false picture of the situation or may be trying to delay the decision-making process. (For the relation between social scientist and the employer, see Kruijer, 1969; Archibald, 1970; Gouldner, 1975; Lazarsfeld and Reitz, 1975.) Another possibility is that a client consciously refrains from using results, which is one of the causes of the limited use of research, so often objected to. According to Lazarsfeld and Reitz (1975), several types of clients also exist. One can be dealing with public institutions or private companies, clients with much or with little experience with research, simple or complex organizations, etc.

During the translation process in which the gap towards recommendations is to be bridged, Lazarsfeld and Reitz (1975) see three actors playing a catalysing role. The first one is the general sociologist who writes books, teaches students and carries out research on independently chosen subjects. Secondly there is the employer, in most cases the government or the institution that finances the research. Thirdly there is an intermediary between the sociologist and the client, who must be able to understand both parties and also has to be well up in the practical problem the client is tackling. It is however striking that in treating the research process and the relations between the parties concerned little attention is given to the role of the target group.

In the relationship between the sociologist, the client and the target group regarding the use of research results, the role of the researcher in policy-making is of great importance. Freeman and Sherwood (1970) distinguish four types: full participation, partial participation, external participation and incidental participation. In the same context Van de Vall (1980) states that results from research that has been carried out by employees of policy-making institutions are more influential than the results of policy research carried out by external consultants. The relationship between client and sociologist is also affected by their mutual judgements and prejudices. Maan, Nas and Pols (1980) show that policy-makers have many criticisms to make of researchers, such as scientific hobbyism, insufficient management of research, little useful results and communication problems because of the high level of abstraction, unnecessary use of complex formulations and the presentation of triviality in numbers. In their turn researchers often accuse their employers of an approach that is too technocratic, absence of a real vision on their own policy, absence of research programmes, rigid time limits and in the case of development co-operation the subordination of the receiving countries to the policy. The social scientist is often confronted with ethical problems with respect to his or her client and the target group. These problems also belong to the subject-matter within the methodological branch of praxeology.

Concerning the study of techniques for planned social change we will limit ourselves to claiming a specific position in praxeology and to stress the need for further study. A classification and exploration of the most promising techniques, and especially of evaluation (including short-term evaluation projects) and rapid techniques, is important. Rapid techniques such as the mini-survey are especially relevant for applied research where the tension between employer and researcher is so strongly felt. However, one must keep in mind that tension also exists between the rapidity and the reliability of data-gathering.

We have now drawn the outlines of praxeology, which in fact constitute a working programme for the future. We conclude at the end of this section that as the 1960s might be seen as the decade of methodology and the 1970s as the decade of ethics, the 1980s might become the decade of praxeology.

Applied Research

We have already defined applied research as research directed towards practical use within certain problem areas. In other words: 'When sociology is not an end in itself, but becomes a means to some other end, it is applied sociology' (Angell, 1967, p. 725). In this respect we distinguish three types of research: thematic, policy and action research. These three types have been developed in this order, mainly in reaction to each other, and because of changing conceptions of planning.

Thematic Research

Academically oriented thematic research is the oldest form of applied research. Primarily, it is aimed at describing a certain problem on which recommendations can be based. Because of its looser ties with intervention the distinction between thematic research and science-oriented research cannot always be rigorously maintained. Within this branch of applied research a number of specializations have developed. Increasing specialization by researchers on a relatively small sub-field has become a general phenomenon in the social sciences, and sociology and anthropology are no exception. In the old days one researcher could be an authority with regard to all social and cultural aspects of one society or region. The anthropologist took on the role of economist, political scientist, historian, etc. Nowadays his or her statements tend to be limited to one or two sub-fields. In most cases researchers have a regional and a thematic specialization.

We have already suggested that within science-application general theories are increasingly applied to sub-fields. In the practice of applied research this thematic specialization has also occurred. Examples include medical, urban, educational, economic and historical sociology and anthropology. The result of these thematic and problem-oriented specialisms is a more intensive co-operation between scientists from various disciplines, both within and outside the social sciences. This has resulted in multi- or inter-disciplinary research. An important advantage of this development is that the analysis of a certain problem from several perspectives will gain a better insight into the matter. But this development also means a loosening of the ties between the various sub-fields within anthropology and sociology. In our view this development towards thematic specializations has to be considered positively. Becker (1972) nevertheless warns against a one-sided organization of scientific knowledge according to problem areas. According to him, this organization demands the use of a great number of approaches which cannot all be covered by one researcher. Moreover, the use of several approaches will lead to problems of comparison. Becker therefore pleads for a double system, in which approaches (or disciplines) as well as problem areas play a role in systematizing knowledge. We share this perspective and also want to point out that praxeology creates the possibility and incentive to compare the results of various thematic researches and the integration of these results within the context of science-application and basic research.

There are a number of causes that have led to specialization within anthropology and sociology. Science itself provides for the first cause.

The amount of knowledge has grown to such an extent that one researcher can no longer survey the entire field. Specialization on sub-fields results logically from this. A second reason lies in the clear definition of the research areas of the various disciplines. Especially in topics where various disciplines overlap or in topics which are not really covered by any of them, many interesting problems or relevant factors are observed. Additionally the processes of rapid social change in developing countries are of importance. Society is becoming increasingly complex, and the questions put forward by society are continually undergoing change. Therefore in this respect the researcher is no longer able to obtain a total picture. (For causes and negative effects of specialization within sociology and anthropology, see Becker, 1972; Voget, 1975.)

Policy Research

Academically oriented thematic research as described above is the oldest form of applied research, but it cannot always be easily separated from science-oriented research. Thematic research is to a large extent separated from policy formulation and planning. None the less available sociological and anthropological knowledge is often used. To make research results more useful for policy-makers, policy research came into existence.

Following Hoogerwerf (1972) we can describe policy as a more or less well-considered striving to reach goals by the use of certain means. Policy, thus defined, is of growing importance to modern society. In this respect, Becker (1972) stresses the increasingly reflexive character of policy, which means that an organization is both making and made by policy. Furthermore, policy is getting more organized and institutionalized, and the use of specialized techniques such as computerized analysis is increasing. Growing rationalization is one of the main factors behind that tendency in which humanity intentionally chooses certain goals and tries to obtain them by means of a preconceived plan.

In this respect Van de Vall (1980) points out the substitution of the free market mechanism by planned regulation or policy in the modern Welfare State. The central issue is the mutual adaptation of demand and supply of products, labour and services to avoid the squander resulting from the price mechanism. This curtailment of the market process generates, according to Van de Vall, new problems. Especially in the field of public services the mutual adaptation of demand and supply has become difficult. By the absence of the free market system communication between policy-makers and clients is defective. Therefore a gap developed between demand and supply, influenced by the high expectations in the field of public services raised by the Welfare State. Social policy research plays a significant part in identifying related problems and in their feedback into policy development. This function is also fulfilled by protest actions, which are often less effective. Policy research has to be considered as research on behalf of planned social change. The researcher gathers and analyses data and offers the policy-maker information on which policy can be based. Because of its focus on social problems and change, policy research can be classified under applied research. An important characteristic is its top-down approach, which makes it quite distinct from action research, in which the target population itself is intensively involved.

The problem of the relationship between researcher and policy-maker and the advantages and disadvantages of policy research belong also to the field of interest of praxeology. They have already been discussed in this context and can therefore be omitted here. The same applies to the potential contribution of policy research, and more generally of applied research, to basic research through the introduction of new questions and insights from practice.

Policy research is mainly viewed as research on behalf of policy. We must however stress that policy itself also has become an important field of study. In both cases – research on behalf of policy and research on policy – evaluation research is of great importance. Description, causal analysis and prediction are the most important functions of evaluation research in this context. Also in thematic and action research, evaluation is of great importance.

Action Research

Action research as such has been conducted since the 1930s and is primarily characterized by two components: knowledge and influence or change. Gadourek (1972) considers it a forerunner of cybernetic thinking which is becoming popular in open systems theory. Action research developed in reaction to policy research and to a lesser extent to basic research. In both cases policy and planning were seen as being imposed top-down with little participation of the target population. It also presupposed a harmonious society with a well-defined common interest, as well as a social science with a high level of accurate prediction. Action research in contrast implies a bottom-up approach based on a conflict model of society and short-term planning.

An exploration of the literature concerning action research, however, yields a wide variety of definitions. We will attempt to systematize the main characteristics of this type of research. First we will mention Rapoport's definition, which is formulated as follows: 'Action research aims to contribute both to the practical concerns of people in an immediate problematic situation and to goals of social sciences by joint collaboration with a mutually accepted ethical framework' (Rapoport, 1970, p. 499). Contrary to this we can take Gadourek's definition (1972). In his view, action research is a heuristic principle for decision-making problems of managers, administrators, or other people responsible for the policy of organizations. From these definitions we can conclude that action research is directed at the solution of a variety of problems. It is practically oriented and to a certain extent directed towards intervention.

None the less the two definitions show considerable differences. First, there are differences in the target population. Rapoport attaches to action research a general usefulness, because it contributes to the practical concern of people in an immediate problematic situation. Gadourek, on the other hand, limits action research to decision-making problems of policy-makers in various organizations. Second, both definitions differ in the orientation of action research. Rapoport explicitly mentions its scientific orientation, which is lacking in the second definition. Gadourek even states that policy-makers should carry out research themselves to systematize their experiences regarding a certain policy and to predict and formulate the effects of actions. The testing of formulated predictions against the effects of action will have to lead to changes in action. This means that new lines of policy have to be introduced until the intended result is achieved. In this approach action research is similar to process evaluation. Van de Braak (1975) views action research as the total of short cyclical activities and therefore also implies a process approach. He distinguished the process of data-gathering, in which the data are used not just for feedback to the target group but also as a basis for planning and action to solve the formulated problem. From the process of data-gathering in order to evaluate the intended or attained effects of those actions, Van de Braak also distinguished between two approaches in action research: the principle of co-operation and the principle of trial and error. Relating to the theoretical orientation of this type of research, he remarks that action research is directed towards both theory and policy development, but that the former is only a by-product.

We have seen that, in the view of a number of authors, action research, policy research and applied research are to a large extent synonymous. Although all of these types of research are directed towards intervention and application, we reject this view. The difference between policy and action research as parts of applied research lies in their orientation to the target group. Therefore we consider action research as a type of applied research in which action and research are interwoven in such a way that the design, implementation and intended effects of a programme directed towards change take place in narrow co-operation with the target group. With this conception of action research we recognize the linkage, described by Van de Braak, with the target group by feedback of research and with action and planning. Moreover it stresses that action research is to be carried out through and on behalf of the target group. The researcher's role is to support and evaluate and to raise the consciousness of the target group. Especially in critical sociology, the highly valued linkage between theory and praxis is made by action research.

In this respect, Swanborn (1971) thinks it is obvious that the participants of the social system which is to undergo change should carry out research themselves. He considers the so-called community self-survey and self-evaluation of working groups as forms of action research. The role of the researcher is unmentioned. In our approach, however, the researcher plays a central role although action research is carried out in close co-operation with the target group. Gadourek (1972), on the contrary, contrasts the community self-survey with action research. He considers the latter a type of participant observation and he states that action research is often biased by subjectivity and the wishes of certain people, while the community self-survey is characterized by impersonal work, little guidance and a central clearing-house of gathered information.

Exploring the literature we note that the methodology of action research is little developed. According to Swanborn this is caused by the fact that its problems can be studied in a great variety of areas. Moreover, he adds that action research is now increasingly used in reaction to criticism of the role of the sociologist as an adviser. In the past he or she functioned as an intermediary for gathered and systematized data, but had no part in the use of these data.

The contribution to theory from action research is not to be neglected despite its practical orientation. We agree with Gadourek (1972) when he states that, although they are practically oriented , such relatively autonomous research teams can give an important contribution to science. Mention must also be made of the function of societal criticism of action research. But as with thematic and policy research, action research encounters its specific difficulties. It is based on the conflict model of society in which different groups strive after different goals. The common interests of these groups are not always recognized. Second, it does not allow much long-term planning or exact policy formulation. Furthermore, it assumes democratic decision-making processes within the target group which may be an illusion. Finally, questions can be posed regarding the relation between action and the scientific character of the research. Therefore action research, policy research and thematic research all can have their specific contributions in the guidance of social development. In this respect evaluation research has also a significant contribution to make.

Evaluation Research

Evaluation research as a type of applied research is characterized by its focus on the scientific gathering of data on the effects of an intervention programme. The effects are being related to the implicitly or explicitly formulated goals. Such orientation is related to intervention in an existing situation. When it deals with research or education, we consider it academically oriented. If it is primarily oriented towards the target group we speak of an 'action approach', and when it is oriented to planning we use the term 'policy approach'. Applied research culminates in the evaluation of these three types. Evaluation of the effects of planned social change with the use of empirical scientific methods has been made since the 1920s (Caro, 1971). Since that time, the use of evaluation research has increased as more scientific methods for planned change gained ground.

We refer to two authors for the definition of evaluation research. Suchman (1969) describes this form of research as the use of scientific methods of data-gathering in relation to the degree in which a certain activity has its desired effect. Veld-Langeveld (1972) defines evaluation research broadly as the study of change, in which policy is the stimulus or independent variable and the effect is the dependent variable. Both see evaluation research as research on causality and therefore stress the relationship between cause and effect. At the basis of this causal relationship between independent and dependent variables lie certain hypotheses concerning the factors which can generate desired change, the conditions which make it possible and the potential intervening variables. These hypotheses and their operationalization in a programme are called the impact model. From the second definition it is clear that we are dealing with a situation of conscious influence or intervention. Furthermore, both definitions relate to a specific form of evaluation research, which is named product evaluation. Process evaluation is a second form, which Albinski (1978) attempts to define as the description and evaluation of a purposely generated process from the point of view of the mutual alignment of sub-processes and their expected contribution to the expected goals. In our opinion, it could better be described as the scientific guidance of experiments based on the trial-and-error method, in contrast with scientific experiments. With Albinski we state that process evaluation and product evaluation together form the complete design of evaluation research and have to be carried out in combination. Based on this discussion we define evaluation research as scientific research which is carried out to make a judgement on goals, methodology, instrumental implementation, effects and feasibility of programmes directed towards intervention and the mutual relations between these elements and sub-processes.

The most widely used method for evaluation research is the experiment in all its forms, which means often merely measurement and the before/after measurement, with or without one or two control groups. The experimental nature limits the possibilities of evaluation research. One of those limits is that it lacks the possibility of making measurements in advance because in practice evaluation takes place only after a project has started. Another is the selection of a control group which is representative for the target group, and has to be kept out of the project.

When it is possible to mark the project which is to be evaluated socially and spatially the procedures of matching and randomization can offer a solution. The experiment is however not the only method that can be used. Suchman (1967) considers longitudinal research as very suitable in this respect. A possibility for control in relation to changes initiated by the project then exists, by studying a panel in a certain situation. After some time when the project or parts of it are introduced, this panel is studied again. The first measurement now can be compared with those of the second measurement. Beside these research methods others such as case studies, survey research, time sequences and correlation analysis can play an important part in evaluation research (Albinski, 1978).

The goal of evaluation research implies more than just a judgement on the success or failure of an intervention programme. Suchman (1971) distinguishes four categories of evaluation: the degree of action, the result of action, the way the result is obtained and the efficiency, i.e. the relation between costs and effects. In this view it is clear that causes and the way certain results are obtained have also to be taken into account. Veld-Langeveld (1972) distinguishes similar categories – such as the effect, the range of the effect, side-effects and efficiency –

and stresses the importance of extending evaluation research to an analysis of the total process of policy formulation and implementation.

The performance of evaluation research is more difficult than might be expected. (For an elaboration on these problems we refer to Kruijer, 1969; Suchman, 1969; Veld-Langeveld, 1972; and Albinski, 1978.) Exploration of the literature throws light on a number of problem categories in the execution of evaluation research. The first category concentrates on goals of the project. These are often vaguely formulated. Hypotheses concerning the relation between desired change and the conditions under which this takes place are often lacking or badly operationalized. Therefore the evaluation researcher is forced to infer the goals from all sorts of official and unofficial notes to formulate the criteria for evaluation. The second category of problems concerns the field situation and the range of the intervention programme. Evaluation is possible only when the field is marked socially and spatially and when the target group has a high level of homogeneity. When this is not the case the influence of possible intervening variables is hard to control. The third category is related to the experimental character of evaluation research. We have already observed that it is often difficult to fulfil the demands of the scientific experiment. Often difficulties arise from the selection of a control group in general, and more specifically in excluding it from the stimulus. In many cases it is also problematic taking two measurements, before and after intervention, and therefore to attribute the observed change to the intervention programme. The fourth problem category relates to the time dimension. An intervention programme should have a limited duration, to make possible the measurement of its inherent effects. In a long programme the influence of field variables cannot be controlled, which may lead to contamination in the observed results.

Both because of and despite the problems just mentioned, we urge a combination of ongoing evaluation with all types of applied research. Ongoing or permanent evaluation means that evaluation is taken up in the intervention programme right from the start, which gives it an integral instead of an incidental character. Then it is not limited to those cases in which doubt exists concerning the attainment of the formulated goals. In this respect, the concept of monitoring is used, which differs from ongoing evaluation because the goals of the programme are not reconsidered. Permanent evaluation which does reconsider the goals offers a number of advantages. By making an evaluation part of the programme, its goals have to be exactly formulated from the start, and hypotheses on which the impact model is based have to be precisely operationalized. This results in a deeper and systematic approach to the programme. Moreover it makes it possible to take measurements in advance which reveal the characteristics of the target group. This offers possibilities of a more reliable insight into the attained goals and the accomplished changes. At the same time, when permanent evaluation is used, possible adjustments to the intervention programme can be made. These adjustments may be necessary because of intervening variables and distortive side-effects, changes in the situation and certain goals. Finally permanent evaluation can contribute to the accumulation of knowledge of conditions under which intervention programmes can be implemented and test hypotheses which are deduced from the theories on which the programme is based. Therefore, we make a plea for the publication of the results of evaluation research, especially in relation to development programmes, through which a feedback process can develop through the implementation of similar programmes in several regions.

We conclude that evaluation research has to be placed in a broader framework, not just by including it in all intervention programmes, but also by connecting the evaluation of one programme with the design and evaluation of other programmes. Therefore with regard to applied research, evaluation research is needed that focuses on the application process: one of the tasks ahead for praxeology. Moreover, the contribution from this type of research to theory development within basic science should not be neglected. We join Albinski (1978) when stating that evaluation research is suitable for the development of a realistic, empirical and well-grounded theory of change. With this as one of the pillars on which application-oriented social research rests, the culmination point of applied social research is described.

Conclusion

We have pointed out that in literature generally a distinction is made between basic and applied social research and have presented arguments to substantiate it. However, we are convinced that this dichotomy in itself is not sufficient to cover the whole range of social scientific methodology. The demands of society and developments in science, such as increasing specialization, have clearly shown that an intersectional field of study is needed which is called praxeology. It is defined as the study of the theory of application *and* the study of the application of theory. It includes a theoretical, methodological and action branch. This means that praxeology is directed towards the thematic application of theory, the study of intervention strategies and the study of the research process in relation to the use of results. Praxeology fills the gap between basic and applied research by the combination of science-orientedness and application-orientedness and can be useful both in the formulation of new theory as well as in the practical application of social science research. In this chapter we have presented a tentative programme for the development of praxeology.

References

Albinski, M. (1978), *Onderzoek en Aktie* (Amsterdam: Van Gorcum).

Angell, R. C. (1967), 'The ethical problems of applied sociology', in P. F. Lazarsfeld, W. H. Sewell and H. L. Wilensky (eds.), *The Uses of Sociology* (New York: Basic Books), pp. 725–40.

Archibald, K. A. (1970), 'Alternative orientations to social science utilization', *Social Science Information*, vol. 9, no. 2, pp. 7–34.

Bastide, R. (1973), *Applied Anthropology* (London: Croom Helm).

Becker, A. H. (1972), 'Over sociologen en beleid', in Hoogerwerf, op. cit., pp. 23–38.

Braak, H. J. van de (1975), 'Action-research, plaatsbepaling van een onderzoekstype', *Intermediair*, no. 20, pp. 23–9.

Caro, F. G. (ed.) (1971), *Readings in Evaluation Research* (New York: Russel Sage Foundation).

Foster, G. M. (1969), *Applied Anthropology* (Boston: Little, Brown & Co.).

Freeman, H. E., and Sherwood, C. C. (1970), *Social Research and Social Policy* (Englewood Cliffs: Prentice Hall).

Gadourek, I. (1972), *Sociologische Onderzoekingstechnieken* (Deventer: Van Loghum Slaterus).

Gouldner, A. W. (1975), 'Explorations in applied sociology', in A. W. Gouldner and S. M. Miller (eds.), *Applied Sociology: Opportunities and Problems* (New York: The Free Press, Collier Macmillan Ltd), pp. 5–22.

Groot, A. D. de (1961), *Methodologie. Grondslagen van Onderzoek en Denken in de Gedragswetenschappen* (Den Haag: Mouton).

Hoogerwerf, A. (ed.) (1972), *Beleid Belicht I* (Alphen a/d Rijn: Samsom).

Kruijer, G. J. (1969), *Organiseren en Evalueren* (Meppel: Boom).

Lazarsfeld, P. F., and Reitz, G. (1975), *An Introduction to Applied Sociology* (New York, Oxford and Amsterdam: Elsevier).

Lier, R. A. J. Van (1979), *Discontinuity in the Social Sciences: A Plea for Praxeology* (Wageningen: Agricultural Uni.).

Lier, R. A. J. Van (1980a), *Stuurmanskunst en Sociale Beweging* (Afscheidsrede, Wageningen: Agricultural Uni.).

Lier, R. A. J. Van (1980b), Interview, *IMWOO-Bulletin*, vol. 8, no. 3, pp. 2–7.

Maan, E. E., Nas, P. J. M., and Pols, M. (1980), *Programmering van Sociaal-Wetenschappelijk Onderzoek en Ontwikkelingssamenwerking* (Leiden: unpublished).

Rapoport, R. N. (1970), 'Three dilemmas in action research', *Human Relations*, vol. 23, no. 6, pp. 499–513.

Suchman, E. A. (1967), *Evaluative Research, Principles and Practices in Public Service and Social Action Programs* (New York: Russel Sage Foundation).

Suchman, E. A. (1969), 'Evaluating educational programs', *Urban Review*, vol. 15, no. 4, pp. 15–17.

Suchman, E. A. (1971), 'Evaluating educational programs', in Caro, op. cit., pp. 43–8.

Swanborn, P. G. (1971), *Aspekten van Sociologisch Onderzoek* (Meppel).

Vall, M. Van de (1980), *Sociaal Beleidsonderzoek* (Alphen a/d Rijn: Samsom).

Veld-Langeveld, H. M. in 't (1972), 'De evaluatie van het beleid', in Hoogerwerf, op. cit., pp. 204–24.

Voget, F. W. (1975), *A History of Ethnology* (London: Holt, Rinehart and Winston).

Wippler, R. (1973), 'Het pluralisme van theorieën en van werkprogramma's: een kommentaar op Lammers', *Sociologische Gids*, vol. 20, no. 4, pp. 270–8.

3

Research and Policy Interactions: a Case Study

G. CLARE WENGER,
Centre for Social Policy Research and Development, Department of Social Theory, University College of North Wales, Bangor, Wales

Abstract
The conduct of policy-relevant research can cause ripples which spread beyond the project itself. In this chapter the author describes the reactions of an agency not directly involved in the commissioning or conduct of the research but for which the findings would inevitably have considerable significance. The interest that this agency subsequently took in the research and the effect of this upon the project are discussed. The author suggests that the context of social research is an area of behaviour which social scientists have under-emphasized as a proper topic for study. In this case, the political context of the research contributed substantially to the content of the final report in ways that could not have been predicted. The author suggests that researchers have an ethical responsibility both to conduct their studies scientifically and to study the research context. The question of whether such study could make it possible to avoid conflict or to take account of and plan for the Hawthorne effect (the effect of being studied) as an agent of social change is raised.

Recent shifts in the economic and political context of research have meant that more funds are available for contract, policy-oriented research than for more purely academic research. Traditionally, these two strands within anthropology and sociology have developed in parallel, funded from different sources and publishing findings for

This chapter was originally presented in a symposium on 'Contract Research and the Problem of Customer Interest' at the XIth International Congress of Anthropological and Ethnological Sciences, Quebec, Canada, August 1983.

different audiences through different fora. Contract researchers have tended to be social-problem oriented, publishing primarily in reports to funding agencies and journals focusing on applied anthropology or other applied social science; whereas university and academic researchers have focused on perhaps more esoteric and generally more theoretical problems, publishing in the learned journals of their profession. If we borrow a metaphor from mathematics and refer to these two strands as 'applied' and 'pure' social science, I think we can agree that pure research has by and large enjoyed higher status than applied research. However, if present trends continue more of us are likely to be employed in policy-related research at some time during our professional careers, and it would seem that there is a case for exploring and making explicit some of the differences and problems that contract researchers confront.

This chapter highlights some of the more obvious contrasts between pure and applied research, illustrates some of the effects through the use of a case study and tries to draw some conclusions about the role of the researcher as an agent of social change.

Value-Free Research?

While few social scientists cling to the myth of value-free research many more share the conviction that as anthropologists, ethnologists or sociologists our role is not to effect social change but to provide knowledge which enhances humanity's understanding of society. Such detachment is easier to sustain in pure research, but policy-related research is, by its very nature, concerned with the conscious change of social processes.

Cora Du Bois (1980) has suggested that anthropology is not a social or behavioural science but a humanistic philosophy. As such it embraces values which tend to be universalistic and thus frequently in conflict with those of policy-makers, whose values are nationalistic and political (Hinshaw, 1980). Anthropologists working in the arena of public policy, therefore, often find themselves in an adversary situation *vis-à-vis* the customer or funding agency, and are frequently accused of bias in favour of the powerless (Hoben, 1982). Thus, maintaining a façade of value-free neutrality becomes difficult to sustain.

Most of us, I suspect, if we are honest with ourselves, would like to feel that our discipline can and does influence policy in relevant contexts. C. Wright Mills (1959) went so far as to suggest that social scientists have a responsibility to try to change the world 'in accordance with the ideals of human freedom and reason' (p. 193).

Although anthropologists have over the last decade moved further beyond academia than in the past, there still remain constraints on becoming wholly identified with applied research. On the other hand, there are those who feel that 'anthropology will remain ineffective in communicating policy-relevant knowledge until we encourage and train a professional corps' and see a need for acknowledgement of the policy and administrative context as a valid professional arena (Hinshaw, 1980, p. 499).

While work in this context may not be conflict-free, the arguments which are stimulated may provide a healthy environment for the questioning of assumptions of both policy-maker and social scientist. Certainly, anthropologists working in the policy field learn that their arguments must stand up to criticisms which may include questioning some of the basic assumptions they share with colleagues. At the same time, they must learn an appropriate language for the presentation of findings to audiences other than fellow members of their discipline (Agar, 1982). With the shrinkage of employment openings, within academia anthropologists may look less sceptically at work in applied fields. If the social scientist is to have an impact outside the confines of the university, and if she or he has a commitment to social change, then it would appear that risks must be taken and values must be made explicit.

Methodology

If value conflicts arise between policy-makers and anthropologists, so do different attitudes and perspectives on methodology. Those working in the field of contract research have found that some accommodation often needs to be made to meet the demands of administrative and managerial staff, whose superiors expect 'sound' statistical data on which to base decisions. This has meant that whatever other methods may be used, much research in the policy field has a survey component and a multi-faceted approach to analysis.

The participant-observer role in policy research can also be problematic since the researcher finds it more difficult to avoid being identified with the funding agency and often has an overt evaluation role. There may even be a schizogenic element, in that work often involves the nature of agency–client relationships, and the social scientist may at different times participate in both groups. At the same time, the visibility of the research process has its own scenario providing often a third or fourth dimension of observation. It is this dimension to which I should like to pay particular attention.

Presentation of Findings

In presenting findings, contract researchers are inclined to limit themselves to those factors which form part of the contractual objectives of the original proposal. However, as anyone who has ever conducted detailed research in a social context knows, the research process has its own dynamic. It is opportunistic and inductive, and both short- and long-range goals may shift during and as a result of the research. Because of the expectations and demands of customers, the researcher makes some attempt to prepare a cohesive and well-structured report of findings even where the outcome differs in scope or emphasis from initial plans. However, even in 'pure' research, only the better ethnographer confides to the reader the interactive process between research and context. In the case of applied research reports, prepared for policy-makers, what is sought is a distillation of findings rather than a description of the process. As a result we are usually told little of the dynamics of the research programme; yet because of the political context in which such research is conducted, and because the researcher fills an identifiable role where both policy and recipient population are the objects of study, the potential Hawthorne effect is enhanced. I would like to turn here to a case study to illustrate the way in which research and the political/policy context may affect one another, and how the dissemination of findings can be reflexive, feeding back into the research and even affecting subsequent outcomes.

Dynamics of a Research Project (Wenger, 1980a)

In 1975–6 British trade unions voiced concern about the continued existence of part-time working. This concern was predicated upon the fact that part-time workers were seen to be exploited on various grounds. They had no job security or tenure, were entitled to no holiday pay, no redundancy payments, no sickness or unemployment benefits and no pension rights. At the same time, it was felt that part-time workers were also paid low hourly rates and were seen as a cheap alternative to full-time labour. On these premises the unions were urging the phasing out or stricter control of part-time employment. Discussions of these matters and their implication for the rural economy caused some concern among academics at the University College of Wales at Aberystwyth. The college is situated in, and has a tradition of interest in, the rural areas. The professor of economics felt that the role of part-time work in the rural economy was of a different order from that in urban industrial areas; that it played a vital functional and integral part in the economy of rural communities where markets are small, and that restrictive legislation would strike at the very fabric of a fragile rural economy where employment opportunities were already limited.

Consequently, application was made to the Board of Celtic Studies – a research funding body within the university itself – for money to carry out research to establish the nature of what at this stage was called 'broken-time working' in the local rural economy. This term was used in order to encompass all jobs that might be performed on a less than full-time basis, including situations where the encumbent worked full-time by holding more than one part-time job or where work was seasonal and therefore not full-time. The funding was granted to the heads of Economics and Geography and was administered through the Department of Economics at the University of Wales at Aberystwyth. The department subsequently advertised for a researcher 'in broken-time working in the Mid-Wales area'. The research was described as to be designed 'to extend existing knowledge of the extent and pattern of part-time working – in farming, forestry, tourism, transport, etc. – in an area of sparse population'. Applicants were sought with 'a good honours degree in a relevant social science subject'.

It was made clear that the sociological implications of patterns of working were to be an integral part of the study, which was expected to be completed in two years. Wearing my social anthropologist's hat, I was hired to conduct this research and started on 1 October 1976. The first hurdle was to prepare a detailed plan for the execution of the research.

Certain decisions which I made in consultation with the grantees determined the shape of the subsequent research and modified and expanded the original intent of the project. A progress report on this period written subsequently for the granting body notes:

> due to the difficulties encountered in the precise definition and isolation of broken-time working as a concept, it was decided that the project should be broadened to study employment patterns and problems in general. (This would have been necessary in any event, in order to isolate cases of broken-time working.)

And:

> Since the original remit sought information on the sociological implications of employment problems, it was further decided to concentrate on sample communities, as a blanket survey of the whole region would necessarily miss any community impact.

A final research proposal was presented and adopted in December 1976, describing a study of six selected communities representing a range of specific community types, including interviews with the heads of 20 per cent of households.

The region of Mid-Wales in which the research was to be conducted had a long experience of underdevelopment. The area consists of 40 per cent of Wales's acreage, but contains only 6.4 per cent of the population. It is, therefore, a sparsely populated upland rural area with scattered farms, hamlets, villages and small market towns with few centres of population concentration. Only eight towns have a population of more than 2,500. The first concerted attempts at amelioration of the development problem had taken place in 1957 with the foundation of the Mid-Wales Industrial Development Association, and in 1966 the region had been designated a Development Area (Garbett-Edwards, 1972). This meant that the region could offer financial inducements to industrialists: advance factories with two years rent free; regional employment subsidies (later discontinued); government grants, loans and taxation allowances (Schnitzer, 1970).

In 1968 the Mid-Wales New Town Development Corporation was set up with the goal of creating a new urban centre in the region based on a market town confusingly already called 'Newtown'. This corporation later became the Mid-Wales Development Corporation (MWDC) and extended its brief to other areas of the region. On 1 April 1977 the Development Board for Rural Wales (DBRW) took over from the association and the corporation. The board had wider powers and responsibilities although subsequent events have curtailed these to some extent.

At the inception of the research being considered here, the development board (DBRW) had not yet been established. In determining which communities to study I decided to contact the head of the existing development corporation (MWDC) to discuss its work and to broaden my knowledge of the problems and experiences of the region. A telephone call to the office in Newtown met with a cold rebuff. The response was along the lines that the University of Wales had no right to initiate research within the corporation's region without consultation, and if there was anything to be said the head of the Economics Department should speak directly to the head of the corporation. Subsequently, reassured by the professor concerned that the research was largely peripheral to the agency's remit and that the researcher was a well-qualified professional, the head of this body agreed to an interview and proved to be extremely helpful in supplying historical and background information about the corporation and the region.

The association and the corporation, and subsequently the board, have concentrated their development efforts on developing the towns of the region, and this became known as the 'growth towns policy'. Two of these small towns (populations approximately 2,000) became included in the study: one where development had been relatively successful and one where development had been disappointingly frustrated.

Interviewing and initial exploratory research in the study communities commenced in February 1977 and by the time the DBRW was established in April they were virtually complete. The previous head of the development corporation, which was subsumed by the board, was appointed director of industrial development, and a chief executive was hired from outside the region. The board, however, occupied the same suite of offices and was in many respects an amplified continuation of the corporation. Inevitably, the advent of the board was a topic on which there was a great deal of discussion in the study communities. Everywhere a high level of anxiety and frustration existed with respect to employment opportunities, and expectations about the board's ability to ameliorate the situation were talked about with hopeful anticipation. The general feeling seemed to be that there would now be a body which would at last have the power to do something for the region and its people, who had long felt ignored not only by the British government in Westminster but also by Cardiff, the Welsh capital.

One of the early findings of the research was the discovery that in every community selected for study except the smallest one – and that was mainly agricultural – grass-roots self-help groups had emerged in local efforts to increase local non-agricultural job opportunities. Most of these groups had started out as pressure groups seeking support from existing agencies, but when frustrated in this direction had resorted to localized 'boot-strap' responses including working with district councils and founding co-operatives. At the same time, private entrepreneurial efforts at development were also encountered. It quickly became clear that both these phenomena were not unusual in the region and in one district had been actively encouraged by the Plaid Cymru (Welsh Nationalist Party) Member of Parliament.

Data collection from the household interview survey was completed by the end of April 1977, before the impact of the new DBRW was felt – although, as stated, great interest was being expressed at this time. Frustration was encountered throughout the region with respect to pre-existing policies in the Development Area (most at least initially continued by the board). This was particularly marked with respect to the preferential terms offered to new industry, entering the area for the first time, as opposed to indigenous firms. There was also some antagonism towards the 'growth towns policy', which was perceived as having been superimposed on the region without consultation. This feeling was strongest in, but not limited to, those smaller communities not so designated, which suffered an accelerated loss of population. Most policies for the development of the region had been couched in terms of stemming depopulation to protect Welsh communities. Those which now saw massive depopulation, even if to local centres, felt the policies to be counter-productive.

From June 1977 to April 1978, in addition to analysing data on the work experiences of workers in the sampled households, I closely followed the fortunes of the small firms and businesses of the study communities, as well as maintaining close touch with grass-roots development efforts, local councils and the DBRW. This period coincided with a time of worsening economic fortunes and rising unemployment. Initial anticipation by residents of the new efforts of the DBRW quickly turned to disappointment and in some cases subsequently to bitterness. This in part resulted from an early statement from the board that development efforts would continue to be concentrated on Newtown and to a lesser extent on other growth centres and that the established programme of advance factory building to attract industry in from outside the region would be continued and in fact stepped up. This was despite much local disillusionment with the programme and the fact that many factories had been standing empty. The emphasis remained on selling Mid-Wales to outside manufacturing companies, which meant bringing English-speaking employers into a largely Welsh-speaking area. In addition to this, the board's officials were perceived to remain ensconced in their offices in Newtown, close to the English border (Wenger, 1983).

The final research report to the granting agency was ready and submitted in July 1978, covering data collected in the various communities up to and including May of that year, by which time the DBRW had been in existence for only one year. Upon acceptance, an abridged version was prepared for publication. This latter copy was delivered to the publishers in November 1978. At the request of the funding agency, the findings of the study were to be first published in this proposed monograph. However, in the early autumn of 1978 the head of the Economics Department at Aberystwyth was asked to present the prestigious Cymmrodorion Lecture, given annually in London before a learned society of expatriate Welshmen and -women. In the event, this paper was co-authored by the head of department and myself (by now employed at a different university) and presented in January 1979 (Rees and Wenger, 1979).

The lecture concentrated on the economic problems of individuals, firms and communities in the Mid-Wales region and raised several points critical of the policies of the DBRW. Response from the board was immediate, and a letter from the chief executive demanding a copy of the paper reached the Department of Economics before the lecturer himself could return. This was followed by an angry telephone call from the chairman of the board which essentially challenged the right of anyone to present such a paper without prior consultation with the DBRW. Correspondence between the board and the university continued until March, at which time it was suggested that the board should have the opportunity to comment on the published paper and the authors the right to reply.

The board's major complaints centred on their claim that the paper had been written without consultation. This was in spite of the fact that a dialogue had continued during the research period between the researcher and a board spokesman. The need to protect the confidentiality of sources of material and my subsequent refusal to reveal sources of complaint and criticism of the board also caused ill-feeling. In reply we pointed out that consultations and discussions between the board and the university took place during the research and continued subsequent to the delivery of the lecture, and that several specific suggestions made by the university had been taken up by the board. These suggestions were described in an epilogue (written in October 1979) to the abridged report, whose publication had been delayed due to industrial action (Wenger, 1980a).

The final report and book reflected a wider study than that of broken-time working originally intended. After an introduction focusing on the historical and economic problems of the region, the manuscript went on to describe present demographic patterns and to give a profile of the experience of development and employment in each of the six study communities. It also included chapters on employment and household income patterns; regional attitudes to work, community, leisure and the quality of life; and migration patterns and rural development experience. In its conclusions it made policy recommendations. In other words, the study which emerged differed substantially from that originally intended.

In September 1979, at the invitation of the Plunkett Foundation for Co-operative Studies based at Oxford, I addressed a meeting on community co-operatives which had been arranged to take place at the Aberystwyth University in Mid-Wales. This paper was on the topic of self-help groups in rural Wales (Wenger, 1980b). In the heated discussion of the paper, criticism of the board's policies was expressed by the audience, which included members of local development groups. In spite of the obvious relevance of the meeting to rural development, the DBRW itself was represented by only a junior officer. In the face of such antagonism he indicated that the board was intending to set up an advisory panel to assist those people who were interested and concerned with grass-roots community development. Although this revelation was greeted with a certain amount of scepticism – if it were true, what better forum for its more formal announcement? – it was received with some interest by those who had experienced the board's previous apparent reluctance to deal with such groups. However, inquirers following up this announced advisory service were informed by the chief executive that there was no intention to do any such thing. It had become clear by this juncture that I had come to be perceived as a *bête noire* by the development board.

In December 1979, amidst rumour that Development Area status was to be curtailed in Mid-Wales, the DBRW's budget was cut by £3 million. In January 1980 a regional daily newspaper ran an article based on my research and findings on the attitudes of indigenous business people and on my opinions about the role of the DBRW. The board was invited by the paper to counter criticism and to give its side of the story. It declined.

Some time early in 1980 the board commissioned work for the production of a community co-operative manual to provide advice for grass-roots organizations. The writer of this handbook in due course consulted me about its contents! While the manuscript was delivered to the board later that year, it has never been published in spite of the fact that the 1980–1 annual report of the board states: 'Other achievements of the DBRW's Village Programme include . . . a "Co-operative Manual", on the opportunities for community co-operatives; the launch of a special scheme for community co-operatives' (DBRW, 1981, p. 13).

The Plunkett Foundation conference on community co-operatives did, however, have one organizational spin-off. This was the founding of Welsh Community Enterprise, a loose affiliation of community development groups to facilitate co-operation and information sharing. The most immediate response was the planning and organization of a second conference on co-operatives in Wales to take place in 1980. Speakers from the Irish and Scottish development bodies, together with members of the Irish rural co-operative movement, were invited to this conference to provide background from their experience of co-operative ventures in their own regions. The chief executive of the DBRW was also invited to speak. The original 'broken-time working' researcher was invited to give the introductory address. This discussed the economic and employment background and identified formal attempts at amelioration.

This conference attracted a larger gathering than the Plunkett meeting, reflecting the growing interest in self-help development which was taking place in the region. The representative from the development board was the last scheduled speaker and arrived just prior to delivering his paper. He followed a succession of speakers who had dealt with the problems of overcoming marginality and the successes and problems of co-operators in Ireland and Scotland. His paper was entitled 'Development in Mid-Wales: is the co-operative relevant?' Early in his paper he remarked on the lack of enterprise in the area, claiming that the people were 'not willing to do it themselves' (Skewis, 1980), thus provoking antagonism in his audience. He claimed that, while he did not consider community co-operatives a viable proposition for Wales, the board would be prepared to help co-operatives on the same basis as other indigenous businesses if they met the necessary criteria. At the same time he gave details of a new village proposal to help the development of a cross-section of villages which had been selected by the board for eligibility for a range of resources that could be made available at the request of and on consultation with the villages so chosen. Subsequent questions from the floor and the following discussion were indicative of a high level of frustration and antagonism on the part of an audience which included, as well as local self-help initiators and co-operators, representatives of local authorities and elected representatives from the parish councils to the House of Commons. Indeed, there was some danger of the meeting ending in uproar.

In December of the same year the report of the contracted researcher was published under the title *Mid-Wales: Deprivation or Development* (Wenger, 1980a). Its publication drew attention from Welsh television and radio, particularly with respect to the criticisms of the role of the DBRW. Interviews were broadcast which concentrated on that small part of the report that concerned the activities of the development board, local attitudes towards it and my evaluation of its policies. The DBRW, although again invited to reply, again declined to respond. Some time later the information leaked out that a policy decision had been made by the board to ignore publication. However, throughout the research period and subsequently up to and after the publication of the book I remained in periodic contact with officers of the board, whose primary dealings with me were for the most part genial and collaborative. Information had been exchanged and suggestions were made in both directions. Indeed, many of the suggestions and recommendations made in the study had been adopted by the board by the time the book was published.

Briefly summarized, shifts and changes within the research environment, including the progress of the project itself, resulted in outcomes which could not have been predicted beforehand. In this example, the customer or funding source was a granting agency within the university, but its original brief was policy-oriented and sought to influence attitudes in government and trade unions concerning part-time work. This specific goal, however, was one facet of a broader area of concern, namely, rural development. Partly as a result of the perspectives of the researcher they hired and partly as a result of political and institutional changes within the study environment, the objectives of the customer shifted during, and as a result of, the research process. Consequently, the final study, while encompassing the initial problem, turned out to be broader and more detailed than anticipated.

At the same time, the effects of the known presence of the researcher and her dealings with the development board, together with their response to this, created both their own dynamic and a simultaneous shift in interest on the part of the original grantees. In this chapter, only the interaction of the research role with the development board has been delineated. With less obvious impact, interactions also occurred with various aspects of local government and informal development groups. In other words, a matrix of complex interactions and linkages developed within which the research process was accomplished ostensibly independently of outside forces.

The dissemination of findings, formally and informally, through lectures, publication, consultation and discussions, led to an increased awareness of the processes in the region and probably to a greater degree of self-scrutiny on the part of the protagonists because of the political arena in which policy-related research unfolds.

Hindsight

Readers will no doubt be conscious of the fact that I have said very little about the core findings or directions of the research which gave rise to this paper. This is intentional because it seems to me that, in applied research, the research context, process and dynamic are more visible, debatably more complex, but – because of the hidden agendas involved – perhaps more important than in pure research. It seems to me that if we accept that such research is about social change then we need to acknowledge our role as social change agent.

My experiences lead me to suggest that the research dynamic is part of the change process. We need to know more about the effects and nature of the research dynamic in a systematic way. The context of policy research is in itself a legitimate area for study, one which should be looked at by those involved in the process. Contract researchers often complain of the pressures of customer demand which lead to the use of more quantitative methods than they might instinctively select. On the other hand, the research dynamic itself is a topic to which participant observation is ideally suited. Indeed, studying the process should be an essential component in the objective evaluation of findings. What we need is a systematic ethnography of research dynamics.

As many researchers have no doubt said, if I had known before I started on this research what I know now, I would have done this or that or perhaps the whole thing differently. To play the role of change agent the (small 'p') political context and effects of the research role must be well understood. To this end, there is much to be learnt by looking at the research dynamic and trying to formulate some basic propositions about this phenomenon and to include this dimension of our work as legitimate data on which to build and refine theoretical propositions. Knowledge of the potential impact of research can lead to, for instance, more informed choice of methodology or approach, taking into consideration the various institutions and factions likely to come under scrutiny, and at the same time can indicate a more interactive approach to agencies operating in the research area. This should not jeopardize the position of the anthropologist as researcher in the eyes of funding agencies. On the contrary, by demonstrating an understanding of the possible and even intended effects of the research, the credibility and professional standing of the researcher can be enhanced.

References

Agar, Michael H. (1982), 'Toward an ethnographic language', *American Anthropology*, vol. 84, no. 4, pp. 779–95.

Development Board for Rural Wales (1981), *Annual Report 1980–81* (Newtown, Powys: DBRW).

Du Bois, Cora (1980), 'Some anthropological hindsights', *Annual Review of Anthropology*, vol. 9, pp. 1–13.

Garbett-Edwards, D. P. (1972), 'The establishment of new industries', in J. Ashton and W. H. Lond (eds.), *The Remoter Rural Areas of Britain* (Edinburgh: Oliver & Boyd).

Hinshaw, Robert E. (1980), 'Anthropology, administration and public policy', *Annual Review of Anthropology*, vol. 9, pp. 497–522.

Hoben, Allan (1982), 'Anthropologists and development', *Annual Review of Anthropology*, vol. II, pp. 349–75.

Mills, C. Wright (1959), *The Sociological Imagination* (London: Oxford University Press).

Rees, Graham, and Wenger, G. Clare (1979), 'Mid-Wales: problems of development', Cymmrodorion Lecture 1978, published in *Transactions of the Honourable Society of Cymmrodorion* (London).

Schnitzer, Martin (1970), *Regional Unemployment and the Relocation of Workers* (London: Praeger).

Skewis, Ian (1980), 'Development in Mid-Wales: is the co-operative relevant?' Paper delivered to Welsh Rural Co-operatives Conference, Aberystwyth, organised by Welsh Community Enterprise, 19–20 April.

Wenger, G. Clare (1980a), *Mid-Wales: Deprivation or Development* (Cardiff: University of Wales Press).

Wenger, G. Clare (1980b), 'Self-help initiatives: some Welsh examples', in Colin McCone (ed.), *Rural Multi-Purpose Co-operatives* (Oxford: Plunkett Foundation for Co-operative Studies).

Wenger, G. Clare (1983), 'The problem of value selection in development policy', in Robert D. Graff (ed.), *Communications for National Development* (Cambridge, Mass.: Oelgeschlager, Gunn & Hain).

II

Taking Sides: The Advocacy Role

Introduction to Part Two

Most policy research has as its tangible outcome a descriptive (more or less theoretical) report together with policy implications and recommendations. Other researchers find opportunities to become actively involved in social change.

The tendency for social scientists to identify with the target population has been mentioned. The ethics of the research relationship with informants or respondents were an early concern of social scientists when the research process became an object of study (Hammond, 1964). As noted in the Introduction, more politically aware researchers may fear the way in which their findings may be used against the community they have studied. Researchers have no control of the use of data and have often been dismayed by the way in which their work has been interpreted (e.g. Cain, 1969; Moore, 1977). Because of this potentiality, purists have avoided investigations which assist in the making and implementation of policy, claiming that such involvement is unethical. On the other hand, Payne *et al.* (1980) note that sociologists may see themselves as spokesmen for the underdog, and Bulmer (1978) has pointed out that policy research need not support the *status quo*. The availability of findings to the target population can also further its case (see Wenger's discussion of self-help groups, Chapter 2). Similar concerns have been expressed by anthropologists and other social scientists.

Both of these perspectives, the sceptical and the idealistic, appear to stem from the view of the outsider, the 'objective' or at least detached social scientist who is marginal to the social process. Part Two presents two chapters from anthropologists describing their roles within the social process itself, as part of the social structure they are studying. Both played an advocacy role, acting as interpreter or mediator between groups as part of the social process.

De Treville's chapter describes her experiences working on two development projects in Egypt, both funded by international agencies, in which she played a scientific investigative role and an active facilitator role in the process of social change. For de Treville there is no conflict of loyalty; she states categorically that she seeks always to represent the interests of the target group of development policy. But as Mair (1985) has pointed out, while most anthropologists involved in economic development consultancies are motivated at least in part by their desire to alleviate poverty at the grass roots, they have to function within the society as a whole and may find that their efforts are disrupted by external events and by élite groups at the national and local level. Most governments in the developing world increasingly demand that research projects are relevant to their own policy needs, and the consultant researcher may find that the interests of the governors and the governed are at variance (Benthall, 1985). De Treville's chapter shows clearly the frustrations of the advocacy role but also demonstrates how social scientists might act politically on the basis of their scientific knowledge and understanding of the social context at both micro and macro levels. De Treville was not always successful, but this is a good example of the direction the social scientist's role can take in the design and implementation of policy. What emerges strongly in her chapter is the need to understand networks of patronage in the research and/or policy domain, which may then be used to facilitate the continuance of the project. While de Treville's work was conducted in Saharan Africa, Blackstone and Hadley (1979) used the same awareness of the patronage network to facilitate their research at the London School of Economics.

The other chapter in this part, by McNamara, describes his role as an in-house researcher employed by the Chamber of Mines in South Africa. His disclaimer and the importance he attaches to the researcher's awareness of his own values have been echoed by Van den Berghe (1967), who even as a foreigner in South Africa found he had to work to maintain his own values in the face of pressures for conformity. McNamara's concern about acceptance by the black miners is not unique, Van den Berghe (1967) and Middleton (1978) have faced similar problems working in an interracial context where neither blacks nor whites felt totally comfortable with them, at least in the early stages of their work.

Like de Treville, Van den Berghe and Middleton, McNamara avoids confrontation to achieve both research and reform. He admits that his approach does not challenge the existing structures of the society but seeks to ameliorate the current position of the mineworkers. In this he and his colleagues have had some success. In correspondence, McNamara comments that, of those who read the draft of his chapter, colleagues were concerned about the effect the employee orientation might have if brought to the attention of employers, while academics who tacitly accepted this orientation were concerned about adjustments to the management perspective. As Stretton points out, 'To persuade people to change course it is often hard to judge whether to adapt your projects to their existing assumptions, or, on the other hand, to try to bring their assumptions and purposes into question' (1978, p. 80). Like de Treville, McNamara applies his academic knowledge to the society at large, seeking to mediate between groups in terms that will be culturally acceptable in order to avoid destructive conflict. As he himself recognizes it is a slippery path beset with potential for misunderstanding.

Similar work, sponsored by a mining company in Papua New Guinea, has been conducted by Mamak (1978). Like McNamara, he was conscious of the reciprocity obligations to both employer and employee. Through similar adaptations he too managed an accommodation with his sponsors and, as he puts it, felt it was his responsibility to point out to them the consequences of their actions and urged wage increases and union acceptance. In both pieces of research, the presence of the researcher raised the consciousness of the workers and contributed to social change.

Good relationships, then, can exist between researchers and policymakers even in contexts where conflict might be expected. While de Treville negotiates between élite groups to achieve benefits for the disadvantaged group, McNamara acts as mediator between the dominant group (employers) and the subordinate group (employees). Benthall (1985, p. 1), reporting on meetings in France, quoted a Vietnamese researcher, Trong Hieu Dinh, who stated that the job of anthropologists was not

> to help insurrectionist movements, but to cast a cold eye on the facts, for instance drawing attention to economic development projects that have damaging results; anthropologists have no strength or power, but stand a chance of being listened to in the long run . . . if they try to be as objective as possible and speak the truth as they see it.

Those who agree with this view will be critical of de Treville and McNamara for their direct involvement. The more radical social scientists will see the *modi operandi* of de Treville and McNamara as mere tinkering within established structures. Others will count the concrete benefits which they have achieved for disadvantaged groups, though limited, as successful and responsible professional involvement. The perspective will depend on the political stance of the critic.

References

Benthall, J. (1985), 'Keeping up the flow of overseas work', *Anthropology Today*, vol. 1, no. 2, pp. 1–2.

Blackstone, T. and Hadley, R. (1979), 'A battlefield revisited – problems of social science research in universities', *National University Quarterly*, Autumn, pp. 472–86.

Bulmer, M. (1978), 'Social science research and policy-making in Britain', in M. Bulmer (ed.), *Social Policy Research* (London: Macmillan), pp. 3–43.

Cain, L. D. (1969), 'The AMA and the gerontologists: uses and abuses of "A profile of aging: USA" ', in G. Sjoberg (ed.), *Ethics, Politics and Social Research* (London: Routledge & Kegan Paul), pp. 78–114.

Hammond, P. (1964), *Sociologists at Work* (New York: Basic Books).

Mair, L. (1985), 'Development anthropology: some new views', *Anthropology Today*, vol. 1, no. 1, pp. 19–21.

Mamak, A. (1978), 'Nationalism, race–class consciousness and social research on Bouganville Island, Papua New Guinea', in C. Bell and S. Encel (eds.), *Inside the Whale* (Sydney: Pergamon), pp. 164–81.

Middleton, H. (1978), 'A Marxist at Wattie Creek: fieldwork among Australian Aborigines', in C. Bell and S. Encel (eds.), *Inside the Whale* (Sydney: Pergamon), pp. 238–69.

Moore, R. (1977), 'Becoming a sociologist in Sparkbrook', in C. Bell and H. Newby (eds.), *Doing Sociological Research* (London: Allen & Unwin), pp. 87–107.

Payne, G., Dingwall, R., Payne, J., and Carter, M. (1980), 'Sociology and policy research', in G. Payne *et al., Sociology and Social Research* (London: Routledge & Kegan Paul), pp. 142–59.

Stretton, H. (1978), 'Capital mistakes', in C. Bell and S. Encel (eds.), *Inside the Whale* (Sydney: Pergamon), pp. 67–92.

Van den Berghe, P. (1967), 'Research in South Africa: the story of my experiences with tyranny', in G. Sjoberg (ed.), *Ethics, Politics and Social Research* (London: Routledge & Kegan Paul), pp. 183–97.

4

The Anthropologist as Legitimator: Participatory Development in Egypt

DIANA DE TREVILLE,
Institute for Development Anthropology, Binghamton, New York, USA

Abstract
Anthropologists involved in development studies or projects usually attempt to represent the interests of the target population. This paper reflects on two of the major dilemmas experienced by the author involved in such work in Africa. It demonstrates the need to maintain awareness of the larger society in which target groups exist and of variation within target populations.

The paper describes the problems which can arise when those with power act on their own behalf. In one instance reported here, an international agency, through a need to demonstrate its own success, drew attention to a project which resulted ultimately in damaging interference from locally powerful groups. In the other instance, the anthropologist was able to use her knowledge of local networks of patronage to ensure that locally powerful groups perceived the continued success of a project as contributing to their own prestige thus protecting its continuance and success.

The paper raises interesting questions about the motivations of élites at different levels of society and stresses the importance of the understanding of such potentially conflicting perspectives for the applied social scientist.

Introduction

As an anthropologist, my primary concern in development projects, whether in phases of planning, implementation, or evaluation, has

This chapter was originally presented at a symposium on 'Participatory Development and the Challenge to Anthropology' at the XIth International Congress of Anthropological and Ethnological Sciences, Quebec, Canada, August 1983.

been to represent the interests of the group for which the project was designed. Since development plans in Egypt formally stress goals of decentralization and inclusion of disenfranchised segments of the population in projects, I have sought, first, to work with these groups in understanding how best a project could fit into their particular socio-economic context and, second, then to represent the different interests of the group to institutions involved in different phases of project activity: donors, ministries and bureaucratic structures.

Two of the major dilemmas I have encountered are as follows. First, failure by those involved in the different aspects of development work to disaggregate the target population into its constituent interest groups: it goes without saying that a given 'community', 'village', or 'institution' consists of a variety of groups, each of which will have differential access to goods and services, based on the groups' relation to the power base or patronage relations obtaining therein. However, the tendency is to depoliticize the development process by assuming that the target population is a homogeneous unit. It is not. It consists of a variety of groups having differential access to power and goods and services. Likewise, the instruments of most project implementation in Egypt – the bureaucracy – is erroneously assumed to be a homogeneous and neutral implementing agency. It is no more neutral or homogeneous than the so-called target group.

Secondly, there is often failure to recognize that participants within the different institutions involved in project planning and implementation may have conflicting definitions of project success based on the inherent interests of these different participants. These interests are generally framed in the context of kinship and patron networks. Hence, while the anthropologist may be called upon to legitimize project success in formally defined terms – for example, at least a nominal amount of goods and services reaching the targeted population – in reality participants in these different institutions often informally define project success in terms of their ability to channel project activities and resources in such a way that their own groups are at least partial beneficiaries. Here, the impact of kinship and patron networks on project activities is of central importance.

When the dynamics of a project are examined with a view both to the variety of interest groups seeking to obtain access to project goods and services at the local level, as well as to the often conflicting interests both within and among donor and implementing agencies and institutions, the concept of 'success' does indeed become a multifaceted issue. I intend to examine two projects, showing how donors, members of the target group, implementing agencies and I – as an anthropologist frequently acting as mediator between these different groups – become disparate participants in the development process.

The Nubian Projects

The Nubians are a distinct ethnic and linguistic group which was formerly situated in the area now inundated by Lake Nasser. These people were resettled north of Aswan, where the Egyptian government built a series of villages replete with related health, educational and other public services. In spite of the heavy overlay of Egyptian government influence over the last several decades, the Nubian population retains a strong sense of ethnic identity and presettlement institutional structures.

One of the structures of particular importance is that of voluntary associations. Nubians have been able to continue these associations by grafting them on to the Egyptian Ministry of Social Affairs' private-voluntary-organization structures that exist throughout Egypt. There is a long history of voluntary associations amongst both Nubians and Nile valley residents. In line with the socialist policies of Nasser, these organizations were, beginning in the early 1950s, incorporated into the Ministry of Social Affairs. All private voluntary organizations now must be registered with the Ministry of Social Affairs, receive some funding from the ministry and are subject to ministry scrutiny as regards projects they initiate. The ministry has provincial governorate offices, each headed by a director general, whose staff enforces ministerial regulations. As will be seen, this centralized control of local voluntary organizations can generate considerable friction between the ministry representatives located at the governorate level and those involved in specific associations. This friction is particularly likely to generate problems in Nubia, where the continuation of local autonomy and associated ethnic concerns is embodied in Nubian voluntary associations. These locally defined concerns can be dimly viewed by governorate ministerial officials who may want the associations to implement recipe-formula development projects over which ministry officials can maintain easy supervision.

This dynamic was played out in a series of projects in which I participated. The voluntary association in question had developed two training projects, one working with young women and one with young men. The women were involved in sewing and handiwork, the young men in carpentry. Over the course of a year and a half I worked with this association in project design, participant selection and programme implementation. We obtained funding from the Canadian International Development Association (CIDA) to finance a series of modest improvements that were designed not only to allow increased numbers of students to participate, but also to expand the women's section into fabrication of Nubian handicrafts and develop marketing channels for these goods. This would assure a higher and more regular return for the women than selling goods through the ministry channels, as had formerly been the case, and provided a way for women to train under one of the village elders skilled in Nubian handicraft work. The project was seen by villagers as one method of securing the continuity of certain crafts reflective of Nubian identity. And, as long as the projects continued at a low profile, there was no reason for the provincial ministry to intervene.

It happened that regulations of CIDA at that time required the funding of small projects of this nature to be administered by an intermediary institution which would maintain appropriate accounting procedures. A United States private voluntary organization operating in Egypt acted as this institutional intermediary. Shortly before the assassination of Sadat, the country director of this US organization was in Aswan, and I took him out to visit the Nubian projects. He was impressed with them, and decided these projects should be visited by a group of US private voluntary organization VIPs coming to Egypt the following month. The visit of these VIPs occurred just a few weeks after the assassination, when security was tight. Fearing that the arrival of high-level US donors would generate tensions and anxieties both within the provincial ministry offices as well as in the Nubian association, I urged the visit be called off. However, the interests of the local US country director in showing off local projects of some success to US donors, in order to obtain funding, overrode these objections.

The results of the visit were unfortunate. With a crew of US donors coming into the area, the provincial ministry could no longer ignore the modest project activities that had been taking place. According to protocol, it was not possible to visit these local projects without visits to the provincial director general of the ministry, who would then become (structurally) the responsible party for these projects. I went to Aswan a few days before the visit to make arrangements. Quite understandably, the director general of the ministry immediately set up several visits for the arriving delegation to some of his favourite, non-Nubian projects, announcing that it was his opinion that enough money had been spent in Nubia. Ministry staff were then sent out to the Nubian projects to oversee arrangements and assure all was in order.

From the point of view of the Americans, the visit was an unqualified success. The Nubian community went to considerable expense to provide an enormous banquet, complete with Johnny Walker whisky, Nubian music and dancing, and many gifts given from the handicrafts project. Because of the high tensions still existing after the assassination, the village members were inspected by provincial security forces before the arrival of the US delegation, and we were accompanied by a jeep bearing soldiers armed with machine-guns. From the point of view of the Nubian association, the visit spelled the end to the semi-autonomous projects they had been developing. After this episode, the director general of the ministry placed restrictions on uses of outside donor money. Thenceforth, his offices would be responsible for allocation and supervision of any donor money.

In this way, so-called grass roots motivation was effectively squelched; the Nubian projects were thereafter under close scrutiny by the ministry, and I left the work with the unhappy realization that (1) the very success of these projects had resulted in their demise; (2) my understanding that the inherent tension between bureaucratic interests and those of local institutions would be forced out in the open by the visit of the US donors was ignored by the US country director, whose own interests at that time were guided primarily by desires to obtain funding, even though this would jeopardize the success of the projects.

In short, my initial success in presenting the interests of the Nubian association such that funding could be obtained was reformulated into success on the part of the ministry to secure control over donor money and success on the part of the US private voluntary organization to impress US donors. The outcome of effective participatory development by the Nubian association was to threaten the élite structure of the provincial ministry, which – following the insensitive visit of US donors – stepped in to tighten the reins of control over this association.

The South-Eastern Desert Nomads Project

The second example I want to discuss involves a project funded by the United States Agency for International Development (USAID), aiming to establish primary medical services and improved water sources for Beja and Ababdy tribes inhabiting the South-Eastern Desert of Egypt. The director general of the Provincial Ministry of Health in the Red Sea Governorate had initially gone to USAID asking if it would be possible to implement a programme in this remote and unserviced area. USAID funded an initial study group into the South-Eastern Desert. The team consisted of a physician, a nutritionist, a hydrogeologist and myself. The physician and nutritionist worked together in obtaining body weights and measurements, blood, urine and faecal samples, and administering general medical aid. The hydrogeologist systematically visited all the major wells in the area for purposes of analysis.

Because no anthropological work to speak of had been done with these remote tribes, I spent the first few days finalizing my interview schedules. In addition to basic demographic data, I focused on the economic bases of the different groups and the relation between ecological areas and socio-economic conditions of the groups in the area. The South-Eastern Desert has an extremely diverse geography, ranging from fishing tribes along the Red Sea coast to herding groups inhabiting the mountainous central corridor. All groups are, and have been for generations, intricately linked into the north–south trade route that runs up the Eastern Sudan and terminates at several points in the Nile Valley. The extreme aridity of this region means that tribes have been heavily dependent on this trade for their livelihood. As this trade is receding, tribal members are being forced with greater frequency into seasonal employment in the Nile Valley. Before this project, the only government service reaching the area was a trip, every three months, sponsored by the provincial governorate, during which basic food commodities were distributed and an accompanying doctor treated illnesses.

Our studies indicated that these tribes had (1) the highest levels of malnutrition in Egypt and (2) the highest rates of Hepatitis B of any known population group in the world. Further, 100 per cent of the women and a majority of children 6 and under suffered from anaemia. By co-ordinating our data, we were able to link my ecologically based socio-economic data to the medical and nutritional data, demonstrating that the above mentioned medical problems were directly linked to groups inhabiting specific areas.

USAID in Cairo was pleased with our results, and asked me to submit a proposal for a project in the area, which I would administer in conjunction with officials in the provincial governorate. This seemed a demonstration of the ability, first, of anthropology both to co-ordinate data effectively in a multi-disciplinary study and to provide a cogent understanding of local conditions to USAID personnel; and, second, for this understanding then to be translated into specific project activity. Based on the studies we had done, I worked for several months with governorate officials in designing a project that would include:

(1) building a modest medical outreach complex that would be staffed by a doctor;

(2) setting up a training programme for doctors serving the area that would cover field medicine and techniques of working with local, traditional medical practitioners;
(3) training paramedics selected by project doctors from the local population;
(4) providing a four-wheel-drive project vehicle for the doctors' use;
(5) undertaking modest improvements to one of the major wells in the area on which tribes were becoming increasingly dependent;
(6) training several tribesmen in well maintenance procedures;
(7) supplying sufficient funds for several major interdisciplinary study trips into the area.

The two major issues of contention in this project centred on (1) problems of implementation and (2) precisely where the locus of control over project resources would lie. It became clear that, as is unfortunately the case in many projects having large budgets, officials in the province saw as the final aim of the project securing funds and equipment, rather than the institutionalizing project activity. The reason is quite simple. Institutionalization would require the governorate to develop positions and provide resources – a medical doctor, paramedics, well maintenance persons, driver for the medical vehicle and an ongoing supply of medical equipment – that would then have to be maintained at the governorate's expense after the project terminated. Since the resource base for extensions of this kind is particularly sparse in this governorate, officials were willing to secure the funds that would be used in training and equipment purchase, but were not willing to assure that the positions and associated upkeep and equipment would be continued.

There then ensued a lengthy period of negotiation with Ministry of Health officials in Cairo to secure an additional doctor at the governorate level who would be located in the project area. This doctor completed his training in field medicine. We then worked on-site with various problems encountered in interfacing modern and traditional medical structures and practices. As this work spread and the doctor continued to gain acceptance by tribespeople, he began to select people to work with him as paramedics who would be sent up to the governorate hospital, at project expense, to receive rudimentary medical training. At this point, the governorate director general of health cut off medical supplies to the project doctor, claiming that it was a drain on the governorate supplies and an expense that ought to be covered by the project. It required another series of visits to the Ministry of Health in Cairo to straighten out this problem. Thereafter, the director general of health insisted the project doctor should spend only two weeks a month in the area and the other two weeks serving in a private phosphate mine eight hours' drive north, indicating that if he (the director general) did not personally receive benefits from the project the situation would not improve. He felt that it was unfair for a junior doctor to receive special training and other benefits while he, the superior, received nothing. I was forced again to go to the Ministry of Health in Cairo to get the latest obstacle cleared. The first secretary of the ministry intervened personally, calling the recalcitrant director general to Cairo to impress on him that the project was not to be continually the object of personal intervention for personal gain.

In the meantime, a vocal and powerful member of the local governorate made a bid to draw project resources away from the Ministry of Health and place them under the wing of the Ministry of Local Government. To validate the claim, three members of the Ababdy tribe were brought up to the governorate capital – a fourteen-hour trip – to complain to the governor that a woman had died as a result of medical treatment by the project doctor. For reasons not explained, it was argued that the death would not have occurred if the project had been directly supervised by the Ministry of Local Government's provincial staff. In discussing the incident with tribal members, it emerged that the Ministry of Local Government official, who was responsible for the food delivery every three months to the project area, had spread the word that unless measures were taken to transfer control of project resources to his offices there would be no food delivery in the near future. But if he succeeded in gaining control of the project, he would ensure that project resources benefited the tribal élite – primarily merchants – with whom he had good relations.

By what may have been merely a coincidence, the director general of health was changed at this time, and I then worked with the new director general to re-establish project activities in ways that would skirt the political intrigues within the governorate. Construction plans were finalized for the medical unit. Two more major interdisciplinary team trips were made into the area, one focusing on the livestock population, related disease processes, the economic role of livestock and related class and sexual divisions of labour; the second attempting to set out a more equitable method of food distribution to favour the poorer and more malnourished groups. This brought into the project scenario certain local merchants who had exerted control over some groups in the hinterland. The food deliveries had formerly been made in large allotments to these merchants, who then disbursed them according to their personal ties and associated interests.

But we had not heard the last word from the Ministry of Local Government official in the governorate, whose authority over the food distribution was now being challenged, and hence his links with the tribal élite and merchants in the project area. He had strong ties also with certain governorate religious officials, as well as patronage links with several members of the People's Assembly in Cairo. He set out on a two-pronged course of action. First, he convinced the head of the Ministry of Religious Affairs in the governorate that a secret mission of the project was to proselytize the tribes to the Christian faith. The repercussions of this accusation were quickly felt from the governor's office down into the project area. Second, he gained the support of certain patrons in the People's Assembly in Cairo to exert pressure on the Ministry of Local Government in Cairo to support a resettlement scheme, whereby project activities would be funnelled into a larger project emanating from his offices that would aim to resettle the nomadic population.

Letting the latter issue die of its own inertia, I set out to tackle the first issue – that of proselytizing – by setting up a meeting with the officials in the local Ministry of Religious Affairs. I showed slides of project activity, played tapes recording members of the tribal groups and settled down to a long discussion about the Islamic Brotherhoods represented in the South-Eastern Desert. During the course of the conversation, it emerged that the presumed 'threat' of the project had prodded the local ministry to set aside funds for building a mosque where the medical complex was to be constructed. Telling the religious leaders I thought this was an excellent idea, I suggested we use the same contractors who would build the mosque also to build the medical complex. Since these contractors were under the patronage of the Ministry of Religious Affairs, this provided an opportunity for the project to be supportive of the activities of this ministry and for the ministry itself to legitimize project activities. The governor himself made a trip to the project area to lay the first stone of the mosque and to observe food distribution activities. After that, there were no more efforts by the Ministry of Local Government official to realign project activities.

Throughout the course of project implementation, it was clear that struggles for project control at the governorate level precluded any notion that governorate-related project activities were consciously reflective of locally defined concerns and interests. Also, bureaucratic myopia by all concerned resulted in the attitude that (1) pre-existing organizations in the tribes could not be used to institutionalize any of the project activities and, therefore, (2) the bureaucratic structure as developed in the Nile Valley needed to be extended to this area, thereby assuring direct control of the project resources from centre to periphery. Finally, it was the tribal élite – and in particular the big merchants – that had the pre-existing resources that allowed it to capitalize on project activity. In all instances, my own ability either to represent the disparate interests of these highly stratified tribes or to secure participation by tribal members at the governorate level was generally met with opposition. Nevertheless, we were able to lay down the first medical services for the area and provide training in appropriate field-medical procedures for doctors serving the South-Eastern Desert. We were also able to initiate a more equitable distribution of food goods, though not without considerable effort in reconciling conflicting interests at the governorate level, as well as at the project level between merchant-élites and tribes with which these élites were linked in patronage networks.

Conclusion

In both the Nubian and South-Eastern Desert projects, major impediments arose at the governorate level. Protagonists in both projects sought to channel project activities through their own networks, the frequent rationale being that members of the group for which the project was intended needed to be guided in – or lacked sufficient training for – carrying out projects. In just this way, throughout Egypt, the national goal of decentralization from central ministries to provincial governorates and on to local village councils has had three interesting and non-decentralizing results:

(1) The arena of political activity and related attempts to control resources has been extended from centre to periphery, thereby systematically extending central government influence to the local level; by channelling resources directly to the governorate level, vertical patronage linkages are strengthened, as members of local governorates seek to secure resources from central ministries and other centrally located institutions. Hence, the Ministry of Social Affairs in Aswan sought to cultivate ties with donors in Cairo in order to channel funds directly from these donors through its local offices. Conversely, problems with the Ministry of Health in the South-Eastern Desert project could be solved only by recourse to officials at the ministry in Cairo. This consolidation of vertical linkages does not, however, preclude the existence of patronage networks at local levels which may be in competition with each other over the control of project activity. Furthermore, goals of these lower-level groups may be different from those of central ministries.

For example, in the South-Eastern Desert there existed competition between different governorate ministry officials and their related clientage, as well as conflicting definitions of project activity between certain governorate officials and central ministry offices.

(2) Greater concentration of power and resources at the governorate level leads to a more systematic penetration of village-level institutions by the governorates, again strengthening vertical patronage links, as élites in these local communities seek to cultivate ties with governorate authorities in their efforts to obtain goods and services available through governorate channels. An example here is the linkages between local merchants in the South-Eastern Desert with the governorate offices of the Ministry of Local Government.

(3) At the community level, patronage linkages remain little changed, as the poor and powerless look to their ties with local élites as being the most secure and ongoing sources for obtaining a share of the action. This is exemplified by the control over food distribution in the South-Eastern Desert by local merchants. At this community level there are frequently problems in targeting project activities so that benefits are either gender-specific or linked to a specific economic sector of the population. In the Nubian projects, it was difficult to target the training programmes specifically for poorer young men and women, since those running the projects frequently gave priority to relatives or others with whom they were bound in patronage networks. From the point of view of village patronage networks, this procedure was both understandable and expected. One had to be satisfied with a mix: some really poor participants but many selected because of their relatively high placement within the village patronage system. As mentioned in the introduction, the idea of a neutral implementing bureaucracy is misleading. And this holds true at the local level as well as at either governorate or national levels. In short, for projects to reach women, the poor, or the malnourished, it may be necessary to recognize that projects will be guided by élites and related patronage networks. The concept of 'grass roots' or 'local participation' in projects does not, as is often assumed, automatically result in an increased participation of the poor. Indeed, the expression of 'community interests' in a given project may well reflect only the interests of the local élite structure.

Women, the poor, or the malnourished are frequently those with least access to goods and services. The dispersion of goods and services had traditionally been meted out by local élites and related patronage networks. Hence, it is through these networks that the disenfranchised most frequently obtain important resources. In the course of the kind of 'institution-building' frequently associated with development projects, if a project bypasses these élite structures (as, for example, setting up local councils, women's groups, co-operatives, voluntary associations, or other institutions not indigenous to the local environment), this 'institution-building' may be seen by local élites as an attempt to set up rival structures for the benefit of the poor – hence undermining their own position.

At this juncture élite members of the patronage networks may attempt to direct project activity or, failing that, encourage locals not to participate in the project. 'Success' here will be defined by leading members of these networks to the extent that they are able to secure some measure of control over the management of project resources and participation in project activities as, for example, the tribal merchants in the South-Eastern Desert. At the governorate level, the Ministry of Social Affairs stepped in to supervise both funding and project activities when it appeared that its own power base was being challenged by the outside-funded projects in the Nubian voluntary association. This is not to argue that there exists an amoral political arena in Egypt. On the contrary, implicit in the concept of patronage is the notion that social and economic activity will take place between (politically) unequal partners within a morally defined arena. Part of the legitimacy on which élite networks are based consists of their ability both to control and then to disburse goods and services for their clientage in a manner defined as 'equitable' by the ethos of the community. Hence, as mentioned, projects which provide alternative institutions to the poor will likely threaten these pre-existing structures. Just how these alternative institutions can remain autonomous and hence provide long-term solutions to the problems of poverty, while at the same time coexisting with local or regional élite and patronage networks, is a fundamental issue in participatory development in Egypt. The question is: can such institutions really exist autonomously, or will their working procedures be affected by and ultimately subsumed under the often conflicting interests of élite and patronage networks? This question is by no means unique to Egypt. The patronage paradigm exists in many other developing countries. But the relationship between this paradigm and development programmes is both under-recognized and understudied.

In the Egyptian context, project success is multifaceted, linked to the often divergent interests of the different donor institutions, élite structures and related patronage networks which participate in a project. In many cases, members of the target group will be least involved in active participation, while the role of the anthropologist will be viewed as more or less threatening – or more or less likely to legitimate project activities – depending on the placement and interests of those different groups. Anthropologists involved in development work are in a favourable, if not unique, position to focus on the interrelations between élites/patronage networks and formal governmental and bureaucratic implementing agencies – and hence to inform development programmes of favourable ways to reach and work with the groups for which a project is formally intended.

5

Taking Sides in Conflict: Applied Social Research in the South African Gold-Mining Industry

J. K. McNAMARA,

Human Resources Laboratory, Chamber of Mines of South Africa Research Organization, Johannesburg, Republic of South Africa

---

Abstract

Applied social researchers report that it is difficult to remain disinterested in policy studies as a result of their exposure to influences and pressures originating from both client organizations and the subjects of research. For this reason, it is essential that social analysts lay out and clarify their own likely value orientations in applied policy research.

In this chapter, this principle of value accountability is related to different phases of applied research in the South African gold-mining industry. Certain shifts in the value orientations of the researcher are outlined and traced to influences exerted by subjects (employees) and clients (managers) alike in the context of changing economic and political developments in the industry.

The discussion weighs up these value adjustments against the eventual (desired) outcomes of research. Additionally, it is argued that changing economic, social and political developments, as well as any accompanying value shifts of applied researchers, need to be continuously reviewed in an effort to develop a broadly accepted framework for the legitimate and effective application of social knowledge.

Disclaimer: This chapter focuses on evaluative aspects of applied social research in a privately sponsored institution within the South African mining industry. The arguments and issues discussed represent the personal views of one member of that institution. No conclusions can or should be drawn regarding the views of other members of that institution or of the institution as a whole.

Value Orientations in Applied Social Research

An important concern of social scientists involved in applied policy research is the question of whether such work can be carried out in a disinterested or value-free manner. Applied social researchers report that it is difficult to remain entirely neutral while attempting to develop a legitimate advocacy role in policy-related studies (Bermant and Warwick, 1978, p. 384).

It has also been argued that any attempts at maintaining a neutral stance in social intervention may merely result in a false impression of impartiality (Bermant and Warwick, 1978). The effort to remain disinterested could also be regarded as running counter to the very purpose of applied research, which by definition involves the application of knowledge in the furthering of valued goals in society.

The general goal of applied research can be described as the desire, on the part of anthropologists, sociologists and others, to contribute to the resolution of pressing social, economic, industrial, or political problems in human society. Within this broad framework, policy researchers have assumed various value positions, such as a commitment to the improvement of the quality of life of certain groups, or the preservation of their territorial and cultural integrity. In recent years, for example, anthropologists have submitted evidence in support of claims for the acquisition or protection of territory by indigenous minority groups in larger nation-states, such as the Aborigines of Australia, the Sami of Norway and the North American Indians (International Work Group for Indigenous Affairs, 1983).

In the course of serving goals of this kind, policy researchers have often been drawn into encounters with opposing parties, such as developers and administrators, who operate on the basis of their own valued goals. Despite this potential for conflict, policy researchers have adopted these value positions primarily through the moral influence of the members of the social groups among which they conduct their investigations. For anthropologists, these influences arise from their own growing identification with the community in which they have chosen to work (Saberwal and Henry, 1969; Wintrob, 1969, p. 70; Willner, 1980, p. 80; Whisson, 1981, p. 75).

The same argument could apply in other situations where researchers are expected to be responsive to the problems and priorities of commercial, governmental and other organizations which provide the funds and opportunities for social research. Apart from the purely economic constraints which funding corporations may exert on applied social researchers, the personnel attached to these organizations may also be present within the researcher's field of operations, such as government administrators or managers and supervisors in industry. The question of whether the researcher owes these people a similar obligation and trust has been raised by some anthropologists (Colson, 1976, p. 266; Whisson, 1981, p. 77).

In certain research contexts, the funding organization and the subject (target) population may also be involved in a formal contractual relationship with each other, such as that between managers and employees in an industrial concern. In these contexts, applied researchers enter, willingly or otherwise, into a moral and transactional relationship both with the client funding organization and with the subject population in which they conduct their investigations. Special difficulties are likely to arise when the influences and pressures originating from subjects and clients run counter to each other or are contradictory. The nature of the relationship between subjects and the client organization may also affect the researcher's role and value position, as will any change in this relationship.

The various pressures operating in these situations arise mainly because research information enjoys the status of a strategic resource which can be applied to support the moral or financial standpoints and policies of the different parties. The evidence of North American anthropologists pertaining to the alleged cultural integrity of a particular Indian group may, for example, help to ensure that the group qualifies for federal aid, land grants and so on.

The strategic value of the knowledge and expertise of applied social scientists has also been apparent to governments, private corporations and defence organizations. During the Second World War, for instance, anthropologists applied concepts of culture and national character to assist war-making agencies in cultivating allies and predicting enemy initiatives (Mead and Metraux, 1965, p. 119). In more recent times, the South African Defence Force has employed the services of ethnologists to assist in maintaining relations with indigenous populations in guerrilla war zones in Southern Africa. Mead and Metraux note that military applications of anthropological methods can be destructive, underlining the need for social scientists and policy researchers to consider carefully their value position in each particular advocacy situation, in view of the likely threats and dangers which such involvement could imply for the future viability of their profession.

Since most policy research is likely to involve the adoption of some kind of value position or goal, irrespective of its apparent defensibility, it is essential that social analysts lay out their values and orientations at the outset and clarify how they are derived (Kelman and Warwick, 1978). This principle of value accountability on the part of policy researchers is particularly relevant in the South African context, a society in which the values and goals of different groups are strongly contested. The present discussion will present a brief review of policy studies in that country, followed by an analysis of the (changing) value orientations of the applied researcher in one sector, namely, the gold-mining industry.

Applied Research in South Africa

In the contemporary South African context, social researchers have found it difficult to avoid direct alignment with one or other political interest group in a society characterized by marked racial and class divisions. In this context also, research information is regarded as a strategic resource by different interest groups.

Policy researchers with academic training in the social sciences can be found working in a variety of different settings, each associated with a particular set of social, political, or economic interests which are being played out in a wider national setting. Social researchers have frequently submitted evidence to, or served on, various governmental commissions into education and labour relations, among others. The findings of social research have also played a role in South Africa's foreign relations. A recent survey of black worker attitudes to foreign investment in South Africa, for example, was valuable in supporting the policy of constructive engagement on the part of countries such as Britain (Schlemmer, 1984).

Within industry, the strategy of trade unions has often been guided by social scientists who are active supporters of the labour movement. In some instances, these researchers have also conducted strategic investigations of behalf of black trade unions.

Recently, for example, the black National Union of Mineworkers in South Africa commissioned members of the University of Witwatersrand to investigate work practices in the gold mines and identify areas in which statutory job reservation had allegedly broken down. The aim was to strengthen the union's stance regarding safety practices in the mines and support the advancement of its members into white-held jobs (Leger, 1985).

Industry managers, for their part, have often made use of the services of professional consultants to assist in improving communications, productivity and so on. Policy researchers have conducted surveys of worker opinions in an effort to enhance the image of private enterprise in South Africa (Nasser, 1985). A few of the larger employers have also set up private research establishments to assist in improving market penetration of products, or for reducing conflict in the enterprise, and so on.

The present discussion is aimed at presenting the author's personal interpretation of aspects of applied social research in one such establishment, namely, the Research Organization of the Chamber of Mines. An attempt will be made to outline the different value orientations of researcher, employer and subject and the kind of influence imposed on the researcher by the employer organization and by the subjects of research (in this case, black mineworkers). The discussion will describe how the researcher's value orientations in conflict studies have been influenced by employer and subject alike and how these value orientations have shifted in response to changing economic and political developments in the industry.

The Research Context: the South African Gold-Mining Industry

In 1985 the South African gold-mining industry employed more than 500,000 people, of whom the bulk (over 450,000) were black. The industry itself is highly labour-intensive, with most employees performing unskilled or semi-skilled work in the underground excavations. A particular pattern of labour utilization has become associated with the industry, namely, the employment of black migrant workers drawn from various territories in Southern Africa, and the accommodation of these workers in barrack-type hostels adjoining each mine shaft.

Within this setting, various social and political problems have been evident, particularly the incidence of violent conflict. At the same time, the environmental hazards and difficulties of deep-level mining in hard rock conditions pose further problems, particularly for the future of the industry, which is obliged to locate and remove gold at increasingly greater depths if it is to survive.

For these reasons, the industry has established a large research establishment funded by the six major mining corporations and administered by the Chamber of Mines. Approximately six hundred people are employed directly by the Research Organization, which operates with an annual budget of roughly R38 million (approximately $17 million in 1985). The bulk of the organization's work is devoted to technological research for deep-level mining and the improvement of the underground environment, but some funds are also diverted to the resolution of 'human' problems, particularly those associated with the employment and accommodation of black migrant workers. The responsibility for such research is carried mainly by the Human Resources Laboratory (HRL), which employs about thirty graduates in the social sciences and operated with a budget of R1·2 million in 1985.

The laboratory's present scope can be traced back to an expansion phase after the industry experienced a sudden withdrawal of labour supplies from Malawi and widespread labour unrest in 1974. In an effort to identify and resolve the causes of mine conflict, and to address the related manpower and productivity problems of the industry, the laboratory's budget and staff complement were increased from 1975 onwards. Since that time, the HRL has carried out an annual programme of research which is approved jointly by the six corporations. Apart from this annual research work, the HRL has also conducted occasional (contract) projects into specific problems at the request of individual corporations within the industry.

Phase 1: Defending the Subject in an Asymmetrical Power Situation

The applied research initiated after the expansion of the HRL from 1975 onwards took place within the framework of a particular pattern of labour relations at the gold mines. For most of the industry's history, black migrant employees had not enjoyed the opportunity to associate in trade union organizations. Structures for the representation of employee interests were confined to the domestic hostel barracks context and were modelled on so-called 'tribal' representation on a numerical basis.

Industry management itself operated with supreme authority, employing a style that could be described as paternalistic and benevolent-authoritarian. In this context, black mineworkers resembled a voiceless majority which had developed the reputation for mobilizing on a largely unpredictable basis in spontaneous work strikes and seemingly obscure internal factional clashes (McNamara, 1980).

The incidence of inter-group conflicts, in particular, aroused special concern, and the industry accordingly approved research into this question as part of the annual programme of work. From the employers' point of view, inter-group clashes amongst the workers implied loss of gold production, extensive destruction of mine facilities, injuries and loss of life. From the researcher's point of view (namely, the author), the conflicts deserved attention not only because of their human costs, but also in terms of their implications for worker solidarity in the industry.

The conflicts themselves were ascribed by management to internal 'tribal' prejudices and alcohol abuse. The researcher believed, on the other hand, that it was necessary to examine the conflicts in question against the background of institutional life in mine hostels, and the related social problems present in these settings.

Accordingly, the author and a black colleague conducted an anthropological investigation into everyday life in a mine hostel in 1976, focusing on leisure-time activities and social relationships among mineworkers. In an effort to gain the acceptance and support of these employees, the researcher had to 'take sides'.

This need arose because the subjects of the study, namely, the 4,000 black residents of the hostel, lived daily under the strict discipline of white mine management, which was seen by them to represent a particular ideology of control. The researcher had to demonstrate, on the one hand, that he was not on the side of management and, on the other, that he could accept blacks as equals in their own social environment. These value orientations of the researcher were put to the test in various ways. For example, when the author first visited the hostel and entered the beerhall, he was offered to partake of the beer being consumed by patrons, partly to assess his readiness to drink together with residents. He was also challenged on the objectives and likely outcome of the research project for the daily lives and problems of hostel residents. Finally, some residents aired a variety of critical views which seemed intended to gauge the researcher's own standpoint and values. The following is an extract from such a set of critical remarks delivered by an experienced and educated employee, while seated with the author at an open-air beerhall table and surrounded by other patrons:

> Most people here will tell you they are happy with living and working conditions, but they are frightened . . . I will tell you what we think. We dig the gold out for whites, not for ourselves. We are like soldiers underground but the white men call us 'boys' . . . In the hostel . . . there is nothing to do but drink . . . Tribal dancing bores me, and I don't want to garden for whites . . . I can't eat this food. I usually buy something from the local store, but it's not enough . . . the *indunas* [tribal counsellors] are illiterate. I can't communicate with them.

Through encounters of this kind, the anthropologist was obliged to clarify his value orientation and 'mission' for the benefit of the subjects of research. These experiences had the effect of encouraging the development of an employee orientation in subsequent project work, as will be discussed later.

The establishment of empathy with hostel residents, however, was not sufficient for the development and maintenance of adequate rapport, or for obtaining information on the social networks of migrant workers. The mere presence of a white researcher in a black hostel setting generated tensions and posed the danger of further aggravating the lack of personal privacy characteristic of such 'total institutions'. The research method employed, however, assisted in resolving this problem to some extent, namely, the use of still photography to record social events, particularly the composition of drinking groups in the beerhall. The method aroused the interest of residents, who were later supplied with free photographs in interview settings.

It was clear, therefore, that the research process had been facilitated mainly by the development of a transactional relationship with the subjects of research. This transactional element was evident also in other ways and arose because the research was conducted in the context of certain local political and developmental problems. For example, individual workers sometimes put pressure on the anthropologist to assist them in finding better jobs, not unlike that reported by Gutkind (1969) in West African urban areas in the 1960s. One particular group of workers at the South African gold mine had experienced a reduction in their number in the aftermath of a violent clash with another group. They believed as a result that their future employment status at the mine was in jeopardy, and cultivated relations with the researcher in the hope that he would submit a positive report on their status.

In another instance, a clerical employee, whose own linguistic identity was in the minority among the other clerks, was given the responsibility by hostel management of providing assistance to the anthropologist and his black research colleague. The clerk quickly took this opportunity to strengthen his own position and status in the hostel by accompanying the researchers in walks around the hostel and holding an umbrella over the head of the black researcher.

On the conclusion of this piece of research into hostel life, the results were conveyed to industry management in reports and presentations, and an effort was made to repudiate conventional stereotypes regarding inter-group conflict among workers. The conflict was attributed mainly to the high turnover of migratory labour and the communal tensions of hostel life, and suggestions were made on this basis. (For details of the findings of this research, see McNamara, 1980.)

In subsequent years the industry did take steps to improve hostel conditions and reduce excessive employee turnover, but these measures were employed mainly for other reasons. The reforms in living conditions were part of a policy of attracting and retaining recruits drawn from within South African territory, as opposed to those drawn from neighbouring countries. The reduction of labour turnover, for its part, was effected to improve productivity in the industry and develop a core of career-oriented black mineworkers.

The experiences of the applied researcher in hostel fieldwork continued to guide his basic value orientation in subsequent project work. In 1979 the researcher took part in a team investigation, at the request of one mining corporation, to uncover the origins of a work strike at a newly established gold mine. The strike had originally been ascribed by mine management to 'outside agitation' on the part of certain unemployed, non-mining blacks who had been seen entering the hostel prior to the eruption of the strike. The event itself was described as a 'strike without grievances' in the local press, partly because the mine concerned boasted the most up-to-date accommodation and recreation facilities available in the industry at that time.

The research team and the corporation's senior management, however, believed that it was necessary first to investigate the likelihood of genuine grievances underlying the strike. The team set out to probe beyond the so-called agitation thesis and identify worker grievances in a strike which had involved more than a thousand mineworkers.

In the course of the investigation, the research team uncovered a variety of grievances which stemmed mainly from the fact that the mine had been brought into production well ahead of its planned schedule. This change implied that the construction of social amenities was not completed in time to accommodate the influx of new workers recruited to make up the production workforce. The result was a shortage of beds and meals, as well as temporary deficiencies in other services. The final report was accepted by the relevant corporation's management, and some improvements were effected at the mine concerned.

This same corporation had for some time been devoted to the improvement of the quality of life of its black employees and was involved in the implementation of hostel reforms designed to provide greater attention to the individual resident. Accordingly, a new scheme for the decentralization of food services was implemented. Later, however, black employees at one mine destroyed several of the new dining halls and related equipment. The HRL was given the task of establishing why these reforms were not accepted. The resulting investigation (conducted in 1978) revealed that there were several administrative problems in the new scheme which had not been resolved, resulting in delays in the replenishment of food supplies for waiting workers and cold food for late shift workers. These anomalies were later rectified.

In these and several other similar investigations of conflict between management and employees at mines, the HRL's role could be described as the provision of communication between two parties in an industrial relationship which otherwise lacked an effective formal mechanism for conveying or negotiating issues and problems. In view of the fact that the mining industry at the time was structured on a paternalistic basis, with strong management authority, the laboratory's role inevitably took the form of an employee-oriented consultancy. To some extent, this role orientation was accepted by industry management, who were anxious to obtain a meaningful and accurate perspective on their employees' attitudes.

Investigations of the kind described above represent examples of the first, extended phase of the HRL's applied policy research on conflict resolution in the industry. Since 1982, however, important changes have taken place in labour relations in the industry, resulting in certain subtle but identifiable changes in the orientation and goals of the applied social researcher.

Phase 2: Supporting the Employer in a Changing Economic and Political Environment

In 1981 the recommendations of the Wiehahn Commission into labour relations in the mining industry were published, and trade union activity on mines began in earnest in 1982. A variety of unions sought access to the industry for recruiting purposes, but one, the National Union of Mineworkers (NUM), enjoyed the most success. A recognition agreement was signed between the union and the Chamber of Mines in mid-1983, and the NUM took part that year in the first wage negotiations by a black trade union in the hundred-year history of the industry.

These developments signalled a change in power relations in the industry which received dramatic expression in the first legal strike by the NUM late the next year (1984). By 1985 the NUM's claimed membership was 110,000, or 25 per cent of the industry's workforce.

Apart from the emergence of black trade unionism at the mines, economic recession had taken place in South Africa, and there were retrenchments in industry, especially in the early 1980s. Although mining interests remained relatively unaffected by the recession because the gold price was set in dollars, industry management remained conscious of the need to keep costs down. The industry also began to adopt an increasingly critical attitude to the research programme which it had sponsored over the years. Not only had the industrial environment started to pose new challenges in the form of organized labour action, but decision-makers began to demand more tangible results from research.

These developments placed new pressures on applied social research, with industry management seeking strategic support in an environment of perceived new threats and challenges. Some research now became oriented to strategic problems in labour relations, such as the development of communications policies to minimize the likelihood of strikes on mines. In 1983, for example, the industry requested that the HRL conduct an evaluation of black employees' responses to certain video productions aimed at explaining economic realities in mining and underlining for these employees the value of having a job.

Another important area of strategic communications in which the HRL became involved consisted of the provision of guidelines and materials for conveying changes in formal service conditions to employees. In 1984 South African industries were obliged to introduce a new taxation procedure according to which all employees, irrespective of race, would be taxed on the basis of the same scales and principles. The mining industry and other industries also were concerned that workers and unions would take up political issues in the workplace, and the HRL was approached to develop a comprehensive strategy and appropriate briefing materials for conveying this change clearly to black mine employees.

These various requests from industry management signalled a shift in applied policy research in which new influences were placed on researchers to address management problems more directly, particularly in the context of changes in power relations in the industry heralded by the advent of black unions. The researcher became obliged to adjust his own value orientation in an effort to maintain credibility and in the interests of continuing to influence employment policies in the longer term.

One aim in this respect has been to facilitate the transition to industrial democracy by encouraging management to recognize the reality of the new trade unions. For example, a survey of black employees' attitudes to trade unions was carried out at one mine in 1985. Although there was an unofficial union presence at the mine, some union members believed that the union had no objection to the survey because it constituted a 'consciousness-raising' exercise. The results of the survey indicated the need for management to compete effectively with the trade unions in regaining the attention and loyalty of employees.

By mid-1985 the nature and scope of applied research into industrial relations issues had not yet been fully clarified. The NUM, however, had already expressed interest in the work of the Research Organization and requested access to findings dealing with health and safety at the mines (Leger, 1985).

The likely future role of the HRL depends to a large extent on the way in which the question of access to research information is resolved. Should the union obtain access, subsequent research could play a mediatory role between both parties in the industrial relationship. If the union is not successful in gaining access, there is the danger that it may advise its members to withdraw from participation in research. The role of the HRL could thus become heavily restricted in future with respect to studies involving these employees.

Conclusions

This chapter has attempted to demonstrate the importance of the social, political and economic context in influencing the role and orientation of applied social research. This influence is particularly evident in the South African setting, a society characterized by powerful racial, political and economic cleavages.

Referring to South Africa, Heribert Adam suggests that few sociologists would claim objectivity or neutrality in a polarizing conflict which affects them directly (Adam, 1981, p. 122). His observation seems to be borne out in the context of applied social research at the South African gold mines, where the social researcher's value orientation has been influenced by the nature of the power situation in industry and by changes in that situation.

Before the advent of black trade unions in mining, the anthropologist had developed an employee orientation and provided an indirect channel of communication between management and black employee. Once these employees began to articulate their own demands through formal representative structures, the employer began to face new economic and political threats and placed increased pressures on researchers to provide strategic support for management.

The dilemma for applied researchers in this changing context lay in the fact that an opportunity was presented to exert a substantial influence on policy, but within the narrow terms and constraints of the employer's own strategic goals. Whereas the earlier, subject-oriented period of research activity had not been constrained in this way, it nevertheless remained relatively weak and remote in terms of its potential application to labour policy as such. These experiences indicate that, for applied policy research to succeed, it is necessary for researchers to adjust their own goals to accommodate the perspectives of the employer or client in the interests of maintaining a longer-term influence over policies and decisions.

These problems in the role orientation of applied policy researchers do not appear to be unique, although they may be more apparent when policy researchers are directly employed by the organization providing funding for research. The practical realities confronting applied researchers in this context underline the need for these researchers to clarify their own goals and values and weigh up the adjustments made against the eventual outcomes of such research. This approach would seem to be most appropriate, in view of the fact that the contemporary practice of applied policy research is characterized by the 'absence of an accepted formulation for the scientific utilization of . . . knowledge' (Zuniga, 1975, p. 99).

The outcome of applied social research in the mining industry can be described mainly in terms of the enhancement of the quality of life of black mine employees, including contributions to the improvement of hostel accommodation and the reduction of inter-group conflict in these settings. Another example of such work was a project to assist in improving contact between migrant mineworkers and their families in the rural sending areas, by means of speedier communications techniques.

Most of these improvements represented incremental reforms within an established structure of labour utilization, which remained largely unchanged, such as the migratory labour process. The pragmatic goals of applied researchers in this respect reflected their interest in the 'concrete needs of individuals rather than some abstract notion of what is good for society' (Kelman and Warwick, 1978, p. 8).

Some observers, particularly radical sociologists, hold the view that incremental reforms merely serve to blunt the revolutionary consciousness of subject populations (Sandbrook and Cohen, 1975, p. 7), or regard such improvements merely as means for the modernization of existing systems of domination (Rex, 1981a). A thorough assessment of the historical relationship between reform and revolutionary change is beyond the scope of the present exercise, but it is sufficient to note that the incremental reforms of the 1970s at the mines did not visibly impede the rapid growth of black trade unions, or reduce the general pattern of contemporary strikes in the industry, which took place mainly in the aftermath of improvements, such as the wage increases of the early 1970s.

The primary role of the HRL has been to facilitate reform from within, by orienting industry management to employee needs and problems. An effort has been made in this respect to uncover the views and experiences of black workers who had otherwise been subordinated and rendered invisible and, consequently, dehumanized in a white-dominated society (Gordon, 1977, p. 3). The HRL has also strived to modify management stereotypes regarding the behaviour of black employees, such as white perceptions of the 'causes' of intergroup conflicts among hostel residents and claims of 'agitation' as an explanation for work strikes. In some respects, the HRL could also be said to have made it easier for management to accept the advent of black trade unions at the mines, although such an influence is difficult to demonstrate.

The extent to which the practice of research among mineworkers stimulated their awareness also deserves consideration. More than twenty thousand mineworkers have been interviewed since 1975 on their views regarding work and living conditions in the industry, and in some instances there has been reluctance to allow such interviewing to take place at certain mines on the grounds that it may stimulate worker expectations.

Applied social research in the mining industry is at present in a formative stage involving new adjustments. This fact indicates that the value orientations and goals of applied researchers are constantly adjusting to new challenges and contextual changes. These changes, and their origin, need to be given continuous attention by those involved in policy studies in an effort to develop a broadly accepted formulation for the legitimate and effective implementation of social knowledge.

Postscript – February 1986

Since this chapter was first drafted, there have been a number of political developments in South Africa, particularly the eruption of violent revolts in black townships and the imposition of a state of emergency in many districts. In the mining industry itself, a threatened strike by the black National Union of Mineworkers was averted late in 1985 after a final wage offer by certain mining employers. A feature of the near-strike was the emergence of political issues in union demands, prompted in part by the state of emergency and in part by the state President's threat to expel foreign migrants, who constituted a significant proportion of union membership.

These developments have been viewed with concern by policy researchers within the industry, who expect that the country's spiral of violence may spread to the mining labour force. Such a development could have serious consequences for employer–employee relations already strained by the 'growing pains' of the new industrial democracy at the mines. One important way of minimizing the likelihood or severity of these political tensions in the workplace is to ensure that appropriate reforms are introduced into existing service conditions and human relationships at the mines.

The focus of applied research has accordingly included the execution of regular surveys of black employee opinion towards industrial relations and employment conditions. In these surveys, mineworkers have noted an improvement in relationships with supervisors and managers at some mines, but still profess to mistrust these authority figures in terms of safeguarding employee interests. Their growing knowledge of and trust in black trade unions, however, is clearly evident. Certain problematic service conditions have also been identified, such as the perceived lack of job security and restricted promotional opportunities for black mineworkers.

These various findings have been conveyed to industry management, and proposals have been made for improving employer–employee relations at the mines. Management has been urged to address the question of job security and to adopt a general policy of disclosing, rather than withholding, relevant information to employees as a means of restoring mutual trust. It has also become clear that employers in South Africa need to develop a distinct identity and mission that is independent of existing forces of control if their enterprises are to survive. This broad motivation was illustrated, for example, in the meeting between senior industrial executives and the African National Congress in Lusaka in September 1985.

The direction which research is taking in this changing context indicates the strategic role of applied policy studies in safeguarding industrial relations in a polarized political and social environment for the benefit of both employer and employee. Policy researchers in this context have had to define their role in terms of the vital objective of ensuring that the economic structures of the country survive this difficult period in its history. This continuity of productive industry and jobs is essential, not only to provide employment, but also to finance the process of social reform in South Africa.

References

Adam, H. (1981), 'The vocation of a sociologist in South Africa', in Rex, op. cit., pp. 116–27.

Bermant, G., and Warwick, D. P. (1978), 'The ethics of social intervention: power, freedom and accountability', in Bermant, Warwick and Askelman, op. cit., pp. 377–418.

Bermant, G., Warwick, D. P., and Askelman, H. C. (eds.) (1978), *The Ethics of Social Intervention* (Washington: Hemisphere Publishing Corporation).

Colson, E. (1976), 'Culture and progress', *American Anthropologist*, vol. 78, no. 2, pp. 261–71.

Gordon, R. J. (1977), *Mines, Masters and Migrants* (Johannesburg: Ravan Press).

Gutkind, P. C. W. (1969), 'The social researcher in the context of African national development: reflections on an encounter', in Henry and Saberwal, op. cit., pp. 20–34.

Henry, F., and Saberwal, S. (eds.) (1969), *Stress and Response in Fieldwork* (New York: Holt, Rinehart & Winston).

International Work Group for Indigenous Affairs (IWGIA) (1983), 'Symposium on Anthropology and Indigenous Movements', XIth International Congress of Anthropological and Ethnological Sciences, Vancouver, personal communication.

Kelman, H. C., and Warwick, D. P. (1978), 'The ethics of social intervention: goals, means and consequences', in Bermant, Warwick and Askelman, op. cit., pp. 3–33.

Leadership South Africa (1984), 'Interview: Malcolm Rifkind'. Fourth Quarter, vol. 3, no. 4, pp. 10–16.

Leger, J. (1985), *Towards Safer Underground Gold Mining* (Johannesburg: Department of Sociology, University of the Witwatersrand).

McNamara, J. K. (1980), 'Brothers and workmates: home–friend networks in the social life of black migrant workers in a gold mine hostel', in P. Mayer (ed.), *Black Villagers in an Industrial Society* (Cape Town: Oxford University Press), pp. 305–40.

Mead, M., and Metraux, R. (1965), 'The anthropology of human conflict', in E. B. McNeil (ed.), *The Nature of Human Conflict* (Englewood Cliffs, NJ: Prentice-Hall), pp. 116–38.

Nasser, M. E. (1985), 'Perceptions of free enterprise: the key to continued economic prosperity', *South African Journal of Labour Relations*, vol. 9, no. 1, pp. 26–9.

Rex, J. (1981a), 'Introduction', in Rex, op. cit., pp. 1–26.

Rex, J. (ed.) (1981b) *Apartheid and Social Research* (Paris: UNESCO).

Saberwal, S., and Henry, F. (1969), 'Introduction', in Henry and Saberwal, op. cit., pp. 1–5.

Sandbrook, R., and Cohen, R. (1975), 'Workers and progressive change in underdeveloped countries', in R. Sandbrook and R. Cohen (eds.), *The Development of an African Working Class* (London: Longman), pp. 1–9.

Schlemmer, L. (1984), *Black Worker Attitudes: Political Options, Capitalism and Investment in South Africa* (Durban: Centre for Applied Social Sciences).

Whisson, M. (1981), 'Anthropological research in contemporary South Africa', in Rex, op. cit., pp. 67–83.

Willner, D. (1980), 'For whom the bell tolls: anthropologists advising on public policy', *American Anthropologist*, vol. 82, no. 1, pp. 79–94.

Wintrob, R. (1969), 'An inward focus: a consideration of psychological stress in fieldwork', in Henry and Saberwal, op. cit., pp. 63–76.

Zuniga, R. B. (1975), 'The experimenting society and radical social reform', *American Psychologist*, February, pp. 99–114.

III

Getting the Message Across

Introduction to Part Three

One of the logical and expected end-products of research is the publication of findings. In some instances publication may be limited to a report to the sponsor or customer of the research. In some cases, reports may be initially confidential. Freedom to publish is not usually a problem, although the content of the report and interpretation of findings may be (Orlans, 1967). Conflict between researcher and sponsor, however, may often focus on publication. In this collection, the sponsors of Warwick's research suppressed publication; in Jaeger's case publication was delayed and covertly restricted; while in Wenger's case the relevant policy body made a formal decision to ignore publication. In other words, the dissemination of findings is a common area of tension.

In Part Three, however, it is not intended to explore the problems of publication or dissemination as such, but to discuss the problem faced by researchers whose concern for social issues moves beyond dissemination to the desire to see action based on their findings. In Part Two taking sides in an advocacy role was discussed; in this part, it is the researcher's active promotion of the theoretical validity of his or her findings rather than the position of the target population that is described.

Many researchers may agree with the anthropologist quoted by Benthall (1985) and referred to in the introduction to Part Two, who sees his role as merely to report the facts. However, some have suggested that researchers have a responsibility to disseminate findings as far as possible, out of respect for informants or respondents, to enhance the credibility of the social sciences and to maximize the effect on an élite audience through stimulating consumer pressure (Roberts, 1984). Other social scientists take this commitment further. They agree with Mills (1959) and consider themselves to have a moral or ethical responsibility to exercise the sociological imagination to push for social change and the betterment of the human condition. Hadley and Gupta, whose chapters follow, belong to this school of thought. Findings in the policy field are arguably of more popular interest than those from basic research. The popularization of research findings, however, is frequently beyond the direct control of the researcher, and the dangers of misinterpretation, distortion, or misunderstanding are maximized. More than one social scientist has had grounds to regret public interest in their study (e.g. Platt, 1976; Moore, 1977; Roberts, 1984).

What researcher in the policy area, during the hard days of data collection and analysis, has not harboured fantasies of the impact of his or her findings resulting in positive social change! Unfortunately, as Payne *et al.* (1980) have observed, 'It remains problematic whether policy research actually influences policy making' (p. 148). Wittrock (1985) goes further to suggest that little policy is soundly based on scientific knowledge. Bulmer (1978), apparently endorsing the 'presentation of the facts' stance, comments, 'The task of policy research is to examine . . . alternative means and goals in a value-critical way.' This view reflects the normative attitude, and societal expectations about social researchers are that they will not engage in public controversial policy discussions. However, there are signs that attitudes may be shifting in this regard. Lambiri-Dimaki (1985) has recently argued that social scientists have a 'strategic and responsible role to play in examining values and identifying policy alternatives'. The two chapters in Part Three highlight some of the problems faced by researchers who attempt to play this non-traditional role. Neither Hadley nor Gupta actively sought public debate on the implications of their findings, but both discuss their frustration at the lack of implementation of the results of their research. In both cases, the discussion of the research findings in the wider forum of debate served to undermine rather than reinforce their acceptability to those main-stream policy bodies whose actions their findings brought into question.

References

Benthall, J. (1985), 'Keeping up the flow of overseas work', *Anthropology Today*, vol. 1, no. 2, pp. 1–2.

Bulmer, M. (1978), 'Social science research and policy-making in Britain', in M. Bulmer (ed.), *Social Policy Research* (London: Macmillan), pp. 3–43.

Lambiri-Dimaki, J. (1985), 'The difficult dialogue between producers and users of social science research: some comments on the theme', in H. Nowotny and J. Lambiri-Dimaki (eds.), *The Difficult Dialogue between Producers and Users of Social Research* (Vienna: European Centre for Social Welfare Training and Research) pp. 15–25.

Mills, C. W. (1959), *The Sociological Imagination* (London: Oxford University Press).

Moore, R. (1977), 'Becoming a sociologist in Sparkbrook', in C. Bell and H. Newby (eds.), *Doing Sociological Research* (London: Allen & Unwin), pp. 87–107.

Orlans, H. (1967), 'Ethical problems in the relations of research sponsors and investigators', in G. Sjoberg (ed.), *Ethics, Politics and Social Research* (London: Routledge & Kegan Paul), pp. 142–59.

Payne, G., Dingwall, R., Payne, J., and Carter, M. (1980), 'Sociology and policy research', in G. Payne *et al.*, *Sociology and Social Research* (London: Routledge and Kegan Paul), pp. 142–59.

Platt, J. (1976), *Realities of Social Research: An Empirical Study of British Sociologists* (London: Sussex University Press).

Roberts, H. (1984), 'Putting the show on the road: the dissemination of research findings', in C. Bell and H. Roberts (eds.), *Social Researching: Politics, Problems, Practice* (London: Routledge & Kegan Paul), pp. 199–212.

Wittrock, B. (1985), 'Knowledge and policy: eight models of interaction', in H. Nowotny and J. Lambiri-Dimaki (eds.), *The Difficult Dialogue between Producers and Users of Social Science Research* (Vienna: European Centre for Social Welfare Training and Research), pp. 89–109.

6

Publish and Be Ignored; Proselytize and Be Damned

ROGER HADLEY,
Department of Social Administration, University of Lancaster, England

Abstract
This chapter draws on the personal experience of the writer to examine problems involved in the active dissemination of research findings. Failure to disseminate the policy implications of several projects in which the writer has been involved is explored in terms of four main factors: the nature of customer motivation, the time-lag between the inception and completion of the studies, project succession and the political isolation of the researchers.

In contrast, a more recent project funded by a government department is described in which circumstances combined to make it possible to adopt a more proactive role in disseminating findings. It is concluded from the results of this experience, however, that such involvement may be viewed unfavourably by governmental research customers and may lead them in consequence to be reluctant to enter new contracts with the researcher. If this example can be generalized, the active dissemination of work contracted by more conservative institutions may be a once-off episode in the career of the academic.

Introduction

This chapter is concerned with the relationship between the researcher and the customer of his or her research. I originally proposed to confine examination of this relationship to the context of a government-funded

This chapter was originally presented in a symposium on 'Contract Research and the Problem of Customer Interest' at the XIth International Congress of Anthropological and Ethnological Sciences, Quebec, Canada, August 1983.

study I had recently completed. However, when I came to expand on my abstract I felt that its focus on the minutiae of a particular episode of researcher–customer interaction made it difficult to address more significant aspects of the responsibility of researchers for disseminating the findings of their research, the subject which had led me to contribute to the symposium in the first place. I have therefore decided to take a broader perspective which looks beyond the bounds of a particular research project, includes other customers as well as government and considers responsibilities to other constituencies as well as the customer.

My starting-point is the assumption that researchers working in fields which impinge on social, economic and political issues have a responsibility actively to promote the dissemination and discussion of their findings not only with the customer but also with others for whom they may have relevance. If we accept the centrality of the values of rationality and freedom in our society, then, as Mills (1959) showed so clearly a quarter of a century ago in *The Sociological Imagination*, the academic researcher has a vital role within an increasingly complex world, in helping people understand the operation of social institutions, the power relationships within them and ways in which change may be brought about. Mills spelt out what he saw as the responsibilities of the social scientist for dissemination and education in terms of three target groups or 'types of men':

> To those with power and with awareness of it, he imputes varying measures of responsibility for such structural consequences as he finds by his work to be decisively influenced by their decisions and their lack of decisions.
>
> To those whose actions have such consequences, but who do not seem to be aware of them, he directs whatever he has found out about those consequences. He attempts to educate and then, again, he imputes responsibility.
>
> To those who are regularly without such power and whose awareness is confined to their everyday milieux, he reveals by his work the meaning of structural trends and decisions for these milieux, the ways in which personal troubles are connected with public issues; in the course of these efforts, he states what he has found out concerning the actions of the more powerful.

I accept the desirability of adopting such an approach and want in this chapter to explore some of the problems of putting it into practice. A distinction needs to be made at the outset between the tenured and non-tenured researcher. The vulnerability of the latter if he or she pursues a strongly independent line in disseminating his or her findings is evident enough, even at the best of times. Now, with sharp cut-backs in funding and tighter and more specific research contracts, it is greater than ever. Tenured researchers, however, can still, at least in theory, risk the displeasure of customers and others to whom they address their work, and it is to them that I shall confine the present discussion.

My discussion is exploratory and tentative, being based on my personal experience as a researcher over the last seventeen years, in two British universities, holding first a tenured lecturing post and subsequently a professorial appointment. I have two main themes. The first concerns my first thirteen years as an academic researcher in which I believe I and my academic colleagues, collaborating on a number of different projects, failed to disseminate our findings effectively, in the various relevant constituencies involved. The second deals with the experience of becoming actively engaged in dialogue with at least two of Mills's three target groups and the consequences of such involvement.

On Not Being Heard

During the period 1966–78, together with a number of different colleagues, I undertook five separate research projects. The projects covered a wide range of subjects but all concerned social services institutions and all included dimensions concerned with organizational structure and staff and/or user participation in decision-making. All included field research within the organizations involved. In sequence, the topics were student conflict at the London School of Economics in 1967; the effectiveness of a voluntary organization recruiting and allocating volunteers to visit and help old people; a nursing experiment in a psychiatric hospital; the use of ancillaries in a social services department; and retired people as volunteers. The customers were a university, a government department (for two projects), a regional hospital board and a national intermediary body promoting the use of volunteers.

Each study concluded with a report to the customer and/or the publication of a book or articles (Blackstone *et al.*, 1967; Hadley, Pharoah and Tate, 1972; Hadley and Webb, 1974a, 1974b, 1975; Hadley, Webb and Farrell, 1975; Webb and Hadley, 1975; Hadley and Scott, 1980). I and my co-researchers on each project were keen that our work should make an impact on policy and practice. Our publications emphasized what we believed to be the implications of our findings. We welcomed opportunities to discuss the research with our customers and other interested people. We sought to widen our audience by writing popular versions of our findings for newspapers and journals. Customer response to our work was invariably polite and sometimes complimentary. But in the end there was very little evidence that it engaged the minds of those in our target groups or measurably affected the policies of the organizations concerned.

Assuming I am correct and our work failed to make much impact, why was this the case? In retrospect I think four factors are of particular importance in explaining this: customer motivation for funding the research; the time-lag between project inception and report publication; project succession; and the isolation of the researcher.

Customer Motivation

The customer's motives for commissioning a research project may not necessarily be directly related to an interest in the topic concerned. For example, sponsoring research may be seen in some organizations as a desirable activity because it enhances the image of the organization, or a study may be backed as a part of internal political manoeuvrings, perhaps to provide reasons for delaying a decision or as means of heading off a conflict. Whatever the reasons, however, if the customer did not have an active interest in the subject of the research at its outset it would scarcely be surprising if he or she remained uninterested at its conclusion. There were probably elements of such indirect motives for backing research in four of the five projects I have described here. The problems facing the researchers in stimulating a meaningful dialogue with the customers, therefore, were likely to be all the greater.

Time-Lag

All social research is likely to run into problems created by the time-lag between initiation and completion. The context in which the research is carried out may change; the customer's interest in the project (assuming it existed in the first place) may have shifted, and it may no longer seem relevant or may be relevant in a way that is now unwelcome.

The time-lag in each of the pieces of work in which I was involved was between two and four years, long enough in three of the five projects to see substantial changes in the political or organizational context concerned. The student movement in Britain had sailed through the storms of 1968 to quieter waters beyond by the time our report of the upheavals of 1967 appeared. The voluntary organization we began to study in 1971 had got through three different directors and adopted substantial changes in practice by the appearance of our report in 1974. The hospital board that commissioned our study of psychiatric nursing had altered related policies and practice before our study was complete.

Project Succession
The researcher's interests and outlook may also change and move on. While wanting to promote the findings of one's current research project, both the need to nurture one's academic career and the intrinsic attraction of setting off on the next voyage of discovery mean that one is likely to be actively engaged in identifying and seeking funds for new research well before the current inquiry is completed. A dissemination phase, apart from the time needed to produce a report, is seldom built into project programming, and the studies considered here were no exception.

Political Isolation of the Researcher
While the independence of tenured researchers is their strength, it can also be a source of weakness. They have no lasting place in the organization or institution they study and, once their work is complete and they have withdrawn, can be quickly forgotten. If the findings of their research are not acceptable they can be labelled as unrealistic, the product of the academic gadfly who can recommend change and then depart without having to live with its consequences. Only if researchers have already established a considerable reputation in their own right is their influence likely to be more durable. The researchers responsible for the studies described in this chapter were, in the main, still in the earlier stages of their academic careers and without this advantage.

The consequence of these factors, it would seem, is that in spite of adhering in principle to the notion of the wider responsibilities of the social scientist, in practice the process of disseminating research findings can all too easily become largely ritualistic in character. We do our duty by presenting a report to the customer and letting off a few salvoes of findings in the general direction of other publics. But serious dialogue is only really expected with other academic colleagues, and meaningful consequences in terms of our academic careers.

On Being Heard

Until a few years ago this ritual had been my predominant experience of the process of disseminating research. However, the most recent project which I have undertaken quite unexpectedly offered opportunities for serious dialogue both with those who had power in the field concerned and with some of those affected by the way in which that power was used. The situation offered the opportunity to take on the proactive role urged by Mills, which I felt by this time I wanted to adopt. As a case study, an account of the project may be of some value in helping to identify both the conditions which may facilitate this process and some of the consequences which can follow from assuming an interventionist stance.

The Research Project Outlined

The research project concerned involved the pilot study of an innovation in decentralized social welfare services. In Britain these services, covering care of the elderly, the physically and mentally handicapped and chronically sick, and children at risk, are organized by local authority social services departments. Typically, these are centralized organizations, divided into specialized sections covering field, domiciliary, day and residential services and with separate specialisms by client groups within the last two.

In the early 1970s research which I had undertaken in a voluntary organization alerted me to the negative consequences of this kind of organizational structure for attempts to interweave voluntary and statutory welfare, a view which was confirmed by subsequent membership of a national committee considering the role of voluntary organizations over the country as a whole. In 1978 I learned of a social services team which, against the general trend, was experimenting with a very decentralized system of organization and seeking to build close ties with its local community. This team located, in the small Yorkshire town of Normanton, had deployed staff in small neighbourhoods or patches covering populations between five and eight thousand; it had integrated different staff – social workers, home helps, ancillaries and street wardens – in teams serving these patches; and it had encouraged all workers to adopt flexible roles, responding to the demands of the situation rather than to the guidelines of their job descriptions.

I obtained a grant from the Department of Health and Social Security (DHSS), the central government department with an overall brief for the welfare services, to carry out a pilot study of the team. The research, contracted with the DHSS, was to focus on two principal aims:

> first, to establish if a distinctive system of community oriented services had been set up in Normanton embodying operational features of the kind claimed for it by its originator;

second, assuming sufficient promise was indicated in the first part of the research, to devise investigative tools suitable for application in a larger scale project which would be used to assess the relative effectiveness of community oriented and traditionally organized services.

The field study was begun in January 1979 and completed in July 1980. The final report was submitted to the DHSS in October 1982 and subsequently revised and published in book form (Hadley and McGrath, 1984).

The Widening Debate

Soon after the field research was started I found myself faced with the opportunity to engage in a wider field of research and debate on the issue of community-based social services. When the DHSS research grant was reported in the social services press, a number of other area social services teams contacted me to say they too were organized on community-oriented lines. It seemed that what I had taken to be an isolated case of pioneering might in fact be part of a new trend in organization, taking place in several different parts of the country at once, with the principal impetus coming from field level rather than management. To try to get a fuller picture of these developments, together with the senior research officer recruited for the Normanton project, Dr Morag McGrath, I convened a small conference of representatives of seven teams claiming to operate locally based, community-oriented systems of service delivery. At this conference it quickly became apparent that, although the organizational structures of the teams differed, they were all feeling their way towards similar goals – stressing preventive rather than reactive methods, the local deployment of staff and close collaboration with the communities in which they were sited.

The effect on members of the teams at the conference of discovering that they were not working on their own and that there were other teams attempting to make the same kind of change was cathartic. There was a strong feeling that the common approach being developed by the teams should be shared more widely. The conference organizers suggested that they should write an article about the seven schemes for the social services press and it was also decided that all the teams would contribute a chapter to a book describing their work in more detail. The article was published in the autumn of 1979 and in turn generated more information about community-based schemes and attracted a small flood of inquiries (Hadley and McGrath, 1979). To cope with these we used a small part of our research funds to produce an occasional bulletin which listed all the community-based teams on which we had information, as well as relevant research and publications (Hadley and McGrath, 1980a).

The result of these initiatives was that by the end of 1980 we had identified and to some extent created a new constituency for the research, consisting of members of other social services teams. This process itself contributed to the next stage in engagement, involvement in a political debate.

The Political Dimension

The opportunity to become directly involved in political dialogue with the research customer, and with others holding power to affect service organization, was related to the change of government in Britain which took place in 1979. Following five years of Labour government the Conservatives were returned to power with a mandate, as they saw it, to cut back on government spending. In the first months of the new administration there seemed to be a policy vacuum in the social services as a result of these political changes. To try to stimulate new thinking, an independent research body, the Policy Studies Institute, organized a seminar for politicians, academics and service providers focusing on new directions in the welfare services. I was invited to give a paper on the development of decentralized social services teams.

By this time, although we were little more than halfway through our field research in Normanton, I was sufficiently convinced of the promise of community-based services to feel that a strong case for further research and development could be made (Hadley, 1981). My paper eventually found its way to the desk of the new Secretary of State for Social Services, Patrick Jenkin. The notion of locally based social services teams, serving a neighbourhood or patch, fitted closely with his own ideas for developing closer ties between statutory and voluntary action. He publicly backed discussion of this approach at a specially convened seminar to hear reports of the ongoing research at Normanton and on a related project (Jenkin, 1983), referred positively to patch systems in a government paper on community care and spoke at the press launch of our book on the seven community-based teams who had attended the original 1979 conference (Hadley and McGrath, 1980b). My feelings about this intervention by a member of the government were mixed. On the one hand, it undoubtedly facilitated the dissemination of our work. On the other, it created the risk that our research would be associated with a particular political perspective (which I did not happen to share) and would not be evaluated on its merits.

The prominence given to the issue of community-based social services by the secretary of state almost certainly was influential in leading to the invitation I received at the end of 1980 to serve on a new government-backed national committee set up, under the chairmanship of Peter Barclay, to consider the role and tasks of social workers.

These various developments offered me the opportunity not only to debate the relevance of the Normanton research in a much wider constituency but to share in shaping recommendations on broader policy issues which might in turn affect the movement towards community-based services. However, while committees of inquiry such as the Barclay Committee are often very influential, their methods of collecting evidence and reaching conclusions usually differ substantially from those of academic research. Although some short-term research may be commissioned by such committees, most of the evidence they use is likely to be in the form of written or oral submissions from interested individuals and organizations. This is weighed in debate and, taken together with the opinions and experience of committee members and their assessment of what is politically feasible, forms the basis of their recommendations.

Academics sitting on these committees will often find that the matters at issue soon extend far beyond the areas of their special knowledge and expertise, and that, if they want to share in shaping the wider recommendations of the committee, they too must be prepared to make judgements about preferred ends and means on evidence which is much less substantial than what they would require in their professional work. This was the position I found myself in as a member of the Barclay Committee. On the central question of the future orientation of social work some of the evidence submitted favoured the development of a much stronger community focus. Other evidence maintained the case for a more specialist and, by implication, centralized approach. At that time little relevant research on the comparative effectiveness of the alternatives had been published. The committee's proposals in this area were made largely on the basis of impressionistic evidence and hunch.

The majority of the committee opted for a compromise between the two perspectives, but one that was tilted more towards a community orientation (Barclay, 1982, ch. 13). Their proposals in this area were, in my view, so ill thought out and woolly that they would be open to almost any kind of interpretation that policy-makers and practitioners wished to put on them. As an academic I could not *prove* the case for a more radical form of community social work; but on the evidence of the limited research I had already undertaken and of contacts with other developments in the field, my *judgement* was that it was a much stronger one. Although it meant going beyond argument based on academic evidence alone, I felt the proposals of the majority on this issue should not be left unchallenged. Together with two other committee members, I decided to write a note of dissent to this part of the report of the committee, pressing for more clear-cut recommendations for the adoption of locally based social services (Brown, Hadley and White, 1982). This served to bring the issue still more into the public eye but also inevitably opened my commitment to this policy to the charge that it derived from ideological grounds at least as much as from 'scientific' inquiry.

Discussion

This research project, therefore, provided in ample measure the opportunity to engage the target constituencies defined by Mills, including at least some of those who are without power but who are affected by the policies at issue. Whether my interventions made any difference to these policies is another matter which I do not intend to attempt to address here. The points we are concerned with in the context of this chapter are whether anything can be learned from this experience about the factors which can work to favour the engagement of the researcher and what consequences such engagement may have for his or her future career as a researcher.

On the first question, it is interesting that, in each of the four factors identified in the first part of this chapter as inhibiting the influence of the researcher, the reverse situation applied. Thus, the customer, in the shape of the political head of the department concerned, became very interested in the substance of the research and encouraged me to feed in findings from the study while it was in progress; the problem of time-lag was avoided because interim results were available from the project; the issue of project succession did not arise as I felt the debate on the findings of the current study should take priority over new work; finally, I was not isolated from the constituencies I wished to engage because the research was perceived as relevant to the interests of several of them.

These factors combine the fortuitous, such as the interest of the then secretary of state, and the deliberate choice of strategy of the researcher. It would be pointless to try to generalize from a single case study, but there are a number of indications of tactics which might profitably be explored in examining the experience of other researchers, including planning for interim reports during the life of a project, the deliberate cultivation of relationships with target constituencies at an early stage in the research, and setting aside time in the research programme for the dissemination of findings.

Assuming such tactics are successful, and the researcher is able to communicate his or her findings and their implication fully to the relevant constituencies, is his or her own standing likely to be affected in the process? In so far as the customer expects researchers to be value-free in this approach, or at least to keep their reports strictly to their technical task and remain silent on their own views about the wider implications of the research, then the proactive role may cause both confusion and disapproval.

I experienced both as a result of my involvement in the debate on the wider relevance of community-based services. By the time our report on the Normanton research was submitted to the DHSS the secretary of state who had expressed strong interest in it had moved to another post and had been replaced by a minister with much less interest in the issues concerned. The customer's view, therefore, was represented solely by civil servants and an advisory committee of academics and practitioners. Such was apparently the effect of the developments which intervened between the commissioning of the research and its completion that the committee appeared to have forgotten the original terms of the contract with the researcher and expected a more wide-ranging and definitive study than I had agreed to undertake.

As I have already noted, my contract was to carry out a pilot inquiry as a possible preliminary to further research. The letter sent to me on behalf of the committee, commenting on our findings, said that its 'overall view was that the report has not really established that a "patch" system was necessarily superior to more traditional arrangements. The matter remains non-proven. It was felt that this was a pity since the study was likely to be regarded as the most definitive on the subject for some time' (DHSS, 1982). Was this criticism for failing to complete a task which was not part of the contract – and which, indeed, was well beyond the scope of any pilot inquiry – some kind of collective Freudian slip in which the committee was getting at the researcher for not having substantiated the wider hopes he had expressed in other contexts of community-based services in the future, or just a poor collective memory?

In any case it became apparent that, no matter how objective the research report we had produced, I was by this time firmly labelled as having adopted a particular perspective and in consequence would not be an appropriate person to pursue further the next logical stage of the research programme we had originally sketched out, the more comprehensive comparison of community-based and conventionally organized services. This development hardly came as a surprise to me, for if the emerging commitment of the researcher to a particular course of action is not matched by similar changes in the views of the customer, it is almost inevitable that the two should part. But if this experience is generalized and repeated wherever the proactive researcher identifies him- or herself then it may seem to imply a poor future for the role of social scientists as 'carriers of reason'. Given the innate conservatism of many of our key social institutions and the desire of the powerful to protect their interests, active and effective engagement with the relevant constituencies concerned in research carried out on behalf of such institutions can be expected to be a once-off episode in the career of the researcher.

The consequences of this process, however, need not be merely negative. My own subsequent experience has suggested that, while research backed by conventional interests may be blocked off, new opportunities can become apparent in constituencies identified by the researcher in the course of his or her work which are more open to change. Such constituencies are unlikely to be located in the most powerful organizational settings in our society, but their relevance to the development of rationality and freedom may nevertheless be considerable. Their openness to the challenge of new ideas and their readiness to adapt tend to make them the foci of interest and sources of influence far beyond their own boundaries. For the same reasons they are often ready to welcome the involvement of researchers who conceive their responsibilities in the proactive terms discussed in this chapter.

Neverthless, to be confined in this fashion to work in the more radical and innovatory sectors of our society must inevitably be a compromise for the academic who is seeking to understand the whole. Yet one is led to the conclusion that in politically sensitive areas, when the issue of promoting the conclusions of research have to be faced, the choice is likely to be between passivity and acceptability, on the one hand, and proactive criticism and marginalization, on the other.

References

Barclay, P. (Chairman) (1982), *Social Workers: Their Role and Tasks* (London: Bedford Square Press).

Blackstone, T., Gales, K., Hadley, R., and Lewis, W. (1970), *Students in Conflict: The LSE in 1967* (London: Weidenfeld & Nicolson).

Brown, P., Hadley, R., and White, K. (1982), 'A case for neighbourhood social work and social services', in Barclay, op. cit., Appendix A.

DHSS (1982), Letter from office of Chief Scientist, 1 December.

Hadley, R. (1981), 'Social services departments and the community', in E. M. Goldberg and S. Hatch (eds.), *A New Look at the Personal Social Services* (London: Policy Studies Institute).

Hadley, R., and McGrath, M. (1979), 'Patch based social services', *Community Care*, no. 285, 11 October, pp. 16–18.

Hadley, R. and McGrath, M. (eds.) (1980a), *Patch Based Social Services Teams, Bulletin No. 1 and No. 2* (Lancaster University: Department of Social Administration), January and December.

Hadley, R., and McGrath, M. (eds.) (1980b), *Going Local: Neighbourhood Social Services* (London: Bedford Square Press).

Hadley, R. and McGrath, M. (1984), *When Social Services Are Local: The Normanton Experience* (London: Allen & Unwin).

Hadley, R., Pharoah, C., and Tate, E. (1972), *The Role of the SEN in the Psychiatric Hospital* (South-West Metropolitan Hospital Board).

Hadley, R., and Scott, M. (1980), *Time to Give? The Retired as Volunteers* (Berkhamsted: The Volunteer Centre).

Hadley, R., and Webb, A. (1974a), *Loneliness, Social Isolation and Old People: Some Implications for Social Policy*, Age Concern specialist report No. 25.

Hadley, R., and Webb, A. (1974b), 'Volunteers with the old', *New Society*, vol. 30, no. 63, pp. 356–7.

Hadley, R., and Webb, A. (1975), 'Vindicating the volunteer', *The Times*, 5 September.

Hadley, R., Webb, A., and Farrell, C. (1975), *Across the Generations: Old People and Young Volunteers* (London: Allen & Unwin).

Jenkin, P. (1983), 'Public systems and social services', in I. Sinclair and D. Thomas (eds.), *Perspectives on Patch* (London: NISW).

Mills, C. W. (1959), *The Sociological Imagination* (London: Oxford University Press), p. 185.

Webb, A., and Hadley, R. (1975), *The Role of the Ancillary Worker in a Social Services Department*, unpublished report to the DHSS.

7

Why Poor People Don't Co-operate: Learning from Traditional Systems

ANIL K. GUPTA,
Centre for Management in Agriculture, Indian Institute of Management, Vastrapur, Ahmedabad, India

Abstract
Development planners and academics have wondered why co-operative organizations set up to serve the rural poor fail to elicit their co-operation. In view of the role co-operatives can play in providing patient and peaceful alternatives to more violent revolutionary alternatives in developing countries, the answer to this question seems central to the developmental debate. Drawing upon the principles for co-operation in traditional organizations, the author identifies lessons for modern organizations. The chapter concludes by demonstrating the politics of policy analysis by taking the example of a recent Indian programme of dairy development through co-operatives. The values of academics who question the ethics of organizational designers are made central to the argument. The importance of involving the poor in generating alternatives for their own development is emphasized. Social scientists, it is stressed, must be accountable to those disadvantaged people whose cause they espouse, lest the solutions become worse than the problem.

This chapter was originally written for a symposium on 'Co-operatives and Rural Development' at the XIth International Congress of Anthropology and Ethnological Sciences, Vancouver, Canada, August 1983. Later, a considerably revised and extended version was presented at the IVth international meeting of the Indian Institute of Management's working group on 'Social Development', held at the Indian Institute of Management, Ahmedabad, January 1984. I acknowledge useful suggestions from the late Professor Ravi Mathai, Manu Shroff, S. Paul, Seetharaman, I. G. Patel, R. Gupta, Baviskar, Betteile, Gangadhar, K. Mathur, Doornbas, Homans Aneja, Bardhan and Maru. Editorial comments of Clare Wenger have not only improved the sharpness of many ideas but have led to considerable redrafting of the paper.

Background

Concern about rural development at national and international levels reflects not so much the sudden emergence of an enlightened élite as the realization that, to sustain the developmental process, a rhetoric of rural development helps to maintain the façade of an optimistic future. If revolutionary alternatives to egalitarian growth are to be avoided or delayed, the discussion of frameworks which can contain conflicts becomes imperative for two reasons. First, growing discontent among the poor may rob the system of the stability which is essential for the élitist growth strategy. Secondly, the possibilities of providing a platform for negotiating conflicts of interest between the rich and the poor may sober the expectations of both parties, leading to a more peaceful and patient search for better alternatives.

Galjart, after reviewing numerous international self-help projects, complains: 'There are almost always people who will not join but it is not clear why' (Galjart, 1982, p. 9). This chapter addresses itself to 'why' and questions the contention that the people who do not co-operate or participate in co-operatives are oblivious of their own developmental potential. It also argues that, while there is a need for training farmers leading to upgrading some of their traditional skills, training to impart advantages of participation or co-operation will serve hardly any purpose because humanity is endowed with a basic instinct of survival that continuously guides the human race to seek what will sustain it. The poor's non-co-operation thus does not stem from their ignorance.

Numerous researchers and practitioners have argued that (1) co-operatives cannot eliminate inequities – in fact they may exacerbate them (Bennet, 1978; McGrath, 1978; Harvey *et al.*, 1979; Baviskar, 1980; Guhan, 1980; Gupta 1981a); (2) success in rural development can be achieved only if *all* groups are fully integrated into, and actively support, the developmental process (Ullrich, 1981); and (3) 'cooperatives are a form of self-help that increases the incomes of the rural poor, but not all poor people are in a condition to help themselves' (McGrath, 1978). If the success of co-operative contribution to rural development has to be measured 'principally by their service to members' so as to protect 'their interest against exploitation by others' (Baviskar, 1980, p. 201) then the question is not whether small members gain as much as the bigger ones or gain in proportion to their contribution, but what the determinants of participation are, with some people taking the lead in formalizing a co-operative structure, sustaining it and strengthening it, while others remain outside or do not co-operate even if they are inside it.

When we conceptualize the simultaneous operations of different classes of farmers and agricultural labourers in different markets (land, labour, product and credit), the incentive or disincentive for various people to co-operate around a particular productive economic activity cannot be worked out in a single-market framework (Gupta, 1981a). One of the greatest incongruities of the current search for the co-operative alternative for rural development is its *single-commodity* or *uni-enterprise* focus. Bennet (1978) has observed that 'the poor lack money, and since institutional cooperatives require participants with resources sufficient to carry on *viable* agriculture, it has been difficult to devise an approach which *genuinely* benefits poverty populations' (p. 66; italics added). Sambrani has echoed this concern (Sambrani, 1982, p. 268).

Bennet took stratification into account while discussing co-operatives and the rural poor, but he erred by treating big farmers, small farmers and agricultural labourers as homogeneous categories for analysis. The fact that the majority of marginal farmers, at least in semi-arid regions, are also labourers, craft workers, migrants, or pastoralists was ignored; and thus the opportunity of identifying precise areas of co-operation or conflict among different classes of farmers was lost.

Perhaps it is also necessary to raise another question: if the co-operatives are instruments of collectivizing farmers' individual productive potential through the agglomeration of market channels for their outputs or inputs, so that they can get better prices or higher individual profits, why should co-operatives try to bring together only *surplus* producers whom market forces are also bringing together? In that sense, should co-operatives reinforce agribusiness and the market mechanism and, if so, should they weaken the adaptive potential of those whom the market neglects or exploits? In Western societies the application of anti-trust laws is already raising this question.

This chapter discusses the differences between the traditional forms of co-operation engaged in by members of non-industrialized communities and contrasts the characteristics of those with the dominant Harvard model of co-operative ventures favoured by economic development policy-makers. It is suggested that the dominant model, which may be appropriate in industrial developed countries, is not suitable as a means of engaging poor people with marginal subsistence economies in the development process. This, it is argued, is because the dominant model adopts a business rationale of maximization of profit and viability which essentially excludes marginal members from full participation in the co-operative venture. The chapter explores some of the problems faced by social scientists who question the dominant model and the justifications presented by those who implement development policy.

The Meaning of 'Development'

Rural development, first of all, is not a process of ensuring proportionate return to poor and rich for their respective contributions. Proportionate shares will at no stage bridge the disparities. For development to succeed, the poor must grow at a faster pace than the rich in order to be able to catch up.

Secondly, rural development is not a process of maintaining the disparities at the current level. Development planners frequently claim that co-operatives, by ensuring a fair price for everybody's output, at least do not discriminate in favour of the rich and thus do not exacerbate the disparities. One should note the following points in this regard. (1) Any marketing channel to be viable needs a minimum amount of output. In many instances, poor contributors provide the threshold quantum of output which makes the enterprise viable and participation more attractive for larger contributors. (2) Value addition and surplus accrual, on the basis of viability of the enterprise, are almost invariably ploughed back in diversification of such products or services that help larger contributors more than the poor. Thus the poor pay more and receive less of those services. For instance, veterinary services provided by co-operative dairy organizations as discussed later in this chapter were created out of the surplus accruing from the contribution of all the poolers of milk – small and big. The rate at which these services are charged to users is not only subsidized but is also uniform for rich and poor members of the co-operative. The extent to which different classes of users will benefit from this subsidy will depend on the frequency of use. Crossbreed cattle require veterinary care more than the local breeds; the owners of such cattle, i.e. the richer people, will therefore use the veterinary services more. (3) *Equal or same price* is really not a *fair* price looking at inherent disparities in transfer prices of services.

Thirdly, rural development is not a process of involving the poor in making sacrifices 'now' so that richer people can accumulate capital now, invest it in some enterprise 'tomorrow' and generate jobs and other income-earning opportunities later. At the given level of vulnerability, the capacity of the poor to limit consumption further is very low. They do so only because the options are few. Even the option of exit, silence, or non-participation is not always available. (For example, if big farmers default, the co-operative credit societies become ineligible for further borrowing. The result is that those who repaid loans in time also become ineligible to receive further credit.)

Fourthly, rural development is not a process of decreasing the self-reliance potential of the poor and making them more dependent on markets on which they have no control. Introducing technologies which do not use traditional skills and local resources invariably increases dominance of the market over individuals. Access to markets/bureaucracy, which the rich invariably have, converts an apparently traditional and scale-neutral technology into an industrial and resource-biased technology.

Thus, in co-operatives of unequals, neutral institutions will not promote development because conflicts are bound to emerge whenever the majority (the poor) try to enforce a greater return to the poorer members. Institutions which promote, fund, or supervise co-operatives need to reinforce the strength of the poor who, despite being in the majority, may lack the capacity to influence decisions of the 'co-operative' body.

The image of development which emerges here is not compatible with the dominant myth of development through co-operatives which is promulgated by institutions like the International Co-operative Alliance (ICA), which very genuinely believe in co-operatives of and *for* viable producers – in whom agribusiness, multinational corporations, local market forces, etc. are all interested. In fact, one of the recent ICA project documents voices the above concern vividly, thus:

> Small farmers are reluctant to take risks and are quite rationally more concerned with their own survival rather than development-oriented [*sic*], a fact ignored by the existing developmental institutions including cooperatives whose facilities do not reach small farmers and in which small farmers do not participate in institution building, though these institutions are *geared to serving their interest*.
>
> (ICA/RTI/NCC/CLT Research Project document No. 14, 1980; italics added)

If the survival mechanism of the poor calls for strategies like shuffling options through the operation of a bundle of enterprises rather than specialization in any single output market (Gupta, 1981c), which co-operative institutions of which they are made a member do not try to strengthen, how and why should the poor farmer participate and co-operate in the task of strengthening such institutions? What else is developmental orientation than ensuring one's survival with dignity, self-respect and, if possible, self-reliance?

This discussion should clarify one issue quite unambiguously. The model of co-operatives that has emerged in countries with fewer problems in information flow, infrastructure and related market institutions than in developing countries will not foster co-operation amongst members in developing societies no matter what some co-operative researchers say. For example, 'in general, the poorest farmers are better served by cooperatives that include some members of a higher income group' (McGrath, 1978, p. 48). The question still remains: why don't the poor co-operate/participate in institutions ostensibly designed to serve their interests? Why have co-operatives the world over not been able to include the poor? And, whenever small farmers (not necessarily poor farmers) do participate, their ability to influence the power networks still remains handicapped.

I want to deal further with the following issues. First, what are the basic features of traditional co-operation *vis-à-vis* modern co-operatives? Secondly, how should we conceptualize the role of resources, risks and skills particularly in marginal regions? Thirdly, I want to discuss the way debate on issues of social research and practices has progressed in India in the specific context of the national programme of dairy development through the organization of co-operatives. I also want to discuss the role the poor have to play in validating the perception of their problems by the researchers.

Traditional Co-operation

Taking socio-ecological characteristics into account, one can see why incentives for co-operation will be different for different classes of poolers of resources and skills (Gupta, 1981a, p. 64; 1985a). On the basis of analyses of a number of traditional co-operative ventures amongst food-gathering and hunting tribes, three models emerge in increasing complexity of social organization. In the first model territory is commonly owned; i.e. the area of operation regarding hunting, honey collection or food gathering belongs to everybody in the tribe. *Redistribution is independent of pooling*. No matter how many people participate in a specific task, the produce collected or generated in the process is shared amongst everybody. In the absence of individual ownership, excellence in various skills determines the leadership roles. A leader in one task, say, food gathering, becomes a follower in another task, say, honey collection, where a person skilled in honey collection becomes the leader. The iterative leader-follower-leader process controls or prevents the emergence of autocracy. Each group will do what is generally decided by the traditional leader. Since every activity requires a number of skills, the tendency for any particular skilled person to acquire exclusive authoritarian power is counteracted through interdependence and iterative leadership as well as collective rewards.

In the second model, there is individual ownership of the territories, and the owner gets a share even if he or she does not participate. *Shares* otherwise *are proportionate to the contribution in any specific group activity*. It is generally the owner who initiates the formation of the group. Despite the rights regarding ownership being distributed amongst various sub-groups of a tribe, the group has overall control over the territory.

In the third model, ownership of territory and resources is explicit. The groups are organized by the owner, but *payment is made on a wage-contract basis rather than on a share basis*. The traditional leader extracts a tribute. The kinship network controls the territories. A share is also given to various market functionaries like forest officials, contractors and traders. The share of labour goes down considerably.

One of the important characteristics of modern organizations appears to be the erosion of the primacy of skill as one moves from most primitive to more complex and modern forms of social organization, together with a decrease in the share of labour in the output. Various modern organizational theories (which emphasize de-skilling as a necessary feature of extending managerial control over workers) recognize that, in the process of skill-building and specialization, there may have to be greater interdependence between workers and owners. This may reduce the ability of owners of resources to control various actions of the members of the production process. However, the conflict of interest amongst various members of an organization is conceptually tenable with the emergence of working conditions that need not be necessarily exploitative for weaker partners in the exchange (Gupta, 1985a; 1985c).

The principles of pooling and redistribution are quite ecology- and class-specific. The nature and the extent of market penetration make a significant difference to the optimality of traditional arrangements. Sahlins (1972) has drawn attention to some of these traditional arrangements, but not much research has been directed to understanding the social, cultural and political ramifications of incorporating some of these arrangements into modern organizations.

There are some obvious features which characterize the pooling and redistribution processes. The incentives or disincentives for pooling resources will not only vary for different classes or kinship/ethnic networks of people but will also depend upon various socio-ecological features. The perception of risk of joining any group for different individuals will depend upon past experience, individual endowment, future expectation, accumulated insights, previous losses, etc. If trade-offs under risk vary amongst various classes of farmers, and if the ability of one class of farmers to negotiate risk depends upon its dependency upon another class, then any pooling framework cannot be conceptualized without taking risk into account. The risk-adjustment mechanisms have evolved historically, leading to various traditional forms of pooling. In contrast with modern co-operative organization, they reveal some patterns of disassociation of pooling from redistribution.

The extent to which current and future decisions to pool individual resources are dependent upon past experience, not only with pooling but with redistribution amongst poolers as well as others, will also be influenced by: (1) the rules of the game or social sanctions or customary structures; and (2) the ability of some members who have not got what they think a fair return to opt out or *quit*. The options of quit or exit need not be *voluntary*, just as options for joining a pooling process need not be strictly voluntary. The emergence of the constraining environment in which voluntary choice of the peasant is compromised by agri-business or by expanding cash-crop economy or market control by any particular organization (private, public, or co-operative) suggests that discussion on pooling cannot be restricted only to the *benefits and costs of poolers* but will *invariably* have to extend to non-poolers, free-riders and those who are excluded, thrown out, or ineligible.

Modern Co-operative Organization

When researchers wonder why the poor do not co-operate, perhaps the problem lies not with the poor so much as with the method of research and the paradigm under which the question is formulated. This issue will become clearer when we discuss the case of a modern co-operative enterprise. The politics of model generation, replication and legitimization will be made explicit in the process.

The National Dairy Development Board (NDDB) is an apex organization set up by the Indian Ministry of Agriculture in 1965 at Anand to replicate the Amul pattern of milk procurement, processing and marketing. This is achieved through an organization with a three-tier structure comprising village co-operative society, district co-operative union and state-level co-operative federation. A detailed review of the Anand pattern is available elsewhere (Gupta, 1981a; George, 1983). An exhaustive micro-level study of the process and the impact of dairy co-operatives on rural development in Gujarat has also recently been conducted (Baviskar, 1983). This chapter deals with only the ecological setting in which it evolved and the issues in replication. It briefly discusses how the agribusiness model of promoting milk production leaves the marginal farmer and landless labourer behind. Even though NDDB officers did not agree with the author's contention that their strategy was based on an agribusiness model developed by Harvard University, it is important to note that the consultants who advised the NDDB in the early years in the process of replication were drawn from Harvard University! The paradox of mal-development will become more obvious when it is shown how the semi-arid regions (which were the traditional habitat of most of the good dual- and single-purpose cattle breeds) have been bypassed by the model of co-operatives evolved at Anand and in Gujarat itself, not to mention the rest of India.

Kaira district, where the co-operative under discussion was established, is one of the most prosperous regions in the state of Gujarat. It ranks first in the population of milk cattle including buffaloes; first in intensity of irrigation; second in food-grain production; third in population density; fourth in fertilizer consumption; and fourth highest in the proportion of agricultural labourers in the total workforce. In terms of the allocation of institutional finance, Kaira ranks second in total outstanding credit and ninth in total deposits. Interestingly, despite a most favourable agricultural resource endowment and market infrastructure, Kaira also ranks sixth in overdue long-term co-operative loans and second in short-term co-operative debts. An abundant supply of green fodder and a moderate climate offer the ideal niche for breeding buffaloes, which is a subsidiary activity.

The demand for milk within Gujarat is not very high. Thus distant markets like Bombay pose a very different challenge here compared with regions where nearby markets for milk exist. Competition from private milk traders would be much higher in the latter case where price disparities are also likely to be less. The majority of milk in Anand was processed into by-products.

The Anand co-operative model evolved from below, from village level to district union. The unions comprise elected non-officials and undertake all the three activities, namely, collection, processing and marketing. Federations came about much later when it was discovered that different unions were competing with each other, thus leading to collective losses. Even today Gujarat has a federation comprising unions of better districts. The districts with considerable population of cattle but with low population density and attendant heavy cost of transportation are not included in the federation. A separate corporation looks after dairy development in these regions. The National Dairy Development Board is replicating the Anand pattern in all regions despite the fact it would appear that incentives for co-operation and mobilization would need to be different in different ecological regions (Gupta, 1981a).

Every member of a milk co-operative society contributes milk to the collection centre and receives payment in the evening or the next day. Besides this, all members are entitled to several facilities like mobile veterinary care, subsidized cattle-feed and artificial insemination for cattle. The bonus earned from the value addition to milk and the margin in sales is distributed amongst members in proportion to their collected output. The veterinary services are priced at the same rate for small, landless and big farmers with the assumption that similar price is the equitable price.

Contradictions and Discontinuities

Various issues highlight the contradictions inherent in the process of replication of a pilot project through top-down bureaucratic methods. As mentioned earlier, the co-operative at Anand had evolved from below, but in replicating, the NDDB insisted that a federation should be set up first, followed by unions and primary village milk producers' societies. The historical model was turned upside-down. In the absence of union or primary societies, it was obvious that the federation would comprise only state government nominees.

The major objective of the whole programme of 'Operation Flood' shifted in favour of *outputs* (boosting milk collection) instead of *inputs* (establishment of farmers' organizations). The single most important element of the Amul model, which even its worst critics would admit to be worth replicating, was accountability of organizations to members. Precisely this feature was lost sight of in the process of replication. The district co-operative unions or primary village co-operative societies which I studied in other states as well as in parts of Gujarat revealed this practice to be the rule rather than the exception. A meeting of the general body of some of the oldest unions had not taken place for years. One could imagine how in the absence of such meetings more complex and difficult participative processes or norms of accountability could be developed in the parent organizations.

The methods chosen by the NDDB to replicate were not always

participative, democratic, or flexible. In fact, the NDDB's greatest burden is the success which it has behind it. As Paul (1982) has suggested, 'if one looks for at least one public developmental programme that has achieved its purpose, undoubtedly one could not mention any programme but Operation Flood I, in which the strategy aimed at stabilizing milk supplies to the four metropolitan cities by helping the milk producers to build up their cooperatives' (NDDB, 1980–1). It is another question whether the success of a developmental programme should be measured by *outputs* or by the *process* and the *institutions* established to achieve outputs.

The leadership of village societies in most of the villages is in the hands of high-caste people. The diversification of services through the investment of surpluses is not linked with the interest of poor cattle-owners. For example, the major problem of the pastoralist is the availability of dry fodder during lean months, whereas fodder-related research at the NDDB aims at either improving green fodder production or the nutrient content of available dry fodder. No dairy federation in any of the states has attempted the development of some sort of public distribution system for dry fodder.

Another important feature of the Amul pattern was the assurance of year-round milk collection that organizations provided to their members. However, several milk routes which were not found viable in terms of the cost of milk collection were closed in the lean summer season, breaking this assurance. Given the fact that in low-population-density, high-risk, backward regions the cost of milk collection would be higher, the uniform viability norms prescribed by the NDDB provided no choice for the organizations but to neglect these regions. There was only one case where a dynamic executive officer of a dairy development corporation pleaded with the state government to be allowed to incur losses in the short run (Aurora, 1983). This was done to promote dairy development activities in drought-prone parts of the state where the cost of milk collection was very high. On the issue of flexibility the contention of the NDDB was that, even if flexibility was allowed, the state federations did not pass this on to their district unions, partly because they were dominated by the bureaucrats and not the elected officials.

It is not surprising that the regions chosen by the NDDB for replicating the Amul/Anand pattern in different states were the regions endowed with most favourable natural resources and market infrastructure. In that sense, this strategy continued the bias of Green Revolution strategy where the emphasis was also to concentrate technological change in the most favourable regions and at the landholdings of the best-endowed farmers. When I raised this issue with the chairman of the NDDB the answer was that if they could meet the milk requirements of the metropolitan cities by concentrating on the best one-third of the country, why should they consider any other strategy? The contradiction inherent in the statement was that this best one-third of the country did not have farmers dependent upon dairying as a primary means of subsistence, as was the case in the most backward, semi-arid and arid part (a little less than one-third) of the country. What is also interesting is that many multinational corporations have chosen precisely the area which the NDDB has chosen for replication of the model in the first phase. In a later phase, the NDDB included many backward regions, but the best pockets have been selected even in those districts.

Several other contradictions can be observed with regard to the way the model evolved and the way it was replicated. If the poor in backward regions survive through a diversification of their household activities, through the multiplicity of skills available from the different members of the family and through using varying time-frames for appraising investment choices in different source markets, then any development programme which does not take into account the above features of household economy will leave the poor behind. For instance, if women manage dairy activities, then the predominant bias in favour of training men will not be very useful, particularly when these men are drawn from better-endowed households. If the poor want to process the milk into butter oil so that the butter milk, as by-product can be used by the children and other family members, then a marketing organization based on the collection of milk may not be the most advantageous way of strengthening the survival mechanisms of the poor.

Further, if we believe that no organization should try to achieve viability at each of its branches or production levels, then the implication is that through the mechanism of transfer-pricing or cross-subsidization the organization should generate surplus from certain products/branches/consumers or suppliers in order to help such branches, people, or products which cannot pay back the cost in the short run. There is no other way an organization can be called developmental, if in the absence of cross-subsidization part of the value addition is not used to compensate the cost of those who would not participate or co-operate on the terms the organization may want them to do.

Arid regions are likely to have more fluctuation in any economic enterprise because of ecological and climatic conditions. Therefore, in the lean seasons, when milk supplies are lower and the prices in the market higher, organizations should be able to understand and accommodate the rational response of farmers to avail themselves of better prices in the market rather than supply milk to co-operatives.

The NDDB did not monitor the regular occurrence of general meetings or drop-out rates in the co-operatives. If some members dropped out and other members joined, there was no way by which the NDDB would know the class background of those who dropped out or those who joined later. Any organization which does not institutionalize a process of continued accountability towards the poor invariably shifts its objectives towards the interests of bulk suppliers as the scale of its operation increases. The question really is whether problems of this nature should be analysed by exploring the behaviour of the poor who quite rationally do not co-operate with such an organization, or should the researchers aim at unravelling the dynamics through which such a shift in the organizational objectives comes about?

Politics of Policy Analysis

The Operation Flood programme has been a centre of controversy in India during the mid 1980s. The participants in this debate conducted in the columns of the popular press, have generally made the following allegations. They have claimed that the professionals in the NDDB are deliberately trying to mislead the country or the researchers by offering inadequate or incorrect explanations/data about their activities. They have alleged that the NDDB is not co-operating with the researchers in their fieldwork or allowing them access to its data; that the NDDB's strategy is unique in terms of its bias towards better-endowed regions or richer farmers; and that the NDDB is deliberately doing things which are not in the interests of the country.

One reason why social scientists often find themselves to be marginal in the process of policy reform is that either they assume a self-righteous position against which the other side takes a defensive attitude – thus even the useful findings are not accepted by the government policy-planning apparatus – or they attribute ulterior motives to planners in which all errors are considered intentional and no allowance is made for genuine mistakes. When the first draft of the substance of this chapter was sent to the NDDB for comment, there was no response for almost a year, even after several reminders and telegrams. Finally an appointment was made for discussion of the draft. The author had scrupulously avoided participation in the debate in the columns of the press. My feeling was that, rather than scoring debating points in the media, as a social scientist I could make greater impact on policy direction if I entered into a dialogue with those who were shaping policies. This approach is a frustrating process both because of the patience it calls for on the part of the social scientist and the faith it assumes both sides to have in each other.

The meeting with NDDB executives in their office began in a very tense atmosphere. Almost the first statement by them implied ulterior motives on my part for writing such a paper. However, since they had done their homework very well, we went through sentence by sentence and tried to understand each other's position. On some issues I realized that my position was not sufficiently accurate or even correct; whereas on others I remained convinced and found additional reasons for policy change. I sent the summary of the discussion back to the NDDB with the hope that they would also concede some points and thus continue the debate in an explicit and open manner. This hope proved to be unfounded.

Despite my own professional frustration with regard to policy reform by the NDDB, I must clarify some of the allegations of the critics of the NDDB. While it may be true that some of the data which researchers wanted were not provided by the NDDB, one must concede the right of an organization to provide data only to those in whom it has full trust. However, the right to information justifiably goes beyond the discretion of an organization, when such a right is enshrined in the constitution or enacted as a law by Parliament. Only otherwise can the organization take a techno-legal view of the matter. On the other hand, banks or other public organizations may be as secretive as the NDDB in providing data and yet may not receive criticism on that account. We must not flog the wrong horse.

The argument that the NDDB did not co-operate with the researchers has been advanced by some of the most respected researchers in India. Dr Baviskar of the University of Delhi made this observation in the columns of *Economic and Political Weekly*. My own experience is that when my colleague Professor Indrajit Khanna and I went to Anand to conduct some case studies of village co-operatives, we faced no problems whatsoever either from the dairy organization or from the village co-operative society. However, I do not really understand why researchers should need to seek co-operation from an organization when fieldwork can be done in most parts of the country without any formal patronage or sponsorship. I would go to the extent of suggesting that when researchers do accept hospitality from an organization, they may be tempted to become less critical of its policies than otherwise. Bell and Newby, in *Doing Sociological Research* (1977), provide several instances of this.

The NDDB's policies of development strategy are not unique. They follow the dominant agribusiness Green Revolution type of approach. This perspective is typical of most Indian public policies in the fields of banking, education, health, etc. In that sense the NDDB is as much to blame as other public systems in India which fail to reach the poorest segments of society. When I raised the question of the Anand model of co-operatives being dominated by the rich, and not very democratic in nature, a very senior leader of the NDDB shot back the perhaps justified question, 'Why should co-operatives organized by the NDDB be expected to be more democratic than the national policy itself?'

The allegation that professionals in the NDDB are less patriotic than the social scientists criticizing its policies is a very serious charge. My own position on this is that while I may disagree with the policy bias of the NDDB and the way its professionals may deal with the whole debate, I would not like to pass judgement on their commitment to the national cause. It would imply that all those with whom one disagrees on issues of social policy can be labelled in a similar manner. In a democratic society such attitudes can generate fascist tendencies. Plurality of perspectives must be respected, though at the same time a social scientist reserves his or her right to espouse the cause which he or she thinks serves the country's interests the best.

With regard to the ethical standards followed by the social scientists themselves, two examples will suffice. The first concerns a leading political scientist and social activist who recently published an article on the 'participation of people' in an eminent journal. However, the only references he cited in his paper pertained to either his own writing or that of his disciples. This seems a rather strange way of preaching participation while not allowing ideas of other intellectuals to permeate one's own. The second example concerns the many participants in the Operation Flood debate who have chosen to ignore certain academic works which did not fit their argument, even if they were aware of these, without any qualms about the propriety of such behaviour. There are other examples where social scientists have behaved in much the same way as the people in the organizations they criticize. The pity is that the scientists as well as the policy planners very seldom consider it prudent or relevant to validate their respective positions with the poor people, whose interest they claim to espouse.

The practice of social research, whether in terms of the choice of variables, the causal model, or the methodological premisses used to validate this model, is inevitably political in nature. If we assume that one of the objectives of such research is to change the social structure in favour of the poor and disadvantaged then two conditions seem to be necessary. First, the positions taken by social scientists on behalf of the poor must be validated by those groups of the poor to whom they apply in an open explicit manner so that their *assumptions* about what the poor want will not lead to solutions that are worse than the problems (Gupta, 1985b). Secondly, ethical issues in social science research should be dealt with squarely so that the values of researchers do not invite the same comments which researchers pass on the researched organizations or policy-planning system.

The non-co-operation of the poor with the organizations supposedly set up to serve them is based on rational reasons. If social researchers find it difficult to deal with this phenomenon, they must question their own methods as well as their assumptions about what they think the poor think. If social scientists seek to influence development policy they must also seek a closer partnership and dialogue with those who formulate such policy. The frustrations inherent in such a dialogue call for greater emphasis on networking amongst academics active in the development policy field so that they may learn from one another's failures and successes.

References

Aurora, Dajeet (1983), former managing director, Andhra Pradesh Dairy Corporation, personal communication.

Baviskar, B. S. (1980), *The Politics of Development: Sugar Co-operatives in Rural Maharashtra* (Delhi: Oxford University Press).

Baviskar, B. S. (1983), 'Milk co-operatives and rural development in Gujarat: a case study', paper presented to workshop on 'Co-operatives and Rural Development in India', 4–5 March 1983, New Delhi.

Bell, Colin, and Newby, Howard (eds.) (1977), *Doing Sociological Research* (London: Allen & Unwin).

Bennet, John W. (1978), 'Agricultural co-operation in the development process: perspectives from social science', in McGrath, op. cit.

Galjart, B. (1982), 'Participatory development projects: some research conclusions', unpublished paper, University of Leiden, the Netherlands.

George, Shanthi (1983), 'Co-operatives and Indian dairy policy: more Anand than pattern', paper presented to workshop on 'Co-operatives and Rural Development in India', 4–5 March 1983, New Delhi.

Guhan, S. (1980), 'Rural poverty: policy and play acting', *Economic and Political Weekly*, vol. XV, no. 43, pp. 1938–82.

Gupta, Anil K. (1981a), 'Farmers' response to co-operative project implementation: cases in dairy and sheep-pasture development in arid regions', paper presented at IUAES symposium on 'Traditional Co-operation and Modern Co-operative Enterprises', 23–4 April 1981, Amsterdam.

Gupta, Anil K. (1981b), 'A note on internal resource management in arid regions, small farmers' credit constraints: a paradigm', *Agricultural Systems* (UK), vol. 7, no. 2, pp. 157–61.

Gupta, Anil K. (1981c), 'Viable projects for unviable farmers: an action research enquiry into structure and processes of rural poverty in arid regions' (New Delhi: Indian Institute of Public Administration, and Ahmedabad: Indian Institute of Management), mimeo.

Gupta, Anil K. (1985a), 'Co-operation in co-operatives: contribution of risk, resources and skills', Indian Institute of Management working paper No. 574, Ahmedabad, presented at XVth International CIRIEC Congress, Florence, April 1984.

Gupta, Anil K. (1985b), 'On organizing equity: are "solutions" the problem?' *Journal of Social and Economic Studies* (New Delhi: Sage), vol. 2, no. 4, pp. 295–312.

Gupta, Anil K. (1985c), 'Socio-ecological paradigm for analysing problems of poor in dry regions: an Indian contribution', *Eco-Development News*, no. 32–3, March–June, pp. 68–74.

Harvey, Charles; Jacob, Jake; Lemb, Geoff; and Schaffer, Bernard (1979) *Rural Employment and Administration in the Third World* (London: International Labour Organization and Saxon House).

McGrath, Mary Jean (1978), *Cooperatives, Small Farmers and Rural Development* (Madison: University Center for Cooperatives, University of Wisconsin), mimeo.

NDDB (1980–1) *National Dairy Development Board Annual Report* (Anand, India).

Paul, Samuel (1983), 'The strategic management of development programmes: evidence from an international study', *International Review of Administrative Sciences*, vol. 49, no. 1, pp. 73–86.

Sahlins, M. (1972), *Stone Age Economics* (London: Tavistock).

Sambrani, S. (1982), 'Management of commodity systems: the development of co-operative dairying in India', *Agricultural Administration* (UK), LL, pp. 253–71.

Ullrich, G. (ed.) (1981), *Evaluation of Cooperative Organizations*, report of international conference (West Berlin: German Foundation for International Exchange).

IV

Identifying Hidden Agendas

Introduction to Part Four

In the Introduction to this book the topic of hidden agendas was raised briefly. In Part Four the nature and problems of such hidden agendas are explored in more detail. While the likelihood of actors in the research process having objectives and motivations which are not immediately explicit is present in any research situation, Cox, Hausfeld and Wills (1978) have intimated that these are more commonly associated with contexts where the researcher acts in a consultancy role. It is interesting, therefore, that while neither author of the two chapters in this part was hired initially as a consultant, their roles were extended in the course of the research to include consultancy aspects. While both McDermott and Jenkins are primarily concerned with hidden agendas of the other actors in the research drama, they both mention agendas of their own which were not explicitly part of the proposed activity. McDermott's chapter is concerned mainly with the hidden agendas of the sponsor, while Jenkins emphasizes those of the subjects of his research.

As Cox, Hausfeld and Wills have noted, governments (or other sponsors) may become involved in research for a variety of reasons. The research may reflect commitment to needs-based policy-making; it may be seen as an alternative to action or, in cases where public pressure exists, as a play for time and an attempt to defuse explosive situations. In all of these contexts, however, the first of these alternatives is likely to be the official explanation.

In many if not most instances, the hidden agenda does not result from any machiavellian intent on the part of the sponsor but arises out of conflicting definitions of the problem (McNaul, 1972; Wenger, 1982), which may become apparent only after the research has commenced. In some cases, of course, different definitions of the problem affect the type of research which gets funded (see Hanmer and Leonard, 1984), but that discussion is beyond the scope of this part of the book. Conflict over the definition of the problem is a central concern in McDermott's chapter, and Jenkins comments on a similar aspect of his work. Both writers discuss the shift in emphasis which their research took – away from a policy emphasis on the responsibility of the victim, to look at other factors in the social context.

Hidden agendas may also become apparent where a sponsor hopes for or expects specific results from the data analysis. Cox, Hausfeld and Wills (1978) have suggested one reason for this: 'Research also has the attraction, *provided it comes up with expected answers*, of removing responsibility for action onto the shoulders of more distant and apparently impartial experts' (p. 111; italics added). McDermott's and Jaeger's chapters in this collection illustrate some of the problems arising when expectations are not fulfilled. In these instances, it would appear that research is commissioned not to inform policy but to validate it. The hidden agenda may in some cases remain implicit until negative findings show up specific policy effects which neither sponsor nor researcher had predicted. Evidence that sponsors might accept in support of positive results can often be questioned as tenuous in support of results which a policy body perceives as negative. Payne *et al.* (1980) have suggested that administrators frequently react to negative findings as if they were a personal or political attack rather than seeing such findings as critical to the policy-making process. Such responses may hinge on unfulfilled expectations of some hidden agenda.

While many implicit as well as explicit objectives of sponsors result from the political context in which the research commences, other objectives can emerge during the conduct of the research as a result of social and political change. In other words, different questions may be asked of the data, or the ground rules or definitions of key terms may shift as time goes on. McDermott's chapter discusses this theme, which was also explored in the chapter by Hadley. In effect, the original agenda changes without consultation.

Several writers have urged researchers to be aware of possible unstated objectives of sponsors and other funding bodies with whom they work (Orlans, 1967; Cox, Hausfeld and Wills, 1978). Some researchers have rejected funding where suspicion of vested interest could jeopardize the credibility of research findings (Ferriman, 1986). On the other hand, Moore (1977) has noted that it is possible to do good research even with 'tainted' funds and cautions against overreaction in 'fear of the hidden hand' (p. 90).

Hidden agendas can, of course, also exist on the researcher's side. The ethical problems which surround access to study controversial topics have been discussed at length. Many researchers whose interests have been in the area of racial prejudice or race relations have commented on the way they have concealed the specific nature of their interest to gain access to and acceptance in the research milieu

(Middleton, 1977; Moore, 1977). This problem has already been mentioned in the context of McNamara's chapter. Jenkins's chapter discusses the ethics of the conscious concealment of his agenda in interviewing racists. At the same time, he suggests that it was the hidden agendas held by his respondents which facilitated his research.

As several authors have pointed out, social research usually implies the study of the powerless by the powerful (Bulmer, 1978; Payne *et al.*, 1980; Bell and Roberts, 1984). Study of those with power in developed societies has been limited for a wide variety of reasons. As Orlans (1967) comments, it would be foolhardy for governments to support 'studying up'! On the other hand, it has been argued that, in order to understand the workings of society, understanding power relationships is essential (Mills, 1959). Both the authors in this part discuss the importance of looking at how decisions are made by those with power.

Payne *et al.* (1980) have questioned whether studying the funding body is entirely ethical if this has not been an explicit aspect of the proposed research. However, one side-effect of the relationship between sponsor and researcher, which emerges as a result of the need to keep the communication channels open as the work progresses and adjustments are negotiated (Orlans, 1967), is the inevitability that the researcher will become aware of the way decisions affecting the research are made by the sponsoring institution or agency. As Jenkins's chapter shows, negotiations with subjects are also important, and subjects with power can sabotage the research or hamper the publication of results if threatened by the findings. As a result, studies of the powerful have been few, and those which have been conducted have had to overcome restrictions and to be conducted incidentally to other research or as part of a hidden agenda. In this collection, the normative constraints on studying those with power are apparent; Wenger's interest in the development agency was perceived as a threat, and her authority to be so interested was questioned; McDermott's proposal to study employers was approved only when stated in terms of seeking their views on youth employment; Jenkins's use of unguarded statements as data was questioned even where these were given in the context of a research visit; and Jaeger's request to interview parents and school governors was denied. McDermott stresses the need to extend knowledge of power relations, while Jenkins discusses the problems and ethics of studying up. The problems of power will be discussed further in Part Five.

References

Bell, C., and Roberts, H. (1984), 'Introduction', in C. Bell and H. Roberts (eds.), *Social Researching: Politics, Problems, Practice* (London: Routledge & Kegan Paul), pp. 1–13.

Bulmer, M. (1978), 'Social science research and policy-making in Britain', in M. Bulmer (ed.), *Social Policy Research* (London: Macmillan), pp. 3–43.

Cox, E., Hausfeld, F., and Wills, S. (1978), 'Taking the queen's shilling: accepting social research consultancies in the 1970s', in C. Bell and S. Encel (eds.), *Inside the Whale* (Sydney: Pergamon), pp. 121–41.

Ferriman, A. (1986), 'Tobacco industry snubbed over cash', *Observer*, 29 January.

Hanmer, J., and Leonard, D. (1984), 'Negotiating the problem: the DHSS and research on violence in marriage', in C. Bell and H. Roberts (eds.), *Social Researching: Politics, Problems, Practice* (London: Routledge & Kegan Paul), pp. 32–53.

McNaul, J. P. (1972), 'Relations between researchers and practitioners', in S. Z. Nagi and R. G. Corwin (eds.), *The Social Contexts of Research* (New York: Wiley Interscience).

Middleton, H. (1977), 'A Marxist at Wattie Creek: fieldwork among Australian Aborigines', in C. Bell and S. Encel (eds.), *Inside the Whale* (Sydney: Pergamon), pp. 238–69.

Mills, C. W. (1959), *The Sociological Imagination* (London: Oxford University Press).

Moore, R. (1977), 'Becoming a sociologist in Sparkbrook', in C. Bell and H. Newby (eds.), *Doing Sociological Research* (London: Allen & Unwin), pp. 87–107.

Orlans, H. (1967), 'Ethical problems in the relations of research sponsors and investigators', in G. Sjoberg (ed.), *Ethics, Politics and Social Research* (London: Routledge & Kegan Paul), pp. 3–24.

Payne, G., Dingwall, R., Payne, J., and Carter, M. (1980), 'Sociology and policy research', in Payne *et al., Sociology and Social Research* (London: Routledge & Kegan Paul), pp. 142–59.

Wenger, G. C. (1982), 'The problem of perspective in development policy', *Sociologia Ruralis*, vol. XXII, no. 1, pp. 5–16.

8

In and out of the Game: a Case Study of Contract Research

KATHLEEN McDERMOTT,
Centre for Social Policy Research and Development, Department of Social Theory, University College of North Wales, Bangor, Wales

Abstract
This chapter sets out to describe the constraints of conducting contract research. Using her own experience of directing a research project for the Manpower Services Commission as a case study, the author tries to point out not only the constraints of contract research but the opportunities it can present to study those in power. The case study is of a project that was contracted to evaluate the impact of the Youth Opportunities Programme on the rural labour market. The chapter seeks to show that, by analysing the government's definition of the problem and relating that perception to the framework within which policy decisions are made, the social construction of youth unemployment and training emerges. The hidden agenda of restructuring the workforce with as little resistance from the workforce as possible is uncovered. A plea is made for contract researchers to study the culture of the powerful and its relation to the creation of social policy.

In this chapter I describe my experience of conducting contract research for the Department of Employment in the United Kingdom. I would like to use that experience as a case study to illustrate the kinds of constraints that social scientists must work under in doing evaluative work, the kind of skill we must learn in the process and the opportunities contract research offers to study those in power. Increasingly, governments have

This chapter was originally presented in a symposium on 'Contract Research and the Problem of Customer Interest' at the XIth International Congress of Anthropological and Ethnological Sciences, Quebec, Canada, August 1983.

become the major source of research funds for academics, and there is often a contradiction between the objectives of the government agency and those of the research team. All too often contract research looks only at the defined problem and ignores the actions of the funding agency as being relevant to the research. Only by analysing the perception of those having decision-making power through the process of negotiation between the agency and the research team can this contradiction be understood and perhaps overcome.

A leading anthropologist, Eric Wolf, set out a task for anthropologists to begin a study of power relations in society: 'anthropology has reached its present impasse because it has so systematically disregarded the problems of power . . . we must find ways of educating ourselves in the realities of power' (Wolf, 1974). He suggests that we go beyond looking only at economic power to analysing ideological power, the power of control over policy-making and opinion-making institutions. I shall argue that the contract researcher is in a privileged position to analyse this process and dialectic of decision-making over society's institutions. However, the contract researcher must include the perceptions and social definitions of the agency as an essential element of the study. By studying the culture of power as well as the culture of the powerless a better understanding of their interrelation will emerge.

The study that I directed took part over a three-year period from 1980 to 1983. I was hired to evaluate the impact of a government programme aimed at alleviating youth unemployment (McDermott and Dench, 1983). Our study was located in rural Wales and was one of three longitudinal studies in different local labour markets. Concern over youth unemployment in Britain began in the early 1970s. However, the problem was perceived as a temporary one linked to demographic changes and a short-term recession (MSC, 1979). The Manpower Services Commission (MSC) was set up in 1974 within the Department of Employment to foster training and employment services especially amongst young adults. The first large-scale programme for the young unemployed was launched in 1975 as the Job Creation Programme. Projects under this programme were intended to be short-term and of benefit to the local community. A major criticism by the public was that the JCP projects generally offered little more than unskilled work with no training. What the Job Creation Programme did, nonetheless, was set a precedent for earmarking considerable sums of government money for tackling the problems of the young unemployed and, to some extent, initiate government responsibility for alleviating youth unemployment.

Once it became clear that the recession was deepening and rapid economic recovery was becoming more unlikely, the MSC established a major training initiative in 1976 called the Work Experience Programme, which provided unemployed young people with six months' work experience in factories, shops and offices while receiving a government allowance. The philosophy behind this programme was that young people in the labour market were particularly disadvantaged due to their lack of work experience and discipline. In 1977 a new comprehensive Youth Opportunities Programme (YOP) was proposed to replace existing government provision for the young unemployed. A government report (MSC, 1979) argued that the YOP was more relevant than the earlier programmes because it tackled at *source* the reasons why young people failed to impress employers. The YOP would provide disadvantaged young people with the *qualities* sought by employers and thereby improve their ability to compete more successfully for available employment. The range of opportunities within the YOP included schemes designed to provide work experience on employers' premises, in community service on projects and in workshops, and work preparation in the form of college and work-based courses not too different from earlier programmes. There was, though, a new element added called Social and Life Skills – a course aimed to improve communication skills and self-awareness, qualities it was felt that young people lacked. This brief history shows that the unemployment crisis was defined as a youth problem rather than a job problem and was focused more on the individual, thus individualizing the problem.

Since the Youth Opportunities Programme was established in 1978, it has had to adapt to rapidly worsening employment prospects for the young. Simultaneously it has faced pressures to improve the quality and the scale of its provision. Initially designed to offer an effective bridge to permanent employment, it has now become the only alternative to unemployment for many young people and functions as a holding-station between increasing periods of unemployment. Furthermore, it has not changed the government's basic perception of young people's joblessness as deriving from a lack in the young people themselves and not in the shortage of jobs available. In the evaluation of such a programme, rural Wales presented an opportunity to study government intervention in a local labour market but also exposed the research team to constraints and manipulations by the government agency.

Before examining some of the constraints placed on the research, one very important issue must be stated. In order to conduct any type of evaluation an understanding of just what is being evaluated – that is, the underlying assumption of the programme – must be made clear. In this study, the government's definition of the cause of the problem, that is, the cause of youth unemployment, was the inadequacy of the young people themselves; this determined what the government viewed as the solution and created the framework in which it sought answers from the research.

If one envisions contract research as a drama played out between those who possess resources (the government agency) and those who possess information (the research team) then the setting in which the drama is played out is the steering committee. Unlike many other research steering committees composed mostly of specialists not involved with the research, ours was mostly composed of the government agency: the MSC research director, the chief MSC research officer, the Department of Employment research director and the department's economist. The remaining two members were from our university: the professor of our department and the senior lecturer, who mainly played the role of mediators between the team and the agency. Given the weighting of the committee by the MSC there was little room for objectivity in evaluating and guiding the work of the research team.

The very first obstacle that we met was defining just *who* the research was to study. The MSC wanted the team to study only those young people who entered the programme and what happened to them after leaving – a kind of input-output analysis. The research team argued for the necessity of a control group, i.e. those who did not enter the programme. Only in that way would one know who entered the programme and who did not and whether the programme made any difference to the eventual status of the young people.

While the team's argument was academically sound, we won our case only when the MSC realized that the number entering the programme was so small that a control group was necessary to raise the number of young people in order for the study to be statistically comparable with the other two urban studies. However, we won this point by dribs and drabs, forcing us to include young people at different times of entry into the labour market. Needless to say this led to many methodological problems and a certain amount of contamination of the data.

A second conflict arose out of *what* we were to study. The MSC wanted us to study only the young people since the problem was defined to be with them. The research team claimed that the young people were only part of the process, that the local agency, the sponsors and the labour market itself were part of the context in which the programme was implemented. The conflict was resolved by defining the research on two levels: for the MSC the local agencies and employers were interviewed to ascertain their opinion on the programme and the needs of young people; for the research team these agencies were viewed as gatekeepers and brokers of resources. Furthermore, our use of a more qualitative methodology (such as participant observation and open-ended interviews) devalued the exercise in the MSC's eyes but freed us to gather a richer data base that put some depth on the quantitative data.

A third conflict was the time factor and the need for results. During the course of the study the MSC was under considerable pressure from the Cabinet, Parliament and the press to prove its worth. The MSC's budget was ever-increasing and yet the number of young people unemployed was growing at an even faster rate. The government needed to be seen as doing something about unemployment without having to change its policies. Therefore the MSC was asking for results long before the research was over. The team, on the other hand, viewed the study as an ongoing changing process that needed the time element to analyse that process. All too often we found ourselves quickly writing reports with partial data and statistics that on the surface meant one thing but over time could mean quite another. This need for constant feedback by the agency was the major cause of friction between the research team and the MSC. The research team tried to overcome this by qualifying the data and trying to present it as a stage within the overall study. However, the government just gathered the numbers and used them to legitimate its own role. An example was a report on long-term unemployed young people (those unemployed for more than six months). After writing fairly dreary statistics, we included a number of case studies to try to illustrate just what those numbers meant. At the end of a long steering committee meeting discussing those statistics, the director made an offhand comment on the case studies: 'Oh, what a nice touch, it made good bedtime reading.' So much for relevance and understanding the hidden injuries of unemployment.

Finally, a problem that is inherent in any longitudinal study, no matter how flexible your design, is produced by the changes occurring in society in general that affect your study and were unforeseen. As stated earlier, unemployment dramatically increased over the course of the study (8 per cent in 1980 to 13 per cent in 1983: McDermott and Dench, 1983). This not only increased pressure on the government to do something about it but changed the population towards whom the programme was targeted. At the beginning of the Youth Opportunities Programme young people who were disadvantaged, who left school without qualifications and who were unable to hold down a job were the focus of the programme. However, as the recession deepened, young people who were well qualified and from middle-class backgrounds were not only unable to find the job they wanted but unable to find any job. The outcry from Parliament and the press resounded through the halls of the MSC: 'What are they doing about these young people who *deserve* to have a job?' This was a potential threat to the government's economic policies as the recession and the consequences of Thatcher's policies were affecting her very own constituency.

At the same time, the research team was finding that recruitment on to the YOP and success afterwards (i.e. finding a job or going on to further education) were dominated by those with good qualifications. The disadvantaged young people who were supposedly the target group were deriving the least benefit from the programme, if they entered it at all. We saw this as a major finding of the study and a negative evaluation. However, given the change in the political and social environment, the MSC ignored this finding, emphasized the increasing role the YOP was playing with well-qualified young people and used this data to support its claim that it was helping those who most deserved to be helped. As the society at large disposed of the goal of full employment, the MSC disposed of the goal of helping those most disadvantaged. We had little control over how the MSC interpreted the data or, more explicitly, the *value* it placed on different findings.

For example, the study found that young women, whether qualified or not, were more disadvantaged on the labour market than young men. This was interpreted by the MSC as an example of conservative 'rural' culture even though this was also found in other studies in urban communities (McDermott and Dench, 1983). The study also found that there were many more people looking for jobs than there were jobs available; and this even applied to those young people who moved to find jobs. This was a major challenge to the government's assumption that the problem was a youth problem, or immaturity, a lack of discipline and experience. The MSC and the government explained this finding by claiming that young people lacked 'training' in the 'new technology' where there were or 'would be' jobs.

This justified the need for the MSC to create a new programme to replace the YOP: a training programme that would take all school-leavers off the labour market for two years and train them in the new technology (MSC, 1981). With one stroke it eliminated 16–18-year-old unemployment by taking school-leavers off the labour market entirely.

There would no longer be a promise of a bridge to work either. The new programme would fill the 'training gap' (the newly defined problem) that would allow the young people to compete more competently for the new jobs. Hence, those who did not get a job after training failed to train properly rather than failed to get a job.

Today these policies are irrelevant to the reality of mass unemployment. The government is merely altering pools of unemployment, reshuffling the pack, without creating jobs. All these examples show that the MSC cannot simply be understood as a palliative to unemployment. It is a response to the 'political' problems posed by unemployment but which attempts to 'depoliticize' that response.

The MSC director announced the new programme by stating its goals

> to equip 18-year-olds with the wherewithal for personal survival in the 1980s. This means taking account of the fact that we do not know where they will get jobs, that we do not know whether they will get jobs and that it seems likely that those less competitive will experience unemployment for some time.
>
> (MSC, 1981, p. 3).

Gone is the goal of full employment (Marsden, 1982); gone is the goal of helping those most disadvantaged on the labour market. The New Training Initiative is aimed to expand compulsory education from 16 to 18, relieving pressure on the labour market and the political pressure of rising unemployment statistics. It is aimed at relieving the moral panic brought on by rebellious unemployed youth who threatened a complacent society in the riots of London and Liverpool in 1981 and again in London and Birmingham in 1985. The New Training Initiative is creating a new role for the MSC: a transformative mode of restructuring the workforce; of providing skills in the new technology for jobs that do not exist now but supposedly exist in some future; of providing socialization in the values of a flexible and disciplined workforce while denying access to work; and by altering the distribution and types of work with as little resistance from the workforce as possible.

By altering our focus from the perspective of the young people to the perspective of the MSC, the meaning of unemployment to the government and the social construction of that meaning to the public gradually emerges. The government's explanation for the causes of unemployment has focused on the individual worker's behaviour. It assumes that unemployment is temporary and necessary to combat a more serious evil – inflation. If the market is left alone, free from state intervention, there will be a 'natural' competition which will create 'natural' wages and will leave society with a 'natural' rate of unemployment. This biological metaphor fits well within a social-Darwinist paradigm of survival of the fittest adapted by this government and expressed by its calls to get on your bike and stop being moaning minnies.

Government policy then becomes one of taking down barriers that would interfere with the 'natural' workings of the market, curbing the power of the unions and their demand for 'unreasonable' wages. High unemployment is explained either by a mismatch of where labour is and where jobs are or by the fact that labour does not have the correct skills or attitudes.

This case study shows that government *does* try to use the research data to legitimate its role, as well as trying to control the framework in which the research takes place. Hopefully the case study has also shown that researchers must recognize the constraints placed on them and recognize the power they themselves have in the negotiations. Furthermore, by analysing the whole process of social planning, including the framework within which decisions are made, a more comprehensive understanding of social problems and policy implementation will be achieved.

A few years ago, Laura Nader called for anthropologists to 'study up', to start doing the same research on those in power as we have done on those who are powerless (Nader, 1974). As more social scientists are engaged in contract research an opportunity presents itself to scrutinize the culture of the bureaucracy, to analyse power networks and to discover the hidden functions of social policy and of contract research. However, this can be done only by stepping in and out of the contract research role, by acting as a true participant observer, by viewing the negotiations and the decisions over the research itself as part of the data in a process of an exchange of power relations. Accountability, then, might shift even a little towards those in power.

References

McDermott, K., and Dench, S. (1983), *Youth Opportunities in a Rural Area* (London: MSC).

Manpower Services Commission (1979), *Towards a Comprehensive Manpower Policy* (London: MSC).

Manpower Services Commission (1981), *A New Training Initiative: An Agenda for Action* (London: MSC).

Marsden, D. (1982), *Workless: An Explanation of the Social Contract between Society and the Worker* (London: Croom Helm).

Nader, L. (1974), 'Up the anthropologist – perspectives gained from studying up', in D. Hymes (ed.), *Reinventing Anthropology* (New York: Vantage Books), pp. 284–311.

Wolf, E. (1974), 'American anthropologists and American society', in D. Hymes, *Reinventing Anthropology* (New York: Vantage Books), pp. 251–63.

9

Doing Research into Discrimination: Problems of Method, Interpretation and Ethics

RICHARD JENKINS,
Department of Anthropology and Sociology, University College, Swansea, Wales

Abstract
This chapter is concerned with the problems and opportunities encountered in the course of a research project concerning employers' selection criteria and discrimination against black workers. There are two central issues. First, what are the implications of the methods one adopts, and the access strategies one follows – either by choice, or by simple dint of circumstance – for the grounds upon which we can presume to offer the resultant account as valid sociological knowledge? Second, the ethical issues which arose during the fieldwork and the subsequent writing up are discussed, although – as is the way with ethical problems – no authoritative solutions can be offered. The problems attached to conducting research in the context of consultancy work are also broached. More generally, the chapter argues that methodological, epistemological and ethical issues are, in research practice, routinely implicated each with the others, and cannot be approached as discrete sets of problems.

This chapter discusses some of the methodological, epistemological and ethical (or political) issues which arose during research into discrimination in selection for employment in the West Midlands area of the United Kingdom between 1980 and 1983. The full report of this research has been published elsewhere (Jenkins, 1986). Part of a wider programme of work within the then SSRC Research Unit on Ethnic Relations at the University of Aston in Birmingham,* the aims of the research were to achieve a more comprehensive understanding than previous studies had produced of the processes of discrimination and racism in recruitment to employment. Motivated in part by an

* The unit has since moved to the University of Warwick, as the Centre for Research in Ethnic Relations.

I have discussed elsewhere (Jenkins, 1984), the process of conducting participant observer research in an urban setting in Northern Ireland. That paper addresses issues concerned with the identity of the field-worker, the problem of uneven access, the limitations of participant observation and the ethics of research. These problems surface again in the discussion which follows. Two other issues are also central to this chapter. First, what are the grounds for my being sufficiently confident of the representativeness and validity of my informants' statements to use them as trustworthy data? Second, what are the difficulties or opportunities which arise when, as part of the research process, the collection of information becomes linked to consultancy exercises?

Methodology

Given that I was concerned to understand the *processes* of the labour market, the emphasis was essentially qualitative. I set out to examine a relatively small number of organizations in as much depth as possible. Qualitative research often implies the use of participant observation. However, although every opportunity for the informal observation of routine organizational activity was taken, participant observation was only a peripheral feature of this research, for the following reasons.

First, in the West Midlands labour market of the early 1980s there was little recruitment taking place to be observed, although there was some. Second, although it would have been desirable and in theory possible to videotape or otherwise record selection interviews and panel discussions – and this has been done (i.e. Silverman and Jones, 1976) – it is difficult to imagine a recruitment situation in which an observer could actually *participate* (although this may overestimate the degree to which most participant observation involves participation as a member). Third, given the sensitivity of the 'race relations' or 'discrimination' issues, it is unlikely that an employer would have permitted a researcher interested in such matters to observe or record recruitment occasions. Employing organizations were not even approached with such a request because it might have put them off

---

argument that it was time to shift the emphasis in research from the behaviour of black ethnic minorities towards white society and racism, and in part by a view that within labour-market studies more generally the demand side of the labour market had at that time been neglected, the focus of the project was upon the practices and beliefs of managers and supervisors and the institutional arrangements governing selection, recruitment and promotion within work organizations.

altogether. As it was, hostility and suspicion were at times encountered in response to a much less threatening request for co-operation.

Given these considerations, the primary method adopted was the loosely structured interview, using an interview schedule composed primarily of open-ended questions.

For reasons of convenience and cost the research was carried out in the West Midlands. In order to include as wide a range of employment contexts as possible, it was decided to examine three industrial sectors: manufacturing, the public sector and large-scale retailing. Of the thirty-three large retailing organizations contacted, eleven (33 per cent) responded positively: seven department stores, two supermarket chains and two multiple-store organizations selling a range of specialized merchandize. In the public sector, fourteen (58 per cent) out of twenty-four organizations contacted co-operated: three in local government, one in higher education, five in the health service and five in the broad area of public transport and utilities. In manufacturing, out of seventy-three companies contacted, only fifteen (21 per cent) agreed to co-operate: five companies in metal manufacturing, three in chemicals and plastics, three in engineering, three in food and drink processing and one other manufacturing firm.

It is perhaps worth speculating upon the reasons for the variation in the response rate between these three groups of organizations. Looking at the higher response rate in the public sector, it appears from discussions with members of these organizations that this may have been partly due to some sense of responsibility as public institutions. In addition, it is my impression that the proportion of graduates I encountered was higher in the public sector, and this may have influenced their readiness to co-operate with a university researcher. Third, it is probably the case that public-sector organizations accept inquiries as a routine aspect of their working environment. Fourth, the municipal politics of 'race' are important; some of the local authorities concerned expressed a public commitment to anti-racism or 'equal opportunity' and thus could not reasonably have refused at least an initial meeting.

On the other side of the coin, the relatively low response rate in manufacturing appears to reflect two factors. First, manufacturing has been one of the most important sites for 'race relations' conflicts in employment, rendering managers in these organizations perhaps more sensitive about the issue and correspondingly suspicious of outside investigators. Second, in the present recession, with more pressing matters facing them, managers in manufacturing, possibly the most heavily researched area of employment in the United Kingdom, may not be disposed to co-operate with 'another bloody academic'.

Looking at retailing, there appeared to be no identifiable factors working to produce either a particularly high or a particularly low response rate. Looking at non-responses, at least three organizations – one in manufacturing and two in the public sector – refused their co-operation because they had previously been required to co-operate, in one way or another, with the Commission for Racial Equality (CRE). This experience had apparently been such as to discourage them from further dealings with members of the 'race relations industry'. This was only the first of a number of occasions on which the CRE's activities had a bearing upon the conduct of the research. It served as a timely reminder – if one were needed – of the highly politicized nature of the social field with which the research was concerned.

In contacting organizations I usually wrote to the personnel manager or to some other member of the personnel function. In those few organizations which lacked a personnel function, a reply, if one came at all, came from the manager or, in some public organizations, from the administrator, whose task it was to cover personnel-type responsibilities. In all cases where access was eventually agreed upon, the initial interview was with a personnel specialist. Having got this far, I then requested access to other members of the personnel department who were involved in recruitment, and to those line managers responsible for making selection decisions. The degree to which this request was granted varied enormously, from organizations in which the personnel interviewee was unwilling or unable to allow me further access, to those in which I interviewed five or six people, to the two case-study organizations: 'Midshire Utility,' where I formally interviewed thirty-eight people, and 'King Co', where the number was twenty-seven. In the case of the latter two organizations, access was granted only on condition that I prepared a consultancy report on specific 'race-related' issues for their own internal purposes. It was these *quid-pro-quo* arrangements which afforded me the luxury of case studies. Where the personnel function was unable to afford me further access, this was often a reflection of the personnel specialism's relatively disadvantaged position within the hierarchies of organizational politics. In terms of access to resources and the exercise of influence, it was only rarely that the personnel functions in the organizations studied were central to policy- or decision-making.

It must now be asked: how representative of the wider labour-market situation is the interview material from these organizations? This question cannot be answered with any precision. However, in the absence of indications to the contrary, there is no reason to suspect that these organizations and managers are particularly exceptional or *un*representative. This impression is supported by two other considerations. First, the findings of this study are broadly in agreement with an existing body of research into recruitment practices in the United Kingdom. Second, there is a degree of internal consistency in the data, both within and between the organizations examined. It can therefore be concluded with some confidence that the broad findings of this research project may be generalized to other urban, multi-ethnic labour markets in Great Britain.

However, the further question must be asked: how representative of the organizations themselves is the interview material from the managers and supervisors concerned? To answer this, it is necessary to recognize that research reports are socially constructed. Data and analysis are no less artefactual, no more 'objective', than the lay testimony which provides the basis for their production. However, that testimony was itself produced – with a few exceptions that are the result of informal discussions, chance conversations, etc. – within a particular social context, a research interview. It is therefore worth examining the factors which may have affected the conduct of the interviews, since these, in turn, may have had an effect on the nature of the material gathered and its reliability.

To begin, let us consider the reasons why managers as individuals agreed to be interviewed. This discussion is based largely on hunches which emerged from informal chats with managers before or after interviews, over lunch or during other non-interview occasions. As such, it is merely my personal interpretation of the situation.

There appear to be seven major reasons for co-operation being accorded. First, there were those managers who were content in the belief that there were 'no problems here', a common enough perspective with respect to 'race relations' (Carby and Thakur, 1977). They appeared to regard my visit as an opportunity to have this interpretation of their situation rubber-stamped by an external (and, in their eyes, quasi-official) agency. In such situations, interviews were generally unproblematic, if occasionally uninformative. Their complacency, however, was frequently born of an apparent ignorance about the kind of situation which might be interpreted as a 'race relations problem'. Correspondingly, many of these interviewees were disarmingly frank about attitudes or situations which, to me, indicated that there certainly might be a problem. 'Ignorance' may be the wrong word, however, since many of them were undoubtedly aware, for example, of the CRE and its position on many employment issues. It might be more correct therefore to say that, any alternative to their taken-for-granted model of the situation was, for them, inconceivable among 'reasonable people'. Given that I did my best to present myself as non-threatening, that was clearly the category to which I was allocated by these interviewees.

The 'no problems here' approach was prevalent in the two main case-study organizations, particularly 'Midshires Utility'. In both cases, as part of the *quid-pro-quo* agreement under which I gained access, I was required to prepare consultancy reports, in one case on the implementation of an equal opportunity policy, in the other on the general state of 'race relations' in the organization. In both cases, the reports were critical of the organization's practices and received a hostile reception. Again in both cases, although also most markedly in 'Midshires Utility', despite the fact that the interview schedule and the methodology had been approved by senior members of each organization prior to the interviewing, among the grounds for attacking the reports were that they were either factually wrong or methodologically insubstantial, or that particular questions had been inadequately designed. That may well have been the case. One may, however, be forgiven for wondering whether they would have been so critical of the finer points of method had the reports' conclusions been more sympathetic to their case.

Although these difficulties created a headache for me at the time – particularly in the case of 'King Co', with whose representatives I had to negotiate for a considerable period following the submission of my consultancy report, before I could be certain that they would not attempt to prevent publication of the research – it must be emphasized that they also created opportunities. Most obviously, perhaps, the nature and tenor of their managers' objections were, in themselves, revealing about attitudes and practices. In as much as these sometimes lengthy consultancy 'debriefing' meetings were among the few situations in which I was a full participant, they were also a useful source of ethnography. With respect to 'King Co', the discussions were particularly useful in that the organization's personnel specialists managed to convince me, on the basis of argumentation and evidence, that a central aspect of my interpretation of their equal opportunity policy was wrong. Without our (occasionally acrimonious) exchanges, this error would have found its way into my academic work, unrecognized by me and profoundly misleading for the reader.

The uncomfortable question must be asked: how often do such mistakes creep unannounced into our work? In the absence of routine referring back from the researcher to the researched, it may be more frequently than we care to imagine. An equally uncomfortable possibility – that I may have been right in the first place and was subsequently hoodwinked by 'King Co's' managers – must also be recognized. There is, however, no way of knowing.

Second, related to the above, there were those managers who not only felt that they had 'no problems' but were also actively hostile to the 'race relations industry' or 'do-gooding academics'. Some people in this category appeared to have agreed to see me only in order that they might have the opportunity to pin one of the 'opposition' down in an interview chair and harangue him. Sometimes – very rarely, thank goodness – the situation was so difficult that the only option was to beat as dignified a retreat as possible. In other cases, however, it was possible to conduct an interview. The latter were often among the most interesting and revealing interviews.

The third apparent reason for giving an interview was the opposite of these; here one encountered a manager who felt certain that there *was* some kind of a problem, but either was not sure what it was, or did not know what to do about it. These were among the most difficult interviews, certainly for me, and possibly, I suspect, for the interviewees as well. Our goals and objectives were often at odds right from the moment I walked into the office. I wanted information; he or she wanted advice and help. Unfortunately, I was rarely in a position to be able to offer either, apart from suggesting people to contact or publications which might be useful.

Fourth, there was the situation in which a manager knew what the problem was and often had a good idea what the remedy might be. For a variety of reasons, however, largely to do with the organizational weakness of personnel management, he or she felt – usually with some justice – unable to do anything about it. This inability to act was frequently in conflict with a professional identity (as a personnel specialist) or personal political beliefs. Contact with me provided such a person with an opportunity to talk to a sympathetic outsider about the situation, and the chance to 'strike back' by exposing the problem to external scrutiny (albeit in an anonymous report).

An example of this kind of motivation is presented by 'John', Personnel Manager for 'Butterfield Brass Ltd', a metal manufacturing company. A social science graduate with postgraduate professional personnel training, John had been given explicit instructions by his top management that 'no coloureds can become foremen' and, in the face of blatant managerial *and* shop-floor racism, reluctantly felt he had no option but to comply with these instructions. Given the economic climate at the time, another job might have been difficult to find. His response to my initial letter appears to have been conditioned by his feelings about the situation: 'When I got this [the initial letter], I thought to myself that there are two ways of answering this. I could either give you the official position or I could invite you down here informally and tell you what actually happens.' Despite John's being anxious that the content of our discussions should not get back to his superiors, he did manage to arrange five further interviews in the organization.

A fifth reason for managerial accessibility was a sense of public responsibility. A significant number of managers – in both the public and private sectors – saw the pursuit of 'racial harmony' as desirable and felt that by participating in this research they might make a contribution to that goal. These managers were frequently personnel specialists with a commitment to the liberal professional ideology of personnel management. The political climate of local government was often an important influence as well in this respect.

Following this, there were those managers who I can describe only as convivially motivated to participate; I got the impression that what they wanted was to fill a couple of hours of their day with an interesting chat. Managers who appeared to fall into this category may also have seen me as a legitimate excuse for organizing lunch with wine on expenses or in the executive dining room. One of the worst offenders in this respect was a public-sector organization which sent me home on several occasions feeling very much the worse for wear. The main problem with these interviewees was keeping them (and myself) on the point! In addition, some of them, those with a frustrated academic bent of one sort or another, were apparently keen to talk to someone from the ivory tower.

Finally, and I suspect that this was true for a considerable number of interviewees, there were those, particularly line managers, who were talking to me because they had been instructed or requested to do so by their superiors. This is not to say that they were hostile, simply that they were busy people who had better things to do elsewhere. As a result, some of these interviews were conducted more quickly than I should have liked; conversely, however, some were very revealing, and all the more so since they often took place in the individual's office on the shop-floor or wherever. This gave me a clearer idea about the situations we were discussing than I might otherwise have had.

Discussion of these interviewees highlights a further difficulty with respect to the representativeness of the data. Since I did not select which managers I should interview, once an organization had agreed to my being granted further access there is the possibility that, due to selection by higher-level management or the refusal (unknown to me) of certain individuals to be interviewed, the composition of the resulting group of interviewees might be biased in particular ways. This may well be the case. It is unfortunately impossible to judge the matter without further information. Suffice it to say that on examining the interview material there seems to be a wide spectrum of responses represented; there are no grounds for thinking that a particular body of opinion has been overlooked.

The reasons why managers talked to me (or not) are one set of factors which may have affected the content of the interviews. The practical accomplishment of the interview, the way in which questions were formulated and asked, also has a bearing on this matter. This is particularly important given the sensitivity of the 'race relations' issue for many of these managers. There are two aspects of this topic which are relevant, the first being the nature of the questions and the structure of the interview schedule. In constructing the interview, my aim was to approach the topic of black workers and 'race' indirectly; in order to do so, the questions concerning these matters were placed at the end. Before getting to these questions, therefore, the discussion should have ranged over a spectrum of subjects, from routine recruitment procedures, to the economic recession, to 'young people today'. By that time it was hoped that the interviewee would have relaxed sufficiently for the questions on black workers not to be seen as threatening. As part of this approach, I was always at pains to point out to managers that, although my research was about 'race', I was interested in a much broader range of subjects as well. This is an example of a research approach which Barrett (1984, p. 9) has appropriately characterized as 'deceptive candour'.

In addition, some of the questions relating to 'race' were framed in such a way that issues were touched upon indirectly. For example, instead of simply asking the respondent what his or her views about black people were, the following question was asked: 'Since the Second World War, many immigrants have come to work in the United Kingdom. Why do you think this has happened?' A question of this nature, while allowing for a fairly straightforward 'historical' answer, also gave those interviewees who wished to do so the opportunity to adumbrate their broader views on the 'race relations' topic. Needless to say, many of them did just that.

The second important dimension of the conduct of the interview was the manner in which the tone or ambience of the occasion was managed. Given that I could usually choose neither the time nor the physical setting for the interview, there was a limit to what I could accomplish in this respect. However, I did endeavour to influence this aspect of the interview in at least two ways. First, if the situation allowed, I spent some time before the interview itself in general chit-chat with the interviewee. I attempted wherever possible to establish some sort of 'co-membership' with the individual concerned. Since I have previously worked for short periods in engineering and for a local education authority, this experience was a resource to draw upon in the context of manufacturing and local government. Depending on the manager concerned, there were often other things in common which could be used in this manner. On the same lines, I was always careful to dress appropriately, to be acceptable.

The other interview management technique was a conscious attempt to adopt a 'normal talk' strategy. By this I mean the attempt to conduct the interview as though it were informal, an 'ordinary conversation'. I also tried, in so far as this was possible, to allow the natural flow of the 'conversation' to dictate the order in which the questions were asked, although I did try to keep the 'race' questions to the end. This did not, of course, always happen. A further price to pay for the 'normal talk' approach was that, due to constraints on time, not all the questions were always asked.

Interpretation

The 'indirect' approach to the 'race relations' question and the 'normal talk' interview strategy were designed to lower the guard of my respondents so that they might be more open and honest in their responses. Whether or not the endeavour was successful is best left to the judgement of the reader of the final report (Jenkins, 1986). However, this question and the issues raised in the previous section – i.e. the wide variety of motivations which lie behind the statements of interviewees, the differing rates of response and access between organizations and industries, and the problematic degree to which the interviews actually document what managers 'really' think or know – prompt the question: what do we have at the end of it all? Is it a usable, coherent body of data, or a collection of non-comparable and unreliable individual statements?

There is no final argument by means of which one can either 'prove' or 'refute' the generic reliability of the interview material. One can only reiterate the argument that, given a degree of internal consistency within the data and the reassuringly high level of agreement with the findings of other researchers, there is no reason to doubt the data's reliability *on principle*. On this basis, there is no option but to treat the interviewees' statements as provisionally reliable, as usable data in the absence of contradictions of this nature.

Considerations of this nature made the two organizational case studies important for this research. They allowed me the luxury of a degree of informal observation which was impossible in the organizations studied more superficially, and the possibility of cross-checking one informant's statements against another's. The latter is essential in attempting to make some sort of judgement of 'what is actually going on'. Judgements of this kind can never be authoritative, but that is no excuse for not making them, albeit in a spirit of appropriate modesty.

The fact that the case studies were linked to consultancies was particularly useful in this context, for three reasons. First, in as much as 'race relations' were a controversial topic in both organizations, I had a privileged entrée to internal organizational politics, particularly with respect to relationships between personnel, line and top management. Second, because the exercise was seen by some people within these organizations as being either in their own or the organization's interests, the access and co-operation I received were better than might otherwise have been the case. However, in as much as these respondents were often engaged in departmental or organizational politics, their testimony had to be carefully interpreted. Moreover, the necessity to submit consultancy reports gave me an opportunity to compare my own interpretation of policy and practice within these organizations with the interpretations of senior managers. In one case, as mentioned earlier, I was persuaded to revise my interpretation of a particular aspect of organizational policy.

Issues of this kind raise a further epistemological problem, that of the relationship between the knowledge of lay actors (folk models) and the knowledge of the social scientist (analytical models). It is, I hope, implicit in the above discussion that analytical models should not be seen as the more 'objective' or factual. I have discussed this topic elsewhere (Jenkins, 1983, pp. 9–11), so suffice it to say here that epistemological equality should be accorded to folk and analytical models. They are both generated by actors, as models of people and objects and their relationships with each other in the social world. The difference between the two kinds of understanding lies more in the fact that they are produced and mobilized by different people in different settings for different ends, than in their relative 'objectivity' or facticity.

Epistemological equality does not mean, however, that they are the same or interchangeable. This is important in the context of the present discussion, in as much as my analytical model is, on occasions, in sharp contradiction to respondents' folk models, the statements of interviewees. This is certainly so in the case of the consultancy reports. Such disagreement should not be interpreted as an example of that commonplace academic arrogance which privileges the analyst's understanding of the world as 'true', in opposition to the 'false knowledge' or ignorance of mere actors. It is, however, fully in keeping with the view being put forward here to insist that analytical interpretations of social reality are different from folk interpretations and may be able to make more sense of the social world. For example, analytical models should be capable of including the contradictions between differing folk models within their scope; social scientists often have access to a broader, more heterogeneous stock of information about a given situation than do lay actors; and social science models, unlike most folk models, are explicitly intended to be explanatory and communicative. These are the grounds upon which I offer my account of the practices of the managers under discussion in preference to their own testimony concerning and explaining those practices. While that testimony is an integral and necessary part of my account, it cannot be allowed to delineate the limits of explanation.

Ethics

The issues raised so far in this chapter also have their ethical dimension. Although there is not the space for a comprehensive discussion of all the ethical problems encountered, there are three areas of concern which warrant some attention. The first of these involves the ethical difficulties encountered during the fieldwork process. The second relates to what one actually does with the data once they have been gathered. The distinction between these two sets of ethical problems is not always clear-cut. Third, there is the question of the shift in research from the 'victim' to the victimizer, in this case, as mentioned at the beginning of the chapter, from black minorities to white racism.

Research of the kind which we are discussing must raise problems for a researcher who has an anti-racist political perspective. Perhaps the most minor of these is the need to maintain a neutral pose while interviewing someone whose answers to your questions would provoke an angry or critical response in other situations. This, however, is a small issue; after all, one of the major reasons for conducting the interviews was to gather information about managerial attitudes to black workers, no matter how personally objectionable I might have found them. Similarly, one ought to be able to deal with the (usually even more revealing) 'backstage' conversations before the interview or over lunch without agreeing with, or supporting, what the individual is saying. Once again, to cite Barrett (1984), this is a matter for 'deceptive candour'. The problem became most urgent when I was trying to tread a delicate tightrope between pressing questions home, on the one hand, and attempting not to alienate the interviewee while negotiating for further access, on the other. There were, of course, occasions when such considerations ceased to be important, when the interviewee was either hostile from the start or had unavoidably become so. These occasions, inevitable as they may have been, were fortunately rare.

A more serious difficulty occurred when I came across evidence of either 'one-off' or systematic racist discrimination. Should it be exposed? Such a course of action, however, was unthinkable – even if there was any certainty of effective action being taken, which is unlikely. The conditions under which I negotiated access with organizations were that anonymity be guaranteed, for both the organization and its employees. Without such a guarantee, which is a standard convention in qualitative research, the research would have been impossible. All that can be done in a situation of this kind is to try to convince oneself that the potential value of the research outweighs short-term considerations.

The problem was thrown into sharp relief by a telephone call which I received from the regional offices of the Commission for Racial Equality. One of the CRE's officers, acting on his personal initiative, was keen to see my data on a particular organization. Having an interest in that company himself, he had heard 'on the grapevine' that I had also conducted some research into its recruitment practices. A request of this nature can, of course, only be refused, although that is not how the person on the other end of the telephone saw the matter. His somewhat irate view was that, since we were both in the business of attacking discrimination, I had a moral obligation to co-operate with him. He could not conceive that I might also have obligations to my respondents and to my own (and the Research Unit's) integrity. Fortunately, he had no more persuasive weapons in his armoury than his nuisance value.

Any kind of fieldwork also raises more general ethical issues, two of which seem in retrospect to be important. To refer back to the earlier discussion of interview-management strategies, how defensible is it to attempt to establish some sort of co-membership with an interviewee? There may well be situations, as in much feminist research, in which this kind of temporary relationship-building has a genuine foundation. If I am to be honest, however, this was not the case in this situation. It was simply a cynical ploy on my part, aimed at improving the quality of the research data, and only defensible as such. My own view is that in this case – where the interviewees were very much in control of most if not all aspects of the situation and potentially on the defensive – the means were justified by the end.

One other ethical bone of contention which frequently arises in field research concerns me here: what to do with information which you have explicitly been told is 'off the record'. Regrettably – from a research point of view, that is – I think that on nearly all occasions the subject's wishes must be respected. Such a situation never arose during this research, the guarantee of confidentiality being sufficient to reassure most interviewees that they had no need to speak 'off the record'.

This is not to say, however, that there were no misunderstandings about which statements should be considered appropriate as research data. The issue arose particularly sharply with respect to my use of casual and informal conversational material in the consultancy report to one of the case-study organizations. Among the organization's responses to this report was the view that my recording of this talk was 'eavesdropping' and that it was not 'legitimate material' for my report. Despite the fact that the other members of the particular conversation briefly reported upon knew that I was a researcher interested in 'race' issues, and could have guarded their tongues accordingly when chatting to me over lunch, there was clearly a misapprehension here, for which I must be held at least partly responsible. The individuals concerned obviously thought that only the formal interview was 'research'; I, however, have a much wider view of research as an activity. This kind of situation is probably inevitable. Since the conversation was not, as far as I was concerned, 'off the record' and was used anonymously, I would insist that it remains ethically legitimate research material. Representatives of the organization concerned, however, remain unhappy about its use.

There is also the question of the shift from studying ethnic minorities to studying white society and racism. Stanley Barrett has argued that this switch of attention from the victim to the victimizer, the powerless to the powerful, has been canvassed as the 'only one path open to ethnically-attained anthropology' (1984, p. 4). The same holds good, I think, for sociology. He goes on to argue in the same passage, however, that such a change 'is a dubious solution, partly because innumerable ethical problems remain'. He later writes (pp. 23–4) that it is a false solution for two other reasons: one, because any discipline which seriously attempts to searchingly investigate the powerful is unlikely to prosper, or even to endure; and two, because of the fact that subversive research is unlikely to have any effect anyway.

To discuss the last two reasons first, they seem, if nothing else, contradictory. There appears little likelihood that ineffectual social research should be seen as a threat. There are four more substantial replies which can be made to Barrett's arguments, however. First, he underestimates the complexity of heterogeneity of modern state societies, particularly in the liberal democracies. He does not appear to recognize either the 'usefulness' of the existence of weak oppositional elements to the powerful in their claim to legitimate domination in a 'free society', or the continued perverse power of an established legal framework concerned with the rights, duties and liberties of the citizen to resist the censorial excesses of the centralized state. It seems to me unlikely, therefore, although admittedly possible, that the social sciences will further threaten their already tenuous existence by conducting critical research into the activities of the more powerful strata of society.

Second, given that the social sciences – particularly social anthropology – are fundamentally conservative disciplines, betraying in this their institutional origins and organization, there is little likelihood anyway that they will convert *en masse* to a strategy of subversive, critical research. Nor is it likely that much of what research is done into the powerful will be particularly subversive or critical. This, of course, should not blind us to the possibility that *individual* researchers may be victimized for undertaking this kind of research. This has happened before and will doubtless happen again.

Third, even were Barrett's worst fears justified, it is indefensible to argue that a solution to an ethical problem is dubious simply because of its career consequences for the researcher or its financial or institutional consequences for the discipline. Ethical dilemmas cannot be solved, or their solutions judged, using criteria of economic or political expediency. If they could, they would not be *ethical* dilemmas. It is, of course, necessary to consider such worldly issues in this context, particularly in the harsh climate presently faced by the social sciences. However, it is equally necessary to insist that ethics and pragmatics must not be conflated in our thinking. It is imperative, in the interests of the preservation of critical social science, that we distinguish as sharply as possible between, on the one hand, professional ethics, personal morality and political conviction, and, on the other, economic constraints, institutional survival and political expediency.

While the strategem Barrett is discussing may, in his judgement, be imprudent, such a conclusion has no bearing upon its dubiety as a solution to ethical problems.

Fourth, there is the question of the ability of social research to achieve change. This is a complex issue, too much so to allow an adequate discussion of it here. Suffice it to say, in response to Barrett's argument, that since the effect or applicability of research may be apparent only with the benefit of hindsight, it is unconvincing to argue that a specific research project is unsatisfactory because it is unlikely to have an effect on the 'problem' with which it is concerned. This is particularly true if one accepts that the definition of a satisfactory effect or application is unlikely to be either disinterested or free from ideological influences.

In closing, there is the question of the innumerable ethical problems which apparently remain if one turns one's attention to racism. There are, of course, problems; this section has largely been taken up with their discussion. Some of these, however, are common to *all* research which involves the researcher in face-to-face contact with his or her subjects. As to the rest, it seems to me that they are the lesser of two evils by comparison with the problems which I would probably have experienced had I conducted research, as a white researcher with a commitment to anti-racist politics, into black ethnic minorities. In any case – and this is where Barrett may miss the point in his concentration upon ethics *per se* – given that my research orientation, for example, was based upon a consideration of previous research and a diagnosis of the primary causes of ethnic disadvantage in the labour market as being located in demand-side processes of discrimination, the decision to undertake research into the behaviour of recruitment decision-makers, i.e. the more powerful actors in this context, was motivated by academic judgements as well as ethical constraints and/or political beliefs. Not that these are easily distinguished in most instances, simply that it is both possible and necessary to differentiate between the different sets of criteria which inevitably enter into judgements about research plans and activities, and to be explicit about the reciprocally influential relationships which they have with each other.

I have tried in this chapter to highlight some of the problems which were encountered during a research project concerned with racism and discrimination in selection for employment. These problems are not particularly new; nor did I successfully resolve all of them. It is my intention, in airing them in this manner, to enable the reader to appreciate some of the social processes by which the finished products, a research report and later a book, were produced.

In keeping with the theme of this collection, however, I have also tried to explicate some of the problems involved in doing work on a politically sensitive topic. Internal organizational politics and the activities of organizations such as the Commission for Racial Equality impinged in various ways on the research, often making the work more difficult than it need have been. However, particularly in the context of the case studies, this kind of problem was, perversely, more a source of opportunities than anything else. If my experience on this particular project is a yardstick, applied or contract research, while beset with its own peculiar constraints, may allow the researcher a privileged insight into the workings of the institutions and organizations for or with which they are working. Provided that the researcher is able, as I was, to maintain a distance or independence from the concerns and control of the host or sponsor, this is a situation to be cautiously welcomed.

References

Barrett, S. R. (1984), 'Racism, ethics and the subversive nature of anthropological inquiry', *Philosophy of the Social Sciences*, vol. 14, pp. 1–25.

Carby, K., and Thakur, M. (1977), *No Problems Here: Management and the Multi-Racial Work Force* (London: Institute of Personnel Management/ Commission for Racial Equality).

Jenkins, R. (1983), *Lads, Citizens and Ordinary Kids: Working-Class Youth Life-Styles in Belfast* (London: Routledge & Kegan Paul).

Jenkins, R. (1984), 'Bringing it all back home: an anthropologist in Belfast', in C. Bell, and H. Roberts (eds.), *Social Researching: Politics, Problems, Practice* (London: Routledge & Kegan Paul).

Jenkins, R. (1986), *Racism and Recruitment: Managers, Organizations and Equal Opportunity in the Labour Market* (Cambridge University Press).

Silverman, D., and Jones, J. (1976), *Organizational Work: The Language of Grading/The Grading of Language* (London: Collier-Macmillan).

V

Unexpected Results and Outcomes

Introduction to Part Five

Once agreement on a research project has been reached between sponsors and researchers both sides have their own expectations of outcomes. Broadly speaking, the sponsors will provide the funds and the researcher will conduct the research as laid out in the proposal or application and, upon completion within the agreed period of time, will submit a final report to the funding agency. Beyond this, specific arrangements may be made for continuous feedback, consultancy, other publication, etc. In Part Four unspecified expectations were discussed which were referred to as hidden agendas; attention was drawn to the fact that expectations, mainly on the part of the sponsor but also on the part of the researcher, may change during the research process. In many cases such changes can be negotiated more or less harmoniously between the parties to the original agreement. In some instances, however, the mismatch of expectations can lead to overt conflict and 'moral recriminations' (Orlans, 1967).

Orlans (1967) has suggested that many of the ethical and practical problems of research can be foreseen and should be negotiated and resolved before the work is begun. However, where conflicts arise from incompatible expectations these cannot be foreseen, and as Part Four indicates the mismatch frequently results from different definitions of the problems or from results which are contrary to those anticipated by sponsors.

Part Four also raised the question of power in the research relationship. The power relationship between researchers and target populations has been widely discussed in this volume and elsewhere, Bell and Encel (1978) for instance have said, 'Sociology is done *on* the relatively powerless *for* the relatively powerful' (p. 25). The same can be said of other social sciences. The power relationship between researchers and sponsors has already been mentioned in the context of 'studying up', but the potential exercise of power exists whatever the topic of research. Orlans (1967), in talking about research sponsors, suggested that their 'ineradicable offense is not their wickedness but their power' (p. 20), although the experience of a few researchers might incline them to the view that some exercise of power could be defined as wickedness.

It is when the research process takes an unexpected turn or comes up with embarrassing findings that the exercise of power is most likely to pose difficulties for researchers. The two chapters in this part deal with the responses of very different bureaucracies to potentially embarrassing findings. Both research projects were concerned with values in controversial topic areas: Warwick's chapter deals with birth control, and Jaeger and Wenger's with gender discrimination. In neither case were the motivations or objective of the sponsors clearly articulated by those who controlled the administration of the research, supporting the argument that conflicts are more likely when expectations are not made clear in advance (Orlans, 1967; Cox, Hausfeld and Wills, 1978). However, this is not sufficient explanation for the problems which developed. In Warwick's case, external political pressures and developments impinged on the funding agency's perceptions of the research. In Jaeger's case, unexpected findings raised ethical questions about the agency's own practices. In both instances, publication of the findings was potentially embarrassing.

The context in which the two projects were conducted could not have reflected a greater contrast. Warwick's chapter discusses a large comparative multinational United Nations research programme. Jaeger's research involved a low-budget project studying the secondary schools of one British county. The response of the research sponsors when faced with findings likely to cause embarrassment was in both cases to exercise their power in a number of ways including attempts to suppress publication of the findings and avoid their use in the formulation of policy. In both cases, the nature of the research funded implied a concern to improve policy in the relevant field. It is interesting that in both cases findings which were deemed controversial at the time have subsequently been acted upon either in another place or at a later date.

Warwick's and Jaeger's experiences throw into relief the vulnerability of the researcher in the context of sponsored research. They raise important questions not only about the ethics of the sponsor-researcher relationship but about academic freedom. These accounts, like Hadley's, draw attention to the relative power of different researchers. In Warwick's case, he had the backing of a reputable research institute and an established academic research career. Despite his obvious frustrations with the funding agency he was able to defend the research from a position of relative strength, and as a result his academic stature and long-term career security were not adversely affected. In Jaeger's case, as an employee of the agency commissioning the research and therefore without institutional backing she was in a position where it was difficult to defend herself. Despite the fact that as a woman teacher she was ideally suited for the particular research (Roberts, 1981; Finch, 1984), this academic strength turned out to be a political weakness when faced with the all-male power structure of the bureaucracy. As a result of her powerlessness, she lost her job. There is no reason to suspect that her experience is unique. Neither is sexism the preserve of sponsors. Bell and Roberts (1984) were unable to include a chapter on gender discrimination by a male research director in their collection of studies of the research process because the women involved feared for their employment prospects. Platt (1976) alludes to similar situations.

One further comment on power must be made. The data with which Warwick's funding agency had problems was that relating to population agency personnel and policy-makers in the foreign nations studied. It was clear to Jaeger that it was her findings about staff policies which embarrassed her employers. Jenkins, as discussed in Part Four, ran into difficulty because he was studying employers. Other researchers have faced similar problems with research findings which identified racist attitudes among teachers (Eggleston, 1985). In all these cases, the data defined as problematic related to relatively powerful, articulate groups in society – in other words, groups that would read the reports and respond negatively to the findings. This response shows that the powerful may not only be afraid of 'scrutiny and rigorous academic standards' (Payne *et al.*, 1980) when *they* become the subject of research; they can also feel threatened by the potential response of the powerful subjects of the research they sponsor. This factor must surely affect the type of research that is commissioned, funded or sponsored.

In terms of academic freedom and career security the growing proportion of research sponsored or funded by policy-making bodies, whether public or private, raises anxieties about contributions to knowledge and the future development of the social science disciplines.

References

Bell, C., and Encel, S. (eds.) (1978), *Inside the Whale: Ten Personal Accounts of Social Research* (Sydney: Pergamon).

Bell, C., and Roberts, H. (1984), 'Introduction' in C. Bell and H. Roberts *Social Researching: Politics, Problems, Practice* (London: Routledge & Kegan Paul), pp. 1–13.

Cox, E., Hausfeld, F., and Wills, S. (1978), 'Taking the queen's shilling: accepting social research consultancies in the 1970s', in Bell & Encel, op. cit., pp. 121–41.

Eggleston, J. (1985), 'Low achievement of the young black pupils is often a consequence of the system', *Guardian*, 29 October.

Finch, J. (1984), ' "It's great to have someone to talk to": the ethics and politics of interviewing women', in Bell and Roberts, op. cit., pp. 70–87.

Orlans, H. (1967), 'Ethical problems in the relations of research sponsors and investigators', in G. Sjoberg (ed.), *Ethics, Politics and Social Research* (London: Routledge & Kegan Paul), pp. 3–24.

Payne, G., Dingwall, R., Payne, J., and Carter, M. (1980), 'Sociology and policy research', in G. Payne *et al.*, *Sociology and Social Research* (London: Routledge & Kegan Paul), pp. 142–59.

Platt, J. (1976), *Realities of Social Research: An Empirical Study of British Sociologists* (London: Sussex University Press).

Roberts, H. (1981), *Doing Feminist Research* (London: Routledge & Kegan Paul).

10

The Politics of Population Research with a UN Sponsor

DONALD P. WARWICK,
Harvard University, Cambridge, Mass., USA

Abstract
This chapter explores the history, politics and lessons of the project on Cultural Values and Population Policy, an eight-nation study sponsored by the United Nations Fund for Population Activities (UNFPA). The central question is why the UNFPA decided to publish absolutely nothing from the project when all of the work was completed and thousands of pages of reports were available, including a popular summary. The answer has to do with the sensitivity of the research topic; the climate of opinion among key international population assistance agencies in the early 1970s; the internal politics of the UNFPA; the specific findings from the study; and the relationship between the co-ordinating organization and the UNFPA. The study ran into trouble partly because some of the findings might be considered critical of member countries of the United Nations or of agencies providing international population assistance. The UNFPA itself had great difficulty with the idea of free publication, but vacillated on how best to deal with that question. The main lessons are that UN agencies may not be suitable sponsors for research with this level of controversy; that it is hard to carry out research when agreements with the funding source are subject to change for political reasons; that in studies of this kind it is difficult to draw sharp lines indicating who is responsible for what in publication; and that judgements about the value of new lines of research may require the lapse of a decade or more.

In June 1974 the Governing Council of the United Nations Fund for Population Activities (UNFPA) approved the Research and Training Project on Cultural Values and Population Policy. The core topic was the role of cultural values, including religious and ethical beliefs, in the formulation and implementation of population policies in the developing countries. The project was to last three years, sponsor studies in eight or more countries and cost the UNFPA $475,000. The co-ordinating unit was the Institute of Society, Ethics and the Life Sciences in Hastings-on-Hudson, New York, now known as the Hastings Center. It was a small, privately funded organization that had played a crucial part in developing the field of bioethics and was also publisher of the leading journal in that area, the *Hastings Center Report*.

The project led to studies in Egypt, Kenya, Mexico and the Philippines; smaller projects in the Dominican Republic, Haiti, India, and Lebanon; research on the strategies and values of several leading organizations providing international population assistance; a series of conferences attended by prominent scholars from several fields; published articles; and other activities. At the end there were several thousand pages of reports, including a popular summary of the main findings. Yet the UNFPA decided to publish absolutely nothing. In a letter to the Hastings Center dated 14 July 1981, the official in charge gave the following explanation:

> This review confirmed our earlier assessment, that the proposed publication would not be likely to be useful for guidance in population policy making in United Nations agencies or governments. Furthermore, the text in a number of places stated positions and conclusions with which we could not associate ourselves. We, therefore, are not prepared to publish the proposed brochure, either as an official publication of the Fund, or as a document otherwise officially associated with the Fund.

This chapter analyses the history, politics and lessons of the project. I was Project Manager throughout the study and author of the commercially published book that summarized and interpreted its findings (Warwick, 1982). I do not pretend to be detached in this account, but I will try to present the events as they happened, drawing on the boxes of correspondence and documents that accumulated between 1972 and 1982.

For the Hastings Center the project was an extension of its previous work on population policy. In 1971 it had completed a study on ethics, population and the American tradition for the US Commission on Population Growth and the American Future. When this was finished several of the co-authors, including myself, wanted to explore comparable issues in the developing countries. But the immediate problem was funds, and preliminary contacts on that front were not encouraging. However, in 1972 the UNFPA called a meeting with two organizations interested in the ethics of population control, one of them the Hastings Center. The discussions set the stage for the project finally approved in 1974.

The central interest of the staff from the Hastings Center was in the ethics of population limitation in developing countries. The Center's first proposal to the UNFPA, in November 1972, listed four purposes for research in this domain:

> (1) to gain a better idea of the way in which ethical values affect the creation and implementation of national population programs; (2) to gain a better idea of the way in which ethical values influence response to international population programs; (3) to determine if the information on the influence of ethical values suggests changes in the way international agencies might channel population aid; and (4) to set forth recommendations for future ways in which conflicting ethical values with respect to population among different groups can be resolved or at least reduced.

The proposal mentioned the following as questions needing examination through research:

> Would it be proper for one nation or international agency to condition its foreign aid on the adoption of population control policies by recipient nations . . .? How ought donor agencies to act in situations where the moral and legal standards of the recipient nation differ from those of the donor nation? In the establishment of population programs, what are the moral criteria which might be brought to bear in situations where there is reason to doubt that the views of the populace in a nation coincide with those of the government in power? When it appears, for instance, that the populace would welcome a family planning program but the government would not?

The preliminary methodology for approaching the research questions involved a survey of the literature, establishing an international working group and developing suitable contacts for consultation and interviews. Out of these steps was to come a more specific work plan. After reviewing the proposal and holding further discussions, the UNFPA gave the Hastings Center a grant to start its work. The Center was asked to contact scholars in the developing countries and present a new proposal showing where the research would be done, how and with whose collaboration.

Why was the UNFPA interested in this project? As the project developed there were different answers that reflected the shifting internal politics of the UNFPA, the preferences of its Executive Director, the interests and fears of key staff, and emerging relationships with financial contributors. But this much is clear. The research project would not have developed without the interest and advocacy of one UNFPA staff member, hereafter called the Principal Contact. This person believed that conventional family planning programmes were weakened by inattention to the cultural settings in which they were carried out. He hoped that the research could suggest new ways in which programmes and cultures could be brought into better harmony. In 1972 even that aspiration was controversial within the UNFPA, and the controversy directly affected the reception given to the project.

As time went on other sources of support and opposition developed. On the support side the Executive Director was interested in how population programmes relate to the values of the users. In a meeting with representatives of the Hastings Center he mentioned how these same questions had come up when he was in charge of agricultural programmes in his home country, and emphasized their importance. He and his senior staff may also have seen some political benefits in this kind of research. It might, for instance, counter the view that the UNFPA was just another purveyor of birth control that was insensitive to moral and cultural issues. The sources of opposition will be noted shortly.

From the beginning there was a difference in the focal concerns of the Hastings Center and the UNFPA. Whatever else it might do, the Hastings Center wanted to consider the ethics of population control in developing countries. This emphasis would provide continuity with its earlier research on population policy in the United States and tie in with its central work on ethics. The UNFPA was not opposed to ethics, but its main interest was in the fit between population programmes and local cultures. For this reason it pushed the Hastings Center to explore its ethical concerns in specific developing countries and wanted the project's conclusions to be based on suitable field research. The Hastings Center did not object to work on the developing countries, but this was not an area in which it was particularly strong. However, compromises were made, and the project moved ahead.

The most critical challenge facing the Hastings Center was to select developing countries in which it would work and to recruit collaborators from those countries. Several staff members from the Population

Council provided help in identifying countries and local scholars. On 3–5 May 1973 a critical organizational meeting was held with twenty-five invitees from eleven different countries and the UNFPA. The discussions ranged over ethics, core research questions and the practical problems of organizing a series of country studies.

On 2 June 1973 the Hastings Center submitted its second proposal to the UNFPA. The project was to have major studies in Egypt, Mexico, Kenya and the Philippines; several smaller studies; a duration of two years; a starting date of 1 September 1973; and a UNFPA contribution of $363,600. The specific objectives were:

- to conduct research on the role of values in the formulation of population policy;
- to conduct research on the role of values in the implementation of population policy and programmes; this topic would cover the influence of international assistance agencies as well as the values seen within a country;
- to identify significant value-related areas now being overlooked by international and national population programmes;
- to translate the research findings into appropriate training materials for use by population programmers, national planners and other interested parties;
- to experiment with new ways of sensitizing personnel of donor agencies, local authorities, technicians and others to the implications of national values for population policy; towards this end the project would collaborate with the UNFPA in organizing workshops, seminars and similar events.

Two differences were evident between this proposal and its predecessor. First, the 1973 document put strong emphasis on field-work in specific developing countries. In the 1972 proposal the developing countries were mentioned, but there were no specific sites and no concrete research strategy. Second, in the 1973 proposal concern with ethics is discussed under the heading of values and value-conflicts. This change in emphasis was partly the result of suggestions from potential collaborators from the developing countries, who had difficulty with the topic of ethics, and partly an accommodation to suggestions from the UNFPA, which found it easier to justify field research on values than broader explorations of ethics. There was informal agreement, however, that the Hastings Center could pursue its interest in ethics through conferences and other means funded by the UNFPA.

External Review

Given the internal debates about the project and the likelihood of controversy outside, the UNFPA decided to submit the 1973 proposal to careful external review. The document was sent to the Agency for International Development, the foreign aid agency of the US government and a major contributor to the UNFPA budget; the Population Division of the United Nations Secretariat in New York; two units in UNESCO; the Canadian International Development Agency (CIDA); the International Development Research Centre, an independent development organization supported by the Canadian government; the Population Council; the population section of the Ford Foundation; the head of the Law and Population Project at Tufts University; and others. The Hastings Center was sent extracts from the comments received, and I was shown the entire file.

The reactions ranged from cautious support to outright opposition. Support came from the Agency for International Development and the Ford Foundation. Two different commentators from UNESCO asked for close contact and collaboration between their respective units and this undertaking. The main criticisms were these:

(1) *The project shows too much control, influence and expenditure by North Americans*. This point came mainly from the two organizations in Canada. One wrote:

> The control, design, and execution of the project is to be carried out by North American institutions and largely by North Americans. This is a disquieting departure from the principle clearly set forth by the Review Committee and by ECOSOC (Economic and Social Council), that the Fund exists for the countries. I am sure donors will be disturbed to learn of the major proportion of support in a project going to developed country institutions. This is even more important in the delicate field of population values and ethics. In one sense, I would even question the ethical approach of the project itself.

This person suggested an alternative strategy: begin with a few pilot projects in developing countries that have adequate research capacity and request such a study. 'If those studies are successful, then it would be appropriate to consider at that time enlarging the scope and participation in the research to share results of pilot projects with interested investigators from other countries.'

(2) *The research is unlikely to improve family planning programmes*. This position was stated most strongly by the then President of the

Population Council, who said he was reacting to the proposal as a family planner:

> In many ways, this version is a skillful example of proposal writing but it seems to me to fail just at the point where substance is needed. One never really learns what 'values' are to be inquired into, or on what level of generality; and one is, or should be, put off by the kind of over-general and essentially empty questions or study objectives of that sort which begin 'what is the role of . . .' or 'to what extent do . . .' That is, there seems to me unfortunate lack of a proper sense of the very substance of the study and it has been my unfortunate experience that such 'big' questions do not yield commensurate answers.

It appears that the reviewer had seen earlier proposals on the project. His suggestion was to have the group set down, 'hypothetically but quite specifically, what kinds of findings might be expected to emerge from this study and how such findings could be utilized to inform population policy or improve its implementation'.

(3) *The study's conceptualization and research methodology are flawed.* A Canadian reviewer described the project's objectives as 'wide-ranging and vague' and recommended that they be sharpened through pilot projects. The director of the Law and Population Project stated that the methodology was 'full of imprecision' and wondered how the results from different countries could be made comparable. A commentator from the United Nations Secretariat criticized the proposal for insufficient attention to the developmental preconditions of success in family planning programmes: 'If there is any real growing concern in this regard, however, it is that family planning programmes are failing when socio-economic conditions are such that couples wish to have a relatively large number of children.'

The project was also criticized for its high cost and its assumption that the research findings could be translated into workable training materials. In a meeting on 8 November 1973 a senior UNFPA official also told me that some East Europeans in the UN feared that this project was part of a plot to foist birth control on the developing countries. Some were likewise concerned, this person said, that the Hastings Center had shown an ideological bias towards the left in its previous work.

The formal review and related discussions had three practical implications. One was that I, as Project Manager, should contact the main critics and try to deal with their concerns. Second, funds for country studies should be channelled directly to the participating organizations or individuals, rather than through the Hastings Center.

This expedient answered the complaint that too much money and control were lodged in North American organizations, but it led to a host of problems in obtaining research clearance. Third, because of its controversial nature, the project had to be approved by the UNFPA's own Governing Council. Thus no firm decisions could be made on any aspect of project administration until that body met in June 1974. The Hastings Center assumed that the project would be funded, and won agreement from the UNFPA to cover my time for a year if it was not, but the delay held up field research until the second half of 1974. While waiting we used the time to negotiate with potential collaborators, and I took two trips to visit nine countries of relevance to the project. With colleagues from the Hastings Center, I also began research on the values and strategies of international donors in population and family planning.

The final proposal went to the UNFPA on 1 April 1974. The research objectives were similar to those in the 1973 draft, but the organization and financing were different. This time the funds for the country studies would go directly from the UNFPA to the responsible individual or institution, rather than through the Hastings Center. The Center was now to be a co-ordinating organization rather than the direct manager of the country studies. It would receive funds for its own work, which included the responsibilities of the Project Manager, research on international donor agencies, conferences on the ethics of population control, meetings of the country directors and integration of the findings.

The UNFPA Governing Council approved the request, but strongly urged that the project have regular and real participation from collaborators in the developing countries. In response, the project set up an Executive Committee including the Project Manager, the Director of the Hastings Center and the four directors of the major country studies. This group, which had come together informally in 1974, met in Cairo in 1975, New York in 1976, Nairobi in 1977 and New York in 1978 and 1979. The meetings had a substantial impact on later stages of the research. The discussions were serious, sometimes heated, and often focused on practical problems of completing the field research and interpreting the findings. Each meeting was attended by one or more staff members from the UNFPA, who took an active part.

Country Clearances

The proposal called for major studies in Egypt, Indonesia, Kenya, Mexico and the Philippines. During a visit to Indonesia I had identified a suitable research team, but it later became clear that they could not handle the study. Since no other team was available, this project was dropped. In the other four countries teams were ready to begin work in 1974, but had to get the approval of their respective governments before UNFPA funds could be disbursed. In three of the four cases the clearance process led to local politics creating further delays of a year or more.

In Country A, thanks to an astute UNFPA co-ordinator, permission came almost immediately. In Country B the national population body quickly issued the clearance, but the foreign ministry decided that such research required the concurrence of another government agency. Because relations between the proposed director of the country study and the head of that agency were strained, permission was neither granted nor denied. The project team started work without the clearance, but could receive no UNFPA funds. After a year in limbo, the team sought and received the backing of yet another government department. The price was a minor modification of the research design to obtain information of interest to that unit.

In Country C the country director was a professor in a major university. He argued that it would be a mistake to deliver money to the central administration. Because of internal politics it was hard to have a study be put forward as a university project and, even if that happened, there was no guarantee that the money would ever reach the researchers. For an independent assessment of the university environment I contacted a representative of a major US foundation. This person also said that it would be unwise to have the project run through the university. The foundation itself contracted directly with university staff for their services. Both the country director and I felt that this practice would be advisable for the present study, and the local UNFPA co-ordinator said that there should be no administrative problem with such an arrangement.

The government granted permission, but then withdrew it after a dispute between the country director and the chairman of his university department. The correspondence suggests that government clearance had been granted on the assumption that the project was being carried out under university auspices. When the clearing agency learned that it was not, it withdrew its approval, but said that it had no objection to the study as such. Apparently this change was precipitated by the department chairman's claim that the UNFPA funds were supposed to be going to the university rather than to the project director as an individual. While I know, as the project representative, that such a proposal was never made or even suggested, and made this clear in a conversation with the chairman, the facts did not prevent him from arguing the contrary to his own friends in the government. The matter was resolved a year later when the country director obtained new clearances from other government units.

The clearance process in Country D was the most complicated. In September 1974 a subcommittee of the national population unit reviewed the country team's proposal as a prelude to clearance. Two members insisted that aspects of the project should be specified in greater detail, and had the power to force compliance. There was resentment of the subcommittee's approach, which was considered overly prescriptive and insufficiently respectful of the competence of fellow researchers. Another memorandum was sent by the subcommittee to the research team in October 1975. The country director provided a detailed reply, but final clearance was not granted until 1976.

The research plan for Country D called for a social scientist at another institution to carry out a small project, and that, too, had to receive clearance. In 1976 he submitted a document to the UNFPA describing what he intended to do. The senior member of the research subcommittee, writing in a personal rather than official capacity, sent him a memo raising five questions and offering four suggestions. The researcher found the comments so offensive that he withdrew his proposal. In a note to the UNFPA co-ordinator he said: 'I don't think I am interested in this project any more.' His main complaint was that the memorandum did not show adequate respect for his professional competence (he was a well-recognized scholar in the country).

Clearance requirements also plagued two possible smaller studies. One was to have been in Brazil where an interested research institute had been identified. Here the problems came not from the country but from the United Nations. When asked to issue a service contract for the research, the UN Resident Representative delayed (effectively refused) on the grounds that the topic was too sensitive. There had been a political battle over population control in the 1960s, and this official did not want to see it repeated. When the UNFPA did not press the case, the study died. In another desired site, Pakistan, it became clear that obtaining government approval would take more time than would be justified by the project's scale.

Publication

No issue caused more grief in this project than publication. It was obvious from the beginning that the subject-matter was controversial.

In 1972 the mood among proponents of family planning programmes was a mixture of pride and defensiveness. The pride was rooted in evidence that, despite the pessimism of earlier years, dozens of countries had established family planning programmes, and some of these were going well. The defensiveness came from the recognition that many countries were not particularly committed to having or implementing family planning programmes and from the narrow intellectual grounds on which birth control had been sold. At that time the leading argument for family planning programmes was that they would meet the expressed demand of the people in the country, who everywhere, advocates claimed, wanted to limit their fertility. The challenge was not to worry about the fine points of client demand and the fit between programmes and culture, but to get on with the programmes. Questions about culture, politics, ethics and donor respect for national values were often perceived by family planning activists as intellectual obstructionism.

This project came along just when debate about the conventional family planning model was heating up. Preparations for the World Population Conference in 1974 were bringing out attacks on the simplicity of the established model, and were raising the level of defensiveness among family planning promoters. Though many of the attacks centred on whether family planning programmes should precede, accompany, or follow economic development, questions about politics, ethics and culture were also in the air. It is thus not surprising that a project on cultural values, ethics and donor behaviour would be greeted with some hostility by established agencies. This hostility, and the sources from which it sprang, lay at the heart of the conflicts over publication.

The possibility of disagreements about publication was evident at the major organizing meeting held in May 1973. The Hastings Center took the position that it would not undertake classified research, although it would be open to different modes of disseminating the findings. The Principal Contact pointed out that publication was difficult in the UN system, and a vigorous discussion followed. After the meeting I wrote the Principal Contact a letter emphasizing the need to publish without censorship from the UNFPA. One part stated:

> The main point is that a sponsor cannot have it both ways. He cannot expect to have the respectability that comes from a well-staffed academic study and the restrictions that are common to contracted research. It is perfectly clear that if the UNFPA insists that this study operates on a strictly 'contract research' basis it cannot be carried

> out by the group we have discussed. Our collaborators are basically academic scholars who are interested in policy research, but who would not want to do research that would be essentially secret or classified.

In reply the Principal Contact suggested that the agreement with the Hastings Center contain a legal clause 'which stipulates this question in precise and legal terms so that nobody in the future will raise any problem'. On 23 June 1973 the Director of the Hastings Center sent such a statement, but it did not solve the problem.

As the project took shape the publication question affected not only the Hastings Center but the collaborators on the country studies. Under the project's terms of reference, any major policy question had to be brought up before the Executive Committee, which first met officially in April 1975. The publication question was discussed in some detail at that meeting, and a tentative agreement was reached. The country directors would be free to publish the reports on their own countries, and the Hastings Center could use the same material, as well as other information, for the overall report. The Principal Contact agreed with this recommendation, which was reaffirmed at the Executive Committee meeting in 1976.

In September 1976 the issue came up anew when the UNFPA was asked to comment on a preliminary draft of a report on the Population Council. In a telephone conversation with me the Principal Contact again asked how much of our data should be published. In a memo to the Hastings Center I mentioned this conversation and commented:

> I think we should take a very firm stand against prior right to review or outright censorship. We went through this in the early stages of the project and I thought the matter was settled, essentially with a policy of free publication. But I suppose those matters are never really 'settled' when the politics around them are in flux.

By early 1977 the project's publication plans were well defined. A memo from the Hastings Center to the UNFPA on 27 January 1977 mentioned four groups of reports: papers on different ways of defining population problems; reports on population assistance agencies; reports on the country studies; and papers or articles drawing together the entire study and offering recommendations. The memo also mentioned plans for 'a group of popular-level booklets designed for use as training materials'.

The publication question came to a head at a meeting called by the

UNFPA on 13 May 1977. It was chaired by the Executive Director and attended by the Deputy Executive Director, the Assistant Executive Director, the Principal Contact and the Chief of the Section for Regional, Interregional and Global Projects. Also present were the Director of the Hastings Center, another staff member, myself, one of the country directors and a journalist hired to prepare a popular summary of the project's findings. The agenda included seven items, one of which was 'Overall publication – (a) responsibility of country directors, (b) final report, (c) development of training materials and (d) other publicity'.

The comments from UNFPA staff were largely negative. The Executive Director almost immediately cited sections of reports that would cause embarrassment to the UNFPA. He also ruled that no more of the project's funds could be used for research on donor agencies. We could study the UNFPA itself, but further studies of other donors were out. The idea of research on donors was part of the project from the very beginning, and was mentioned prominently in a brochure describing the study. But the Executive Director was adamant on that point.

The greatest surprise came when the Executive Director proposed that if the findings had to be published, it should be done without mentioning the UNFPA as a funding source. The matter set off a discussion that lasted until January 1978. Within the Hastings Center there was some uncertainty about how to handle the request. I was strongly opposed to this idea for reasons that I stated in three letters to the Center's Director:

(1) It would be a serious mistake for the Hastings Center to accept the principle that sponsorship would not be disclosed. One relevant circumstance was that this was a large study in which the UNFPA played a significant role in design and implementation. It was thus an interested party and one that would benefit from the non-disclosure.

(2) The country studies could not be properly summarized without mentioning the UNFPA, which funded them and helped to negotiate clearances with the government. Failure to disclose the sponsorship would almost certainly cause difficulties for the country directors and probably for the UNFPA.

(3) Non-disclosure might cause more problems than disclosure. Because this had been a visible and controversial study, many people knew about it. If publications were issued without identifying the funding source, critics could rightly say that a project ostensibly concerned with ethics was acting unethically.

(4) Failure to disclose would violate the normal practice of American

universities. For example, the Faculty of Arts and Sciences at Harvard University, with which I was affiliated, would not accept a research contract unless sponsorship could be disclosed. There was some debate on this point within the project, and some evidence that for smaller studies in which sponsors had no vested interest non-disclosure might be acceptable. My point was that for a study of this size and visibility open disclosure of the funding source was essential.

In the end the Hastings Center rejected the idea of non-disclosure. The UNFPA was not pleased with that decision, and sought a compromise. In October 1977, a UNFPA staff member close to the research project wrote a memo to the Principal Contact with this summary of the issues at stake:

> UNFPA wants protection from the possible negative repercussions of not acknowledging its sources of support. ISELS [the Hastings Center] is not trying to embarrass UNFPA; UNFPA is not trying to stop ISELS publishing. Both institutions are bound by complicated rules of procedure and policy-making boards; the UNFPA Board of Governors has endorsed the study, and the ISELS Board has insisted on acknowledgment of sources of support on publications. Thus to the extent that ISELS produces any publications from the project, they are forced to acknowledge UNFPA as a source of support. This is reinforced by the fact that a widely distributed brochure on the project, prepared at UNFPA's request, clearly identified UNFPA as the major supporter.

The memo recommended conceding that the Hastings Center would have to acknowledge UNFPA support and designing a suitable disclaimer notice to go with all publications from the project. It also suggested telling the UNFPA Governing Council that the findings of this project would be controversial and 'that wide (and perhaps heated) discussion of the results of this project is more likely, in the long run, to reflect positively on the UNFPA than negatively'.

In January 1978 the Director of the Hastings Center sent a letter to the UNFPA with these proposals. First, the UNFPA or its delegated readers would read the drafts and offer criticisms. Second, if the author chose not to revise in line with the criticisms, someone from or suggested by the UNFPA could prepare an independent response that would be published with the paper. The letter also enclosed a disclaimer used by another organization in its publications, and suggested it as a model for this project.

The next episode occurred in February 1980, when a book-length manuscript which I had prepared was sent to the UNFPA. Their reviewer commented only on the section on recommendations and was almost entirely negative. Some forty-one points were raised, most of them challenging specific moral principles or conclusions. The final sentence stated that the issues addressed were 'value-laden, ideal and non-practical'. The memorandum did not specify the meaning of 'non-practical', but presumably the author felt that more should have been done to indicate how programmes could be designed differently in light of the research findings. Interestingly, four anonymous reviewers for two publishing houses found the manuscript far less controversial than did the UNFPA. One writer, in fact, suggested that the recommendations were too bland and should have more bite. But the UNFPA was reviewing the draft with a different set of concerns than a publisher might have.

A letter from the UNFPA accompanying the memorandum about the manuscript also contained this paragraph:

> We have recently had called to our attention two articles from the Richmond (Virginia) *Times-Dispatch* making reference to 'a United Nations study to be released this summer.' The study referred to, however, seems to be Mr Warwick's manuscript, which is his product and not that of the United Nations. We would appreciate it if you and your colleagues would make clear this very important distinction.

The two articles were not enclosed, so that we could not check their contents. To my knowledge neither I nor anyone on the project had discussed the findings with that or any other newspaper. But the UNFPA officials were obviously sensitive about how the study would be identified.

The reception given the project's reports in 1981 may have been affected by a fairly visible paper I published on foreign aid for abortion (Warwick, 1980). The invitation to prepare the essay, which was the first on that topic, came from a scholar who was organizing an academic conference on abortion, a subject on which I had not previously written. My thoughts came from several sources, including two within the project. One was findings from the Philippines suggesting the existence of covert foreign aid for abortion in that country. The other was my own research on the Agency for International Development, which had supported abortion but was then prohibited by law from using US foreign assistance funds for that purpose.

In further research I contacted a member of the UNFPA about its policies on aid for abortion. He said that the fund did not sponsor abortion projects as such, but that it did support governmental programmes including abortion among other services. He cited several countries in which that situation was found. Shortly after the article was published another UNFPA official phoned me to say I was wrong about one of the countries listed. I accepted his suggestion, which did not change the substance of my argument, and sent a correction to the journal in which the article had appeared. Later I received a letter from an associate of the first person with whom I had spoken giving yet another version of UNFPA policy on abortion.

This debate took place just at the time that the Reagan administration was taking a hard line against foreign aid for birth control and an even harder line against aid for abortion. As more attention was given to this issue, the UNFPA's definition of what constituted aid for abortion became less inclusive. By 1984 serious proposals had been made by members of the US Congress to cut off several million dollars of American funding to the UNFPA, largely because of its support for the family planning programme in China, which included abortion and allegedly coerced abortion. Some of the hostility to the final manuscript may have been stimulated by my article, though other factors were obviously at work. The main problem, it seemed, was that the UNFPA had difficulty with any publication that explicitly or implicitly criticized a member state of the United Nations or another international organization. The paper on foreign aid for abortion undoubtedly made matters worse, but it is unlikely that the UNFPA would have published anything from the study even if that article had not appeared.

Other Relationships with the UNFPA

This discussion may leave the impression that dealings between the project staff and the UNFPA involved nothing but suspicion and conflict. That was not the case. Throughout the project the UNFPA provided the funding necessary to keep the project moving, even when we were having serious disagreements. We were told informally that in one UNFPA review meeting funds to support my time were cut back, but even if that was true the amount was not great and the inconvenience was minor. In the countries being studied UNFPA co-ordinators were helpful in obtaining clearances and in forwarding money to the collaborators. The only difficulty with UN field missions arose in Brazil, and its source was not the UNFPA but the Resident Representative of the United Nations Development Programme.

Further, the Principal Contact and other UNFPA staff regularly attended the Executive Committee meetings and conferences sponsored by the Hastings Center. There were sometimes debates, often about publication, but their behaviour was reasonable and constructive. The main problems we faced were not financial or administrative harassment from the UNFPA, but the impossibility of reaching a lasting agreement on whether, when and how to publish. In the end the project was completed, and the UNFPA honoured all of its funding commitments.

Some Lessons

What lessons can be drawn from this experience? The most basic is that the UNFPA, and probably most UN agencies, may not be suitable to sponsor this kind of research. UN agencies are typically cautious about publication. The UNFPA had a particular problem in its relations with other donors, for it had to work with several of them in the field and received substantial amounts of money from one, the Agency for International Development. It is thus not surprising that, when it appeared as if the research would have some negative points to make about donor agencies, the UNFPA's Executive Director wanted that line of research ended. My own sense, based on dozens of conversations with UNFPA staff, is that most of them wanted this project to work out. But that could happen only if it did not damage the organization's larger objectives, such as maintaining good working relations with member countries.

A second lesson is that it is difficult to carry out serious research when agreements with the funding source are subject to change for political reasons. On this project the Principal Contact twice agreed with the policy that the findings would be published, but had to back away when his superiors had other ideas. Similarly, we thought we had full support for our studies of donor agencies, but new work was cut off when the Executive Director banned any further use of funds for that purpose. Thus even firm authority at the top became a source of instability when it was used to cancel agreements previously reached between subordinates and a research contractor. The situation was further complicated in the 1980s as the UNFPA came under attack for its indirect support of abortion.

Third, in a project of this kind it is difficult to draw clear lines about who is responsible for what in publication. The fusion of sources is present in most social research, but presents particular problems when opinions are divided and sponsors may not want to be associated with some of the views of researchers whose work they fund. My own writing on foreign aid for abortion is a case in point. The reasons that I was interested in that topic were directly connected to this project; the very idea of such aid had not occurred to me before we began the research. My article drew on project findings, but was not done for the project. Hence the press could rightly say that this publication was based on a UN-sponsored study, and the UNFPA could properly claim that it was nothing more than my own opinions. I see no way out of this problem unless the researcher is willing to suspend writing for a lengthy period on issues not directly under project control. Few active scholars will make that concession.

Finally, judgements about the ultimate worth of a research project may require the lapse of a decade or more. In population studies topics considered impractical, unhelpful and even dangerous in 1972 have now become far more acceptable. The notion that socio-cultural influences are crucial to the success of family planning programmes was thought dubious by many practitioners when the project began. The emphasis then was on getting programmes started and setting up 'delivery systems'. By 1985 it was clear that in countries such as Kenya 'delivery systems' are of little help unless there is client demand for services. Today the question of how client demand relates to social structure and culture is the subject of research by many scholars. In April 1985 the International Union for the Scientific Study of Population, a mainline organization, sponsored a three-day seminar on 'Societal Influences on Family Planning Program Performance'. The seventeen invited papers, including one by me, covered such issues as cultural receptivity to fertility control; impediments to acceptance of fertility regulation in West Africa; and cultural obstacles to fertility regulation in Kenya. Recent literature has also paid considerable attention to socio-cultural questions (see Bulatao and Lee, 1983). The UNFPA may thus have been ahead of the field in what it wanted to support, but was overtaken by bureaucratic and political realities that diminished, if not destroyed, its interest.

References

Bulatao, R. A., and Lee, R. D. (eds.) (1983), *Determinants of Fertility in Developing Countries*, 2 vols. (New York: Academic Press).

Warwick, D. (1980), 'Foreign aid for abortion: politics, ethics, and practice', *Hastings Center Report*, April, pp. 30–7.

Warwick, D. (1982), *Bitter Pills: Population Policies and their Implementation in Eight Developing Countries* (Cambridge University Press).

11

If It's Bad News, Shoot the Messenger

JOSEPHINE JAEGER, retired, and G. CLARE WENGER,

Centre for Social Policy Research and Development, University College of North Wales, Bangor, Wales

Abstract

Considerable literature exists on the topic of gender differences and de facto *gender discrimination in education. This chapter discusses a study of equal opportunities in the secondary schools of one local education authority. It shows how a woman teacher became interested and involved in research in this area as a result of her own experiences as a teacher, carried out a study which came up with embarrassing results, and ended up unemployed. The chapter deals with the difficulties faced by a female researcher in an almost wholly male education department determined to maintain the* status quo *of preference for male teachers in the county's schools.*

Despite considerable literature suggesting the contrary (Whyte *et al.*, 1985), education in England and Wales is usually perceived by local education authorities to offer equality of opportunity to all, from entry at the age of 5 years to further education (Bloomfield, 1984). It is also assumed despite evidence to the contrary (Acker, 1983; Davidson, 1985) that this same equality of opportunity applies to all members of the teaching profession so that all have the chance to reach the highest branch of the professional tree. Any man or woman wishing to enter the teaching profession has to have equivalent qualifications and follow the same courses of training, giving them equality (it is assumed); but here too questions about the facts of discrimination in terms of recruitment, responsibilities and salary levels have been raised (Deem, 1978; Davidson, 1985). Coupled with this is the fact that legislation has been enacted in the shape of the Equal Pay Act 1970 and the Sex Discrimination Act 1975 to outlaw discrimination. In this context it is commonly claimed that there is no discrimination against women teachers. The experience of Josephine Jaeger suggests otherwise.

One of the aspects of gender discrimination in education on which there has been much academic discussion is the lack of role models for girls in positions of authority within schools (Byrne, 1978; Deem, 1978), particularly in the sciences (Smail, 1984). The dearth of women as headteachers and deputy heads is particularly marked (Davidson, 1985). When these facts are cited as evidence of discrimination, the counter-argument is that qualified women either do not apply or that women are unwilling to take on the added responsibilities (NUT 1980).

This chapter is a cautionary tale about a woman teacher hired by an education authority (referred to as 'Broadshire') ostensibly to study the extent of gender discrimination as it affected curriculum choice in the county's secondary schools. The authority confidently believed that discrimination in its county was minimal. This account shows how the researcher became the victim of her research subject and suggests that gender discrimination in Broadshire, far from being a *de facto* effect of intervening variables, is an accepted part of an administrative rationale.

Background

Before discussing her research experience, it is worthwhile to consider how Jaeger's personal experience as a woman teacher led her to an interest in equal opportunities. Jaeger was educated in a co-educational primary school and at the age of 11 moved to a single-sex secondary school. This school had a female headteacher, and most of the staff were female. Women, therefore, held the positions of responsibility. Jaeger decided to enter the teaching profession and from school entered a single-sex teacher-training college where again women held the positions of authority. Because of her personal schooling experience, she was unaware that in the majority of schools men held and still hold most of the senior posts (DES, 1983) and that women teachers were then paid only four-fifths of the pay of their male colleagues even when they carried comparable responsibilities.

The day she took up her first teaching post, Jaeger was joined by three more probationer teachers – two men and one woman. All had similar school and college qualifications and all taught the same classes within the school. At the end of the first month, when they were paid, the differences in salary were apparent. This unequal payment was never explained. During her years as a teacher, Jaeger became aware of many instances of discrimination. Two are worthy of mention, one near the start of her career and one towards the end.

Early in Jaeger's teaching life, the male head of the school in which she was teaching had been informed by the local authority that starting in the next academic year all schools would have to produce stock and inventory books. This allowed him one term to produce the required books. Jaeger was approached by the principal to carry out this work with the promise of a promotion in the September with responsibility for stock control. As there were no records within the school the task was formidable. After spending most evenings and weekends devoted to the work, all was recorded and on display for a visit by the deputy director of education in July. The headteacher was lavish in his praise, and the deputy director was also very complimentary. However, the expected promotion was given to a young man with half Jaeger's experience and similar qualifications. When Jaeger asked for an explanation, the principal replied that he hoped Jaeger would continue to control the stock and records and understand that the promotion had gone to the young man because he had married during the summer holidays and therefore needed extra money to run a home, while she was a single woman who did not need extra finance. Jaeger suggested that in that case her young male colleague should take over the stock records!

Later in her career Jaeger applied for the post of deputy head in the school where she was teaching. Despite the fact that the headteacher wanted her as deputy, she was not appointed because the governors wanted a man in the position. The man they appointed had the same qualifications as Jaeger but far less experience.

In her last teaching post, Jaeger was first deputy head in a large comprehensive school but was the only woman in the top twenty positions in the school. She had applied for a number of headships and reached the interview stage for six, but each time a man was appointed. On two occasions she was told she would make a very good headteacher but the governors felt they needed men in control of their schools. One is tempted to ask why she was interviewed if they held those views! Could it have been to make their short lists look more acceptable and non-discriminatory?

The Broadshire authority for which Jaeger worked knew that she was anxious to have a change of career direction. Subsequently, she was offered the chance of secondment from her teaching position to work in the Education Department, undertaking a piece of research for the authority. She accepted the new role and on the instruction of the authority resigned her school position. In return she received a letter of appointment which was to cover the period of the research and subsequent employment. At this stage she was unaware that there would be an outside organization involved in the research project which would be putting in a considerable financial commitment.

The Research

The outside funding agency had made known its desire to conduct a study of gender discrimination based on a local education authority. Broadshire, confident that discrimination was not a major problem in the county, had been anxious to collaborate. An outline proposal was agreed by the funding agency; Jaeger was appointed and subsequently drew up a more detailed plan of research. The research involved a study of the curriculum of secondary schools, subject choice and allocation of students to identify any possible evidence of discrimination on the basis of gender. Research elsewhere had identified a tendency for girls to be over-represented in the arts and language subjects, while boys were over-represented in the sciences (DES, 1980). The study was based on secondary data compiled by the authority for all schools, questionnaires completed by most schools and detailed case studies of selected schools including interviews with teaching staff. An exploration of staffing in terms of number, gender and salary levels was also conducted. The possibility of including governors and parents in the study was vetoed by the deputy director.

Despite the role of the education authority in the commissioning of the research, the level of interest in its conduct appeared to be low. Although the funding agency had allocated funds for the provision of an office and equipment, no proper facilities had been planned apart from a table and a chair behind cupboards in a corner of a large general office. When the researcher reported for work, other members of the department were unaware of her existence and uninformed of the work she was to undertake.

The funding agency paid for a clerical assistant, but the researcher had no say in the succession of assistants who were appointed. The deputy director of education decided that the time of the clerical assistant should be shared. Whilst accepting that initially there was insufficient work to occupy an assistant full-time, Jaeger found she had to fight for even a minority of time. The (male) employee with whom the clerical assistant was shared told the first assistant she was to work for him 60 per cent of the time and told the researcher that he intended piling on the work until the assistant was working full-time for him to prove he needed a full-time personal secretary – this despite the fact that funding for the clerical post came from the outside funding agency. The deputy director supported his colleague and allocated him the mornings, i.e. 4½ hours, with afternoons (2½ hours) for research work. If Jaeger was not in the office during the afternoons, research work would not be completed, because her colleague used the research time as well as his own. Complaints were dismissed by the deputy director with the comment, 'If he needs the time he will have to have it because he must get his work done.'

While the researcher was in all respects a member of the otherwise all-male staff of the Education Department, she was not invited to become involved with any of the committees or meetings of the department, which would have provided a major source of data on decision-making. One very important area was the advisory team. Since the research involved the curriculum in secondary schools and therefore any recommendations made could have an obvious bearing on the work of the advisers this seemed a marked exclusion. Jaeger's efforts to become involved in this group were blocked on the grounds that she was not an adviser. She was not able to join their meetings, and the meaning of her work was not officially explained to them. Any contact she had was on her own initiative; a few of the advisers were helpful and co-operative, although others ignored her. This did not enhance the status of the work nor imply that the results should be taken seriously.

During the course of the research a committee selected by the deputy director monitored its progress. This committee of twenty members included representatives from the local education authority, the funding agency, the Schools Council, various teachers' associations, the PTA, a university, the schools inspectorate and the county council. The group met regularly before and during the research period and discussed methodology, interim findings and the form the report should take. When the research was completed Jaeger wrote the final report and recommendations for action to be taken by the authority.

Findings and Recommendations

The findings confirmed those of previous studies. It is, in this context, not ungenerous to state that there was nothing new in the report, since its objectives had been to discover the extent of problems in the Broadshire authority's own secondary schools.

The report suggests that girls' experiences and boys' experiences of secondary school are considerably different. It suggests that girls and boys are perceived differently by teachers. Girls are seen as more passive, less aggressive and generally more conforming, i.e. better behaved (see also Stanworth, 1983). Boys, on the other hand, demand and get more (positive and negative) attention from both male and female teachers (see also Adams, 1985).

The report suggested that freedom of choice of subject options and examination results were poor measures of equality or discrimination and urged that the whole of a school's policy and teaching strategies needed to be considered. It was pointed out that crucial choices are made at a stage of development when pupils are passing through the adolescent identity crisis, when they are most susceptible to gender stereotyping (see also Cant, 1985).

Broadshire's pupils, like those in other studies (see Ormerod, 1975), made predictable choices, with the science subjects being dominated by boys. Even within the sciences girls tended to opt for biology, while boys were more likely to study the physical sciences. It was noted that these choices had important implications for career prospects, where success is enhanced for those whose education has concentrated on physical science and mathematics.

Analysis of careers counselling indicated that boys and girls were not equally encouraged to consider all options. The report stressed the importance of women's career orientation in a society where 20 per cent of working women support families alone and where 65 per cent of married women are economically active (EOC, 1985). The authority was urged to consider the need to avoid gender stereotypes in discussions and literature on careers.

The results showed that, while most teachers did not mind whether they taught girls or boys, where there was a preference, it was mainly for boys. Teachers tended to see girls and boys as two separate groups. It was found that, because girls were more passive, problems were more likely to go undiscovered, while boys made their needs known.

The teachers surveyed for the most part found no evidence of change in the roles of men and women in schools. Where male teachers identified change towards greater equality they were critical of this and felt threatened that the position of men was jeopardized. Women felt things were moving too slowly (see also Adams, 1985). Suggested measures to facilitate change were unanimously rejected by male teachers. Women teachers were consistently concentrated in the lower salary grades, and even where women held similar posts they received a lower level of pay.

The report admitted that children come to secondary school conditioned to accept traditional gender roles. It suggested that secondary education policy could either reinforce or counteract and challenge the traditional view. It urged schools to prepare both males and females for shared responsibilities and a career.

In her conclusion, Jaeger suggested that the results gave cause for concern in terms of both sex stereotyping and discrimination. Recommendations were made that the authority should adopt a written policy on equal opportunities in education; should actively endeavour to heighten awareness of *de facto* discrimination; and should consider strategies to eliminate gender stereotyping. In addition, it was suggested that staff selection guidelines should include reference to equal opportunities; that the situation be regularly monitored; and that equal opportunities should become a standard concern of advisory staff. The report suggested that all information circulated to parents should reinforce the policy of equal opportunities.

At the school level it was suggested that schools should develop their own equal opportunities policies reinforced by internal mechanisms for self-monitoring, and that they should develop their own strategies to overcome gender stereotyping. It was recommended that in-service courses for teachers be introduced to sharpen their awareness of unconscious discrimination and that in each school a member of staff should be appointed with a special monitoring brief. The adoption of non-sexist language to describe posts was encouraged: 'headteacher' instead of 'headmaster', etc. The report stressed that all teachers be assigned comparable duties to maximize professional advancement irrespective of gender, and suggested that discussions of equal opportunities be included in induction procedures for probationer teachers. A content analysis of all textbooks, worksheets, etc. was suggested to eliminate overt and covert messages of gender stereotyping and sexist language.

A recommendation was made that, in addition to *allowing* access to all subjects, pupils should receive guidance and counselling to help them to understand the long-term implications of option choices. Where necessary pupils should be encouraged to study non-traditional subjects in which they had shown interest or ability. Possible disadvantages of particular choices should also be explored with pupils.

Subsequently, virtually all these points and recommendations have been reiterated by other writers in the field (see Whyte *et al.,* 1985). Comparable recommendations have been accepted and acted upon by other education authorities (Pratt, Bloomfield and Seale, 1984).

The Aftermath

All members of the research committee were given a copy of the report and asked to submit their comments. Only three members did so – the

National Union of Teachers, the funding agency and the university representatives. All three were supportive of the report. After the two sponsoring bodies had accepted the report and it had been printed, some members became critical. One man in particular, who had been involved throughout the research, publicly attacked the method of the research, the style of the report and its recommendations at a meeting of education professionals called to launch the report! This came as a shock, as he had not offered any criticism (constructive or otherwise) at committee meetings nor submitted any comments prior to publication. It was almost as though he felt he had to distance himself publically, in the eyes of his colleagues, from appearing to agree with the report. A final meeting of the steering committee which had been planned to discuss the implications of the report was never scheduled.

In accepting funding from the outside agency, Broadshire had made a commitment to publish the results of the research. Jaeger's findings and, more critically, her recommendations, were now perceived as embarrassing to the education authority. Various strategies were employed in attempts to delay and limit publication and to avoid further dissemination of the findings. The final sections of the report were edited by a senior official of the department, who toned down interpretation of the findings and recommendations. First printings of the final report were inordinately delayed and when proof copies appeared were in print so small that they were virtually unreadable and had to be reset.

It was decided that the report would make no reference to Jaeger by name as author or in any acknowledgement, since this was a Broadshire report and so unattributed. When the report was at last published a minimum of copies was printed; there was no public announcement of publication; no active attempt to disseminate beyond the authority; and requests for copies were frequently ignored. Jaeger was not allowed to speak when the report was presented to the authority's headteachers and was discouraged from accepting invitations to speak publicly about the research. Indeed, it was suggested that she had no right to do this, leading to contradictory situations where the funding agency was requesting lectures and the regional representative of the funding agency was trying to suppress them.

The general response of the authority's teachers was mixed. The headteachers closed ranks in opposition. Men teachers were mainly sceptical, while women teachers were anxiously looking forward to changes. Several have subsequently taken up cases against the education authority on grounds of gender discrimination.

On three occasions during the course of the research in the Education Department, the deputy director discussed with Jaeger the type of work she would like to do on completion of the research. One possibility was to undertake some further research. Having spent time examining the situation in secondary education, it was suggested that a similar study of primary education might be conducted. This was an area of work which appealed to Jaeger as she had spent several years teaching in primary schools; and, from her reading of the sociological literature, she knew that attitudes developed in those early years influence the attitudes at secondary level. A second suggestion was that she might join the advisory team from whose meetings she had previously been excluded. One thing which was made quite clear was that she would remain in the department and not return to the classroom.

Throughout the research period Jaeger had been aware of the sensitive nature of the study subject. She had therefore consciously avoided adopting an aggressive or confrontational style, attempting at all times to present her data as objectively as possible. Shortly after the dissemination of the final report, Jaeger was called to see the deputy director. There was a long explanation about the budget cut-backs which would have to be made in the authority, and it was announced that therefore there was only one job available for her. The work which was offered was a clerical/administrative job in an establishment which was approximately thirty miles from her home, in contrast to the fifteen she was then travelling, although at a salary at her current level, i.e. approximately three times the scale level for that post! At no time was her competence as a teacher, researcher, or administrator questioned. No reference was made to the previously discussed possibilities of further research or an advisory post. She was advised to go away and think about it but under no circumstances to discuss it with anyone.

Jaeger considered that the offer was insulting and humiliating. With her qualifications and experience of thirty-four years as a teacher, all that the authority had offered was a position which would be seen by the teaching community as one of lower status than a newly qualified teacher. There was some suggestion that a fancy title could be found to give the job status but even the most inexperienced teacher could have seen it for what it was – a severe downgrading. Apart from the quality of the job offered, the distance from Jaeger's home would be doubled.

Jaeger discussed the offer with one of the senior officers of the department, who said he understood how Jaeger felt but that she should understand that the Education Department was in no way prepared to have a women in a position of authority. The all-male composition of the department indicates the likely truth of this assertion. The job was again discussed with the deputy director, and Jaeger expressed her dissatisfaction. It was made plain to her that it was that job or nothing. There were no openings in the Education Department as no extra people were being brought into the office. One of the arguments put forward for this was the fact that there was no money available from any source and that they were cutting back on the numbers of people to be employed there. (This reasoning apparently applied only to female employees. Subsequently, several male appointments to the department were made.)

Her discussions with the deputy director did not become heated, but Jaeger pointed out that the location of the offered employment would mean an absence from home for a minimum of twelve hours a day. This long day would be even longer when evening meetings were required. The solution to this problem must have been already prepared because Jaeger was told that a small one-room flat had been arranged within the building at minimum cost. She was to arrive early Monday morning and stay until Friday evening. At no time was the impact of such an arrangement explored. The rural location of the proposed 'live-in' job would have made it virtually impossible for a single woman to develop a social life, and Jaeger was convinced that she would have been used as the resident housekeeper. She agreed to think about the offer.

Jaeger decided she could not accept the offered job. She consulted with her union, with the legal section of the Equal Opportunities Commission and with her own solicitor. She received the same advice from all three. It was felt that she could challenge the local authority and win. However, it was pointed out that compensation in such cases was averaging £2,000 to £3,000. The authority would have no obligation to give her a more suitable job and was not bound to offer her early retirement. She might win her case of *de facto* dismissal but she could end up with nothing more than £3,000 and no income until she reached retirement age. Added to this it would be unlikely that another authority would employ her. It seemed apparent to Jaeger that there was only one course of action left and that was to apply for early retirement. This would mean a much reduced income, but at least she could salvage her pride. She therefore submitted an application for early retirement, and eventually it was granted. Perhaps someone of a different personality would have fought the authority to expose the injustice and prejudice of the case. Jaeger, however, admits that she is a person who avoids direct confrontation if there is an alternative. At this point the tension in the situation was mounting, and she could not face perhaps a year or more of litigation and at best marginalization within the authority if it was forced to provide suitable employment up to retirement age.

Subsequently, a third interview with the deputy director took place. He was not in the least surprised at her course of action. He felt she had made the right decision and expressed the opinion that she would be comfortably placed financially by taking early retirement. When she explained that this would not be the case because she had a mortgage which would not finish until she reached sixty, he had a very ready solution. He told her that as a single woman she did not need a house to live in and that she should sell her house and apply to the county for a single person's one-room flat. This would be quite adequate, and she could live off the money from the sale. One wonders if such a suggestion would have been thought of, let alone made seriously, for a male professional employee. He also said that a woman such as Jaeger who ran a good home and was a good cook was wasted out at work because she could have made some man a good wife.

Despite attempts to minimize dissemination of the report and the removal of Jaeger's name as the identified author, requests for her services as a speaker increased. No longer employed by the education authority, she was free to accept such speaking invitations, many of which came through the funding agency. The regional officer of the funding agency, however, continued to express concern about these lectures and while no longer able to control Jaeger made his disquiet evident. There seems to be no obvious explanation for this attitude, although he may have been concerned that her findings could undermine his standing with the education authority with whom he seeks to maintain cordial relations. Subsequently, Jaeger has been involved as a consultant to a local authority with a stated commitment to equal opportunities.

At the age of 54, with thirty-four years' teaching experience behind her, to say nothing of a competent piece of published research, Jaeger found herself out of a job on a reduced pension. This was the result of challenging the policies of the entrenched male power structure of Broadshire's Education Department. What factors led to this outcome?

One needs to question the reason behind the initiation of the research in the first place. Were Broadshire's education officials seriously concerned about potential gender discrimination in their schools? Were they convinced and anxious to prove that their schools were free of such discrimination? Or were they anxious to demonstrate enterprise in securing additional funding for the education authority from an outside agency and to be seen to be conducting important research? At this point it is only possible to speculate. However, one would assume that an authority that claims it is not discriminating would react to the report with dismay and would immediately take steps to initiate change. Such an authority would see the value of the research as a guide to the identification of problem areas and potential policy changes. Having conducted a serious and professional piece of research, Broadshire chose not to act on its recommendations. What is clear is that Jaeger's findings and recommendations were unacceptable or embarrassing to the authority and represented a threat to the *status quo*. Her insistence on reporting the facts as she saw them and her confidence in her own interpretation of the findings particularly with respect to staffing led her into head-on collision with the power structure. The university representative on the steering committee has commented that Jaeger probably knows more about gender discrimination in schools than any other person in the United Kingdom. For Broadshire it appears that she knew too much and that the male lobby was too strong in opposition. Having seemingly commissioned research as a symbolic gesture, it appears that the only way that the authority could suppress the bad news was symbolically to kill the messenger. Ironically, while other authorities have acted aggressively to foster equal opportunities (Wells, 1985), and while Jaeger is involved in training school equal opportunities co-ordinators in another authority, Broadshire is fighting legal action from women teachers.

References

Acker, S. (1983), 'Women and teaching: a semi-detached sociology of a semi-profession', in S. Walker and L. Barton (eds.), *Gender, Class and Education* (Barcombe: Falmer Press).

Adams, Carol (1985), 'Teacher attitudes towards issues of sex equality', in Whyte *et al.*, op. cit., pp. 119–30.

Bloomfield, J. (1984), 'Option scheme management for equal opportunities', paper presented at the Girl Friendly Schooling Conference, 11–13 September, Manchester Polytechnic.

Byrne, E. (1978), *Women and Education* (London: Tavistock).

Cant, Andrew (1985), 'Development of LEA policy: Manchester', in Whyte *et al.*, op. cit., pp. 149–56.

Davidson, H. (1985), 'Unfriendly myths about women teachers', in Whyte *et al.*, op. cit., pp. 191–208.

Deem, R. (1978), *Women and Schooling* (London: Routledge & Kegan Paul).

DES (Department of Education and Science) (1980), *Girls and Science: HMI Matters for discussion 13* (London: HMSO).

DES (1983), *Statistics of Education* (London: HMSO).

EOC (Equal Opportunities Commission) (1985), *The Fact about Women is . . .* (Manchester: EOC).

NUT (National Union of Teachers) (1980), *Promotion and the Woman Teacher* (London: NUT/EOC).

Ormerod, M. B. (1975), 'Subject preference and choice in co-educational and single sex secondary schools', *British Journal of Educational Psychology*, 45, November, pp. 257–67.

Pratt, J., Bloomfield, J., and Seale, C. (1984), *Option Choice: A Question of Equal Opportunity* (Slough: NFER/Nelson).

Smail, B. (1984), *Girl Friendly Science: Avoiding Sex Bias in the Curriculum* (London: Longman for the Schools Council).

Stanworth, M. (1983), *Gender and Schooling: A Study of Sexual Divisions in the Classroom* (London: Hutchinson).

Wells, Jenny Headlam (1985), 'Humberside goes neuter: an example of LEA intervention for equal opportunities', in Whyte *et al.*, op. cit., pp. 131–48.

Whyte, Judith; Deem, Rosemary; Kant, Lesley; and Cruickshank, Maureen (eds.) (1985), *Girl Friendly Schooling* (London: Methuen).

12

Conclusions: Establishing a Dialogue

G. CLARE WENGER

The chapters in this collection have emphasized the problems inherent in the relationship between social science researchers and policy-makers. Their selection does not imply that good relationships do not exist but is intended to illuminate inherent tensions in the relationship. Like marriage, it is more difficult to identify what is right with a good partnership than to identify causes of tension in a strained relationship. The contributors have provided us with a cross-section of research projects and at the same time a cross-section of policy-making bureaucracies. Even allowing for descriptions of research projects which are referred to here but published elsewhere, the size and nature of the sample is too small and heterogeneous to allow for confident analysis of what I started out by calling the problematic relationship. Those conclusions which are drawn here must, therefore, be in the nature of hypotheses for further discussion, testing and refinement.

In this final chapter, I want to explore some of the reasons for conflict and its manifestations in the hope that a better understanding of the nature of the problems might help to establish a more constructive dialogue. I also want to look at the problem of power relations in the research context and discuss some of the implications of sponsored research for academic freedom and the creation of knowledge.

The discussion concentrates primarily on the research relationship with policy-makers, both sponsors and other users of social research. It specifically avoids the influence of government and other bureaucracies in the exercise of power that determines which of the social sciences receive most support or are accorded highest status and acceptability. It also does not explore the influence of agencies in determining what topics of research are funded and thus defined as legitimate areas of study. Both of these aspects of the creation of knowledge are arguably more important than the narrower concern of this book. However, their treatment in this volume will be peripheral to the problems of the problematic relationship.

I make two basic assumptions in this analysis. First, it is assumed that 'The sponsors of research are not only as human but as moral as we who ask for money', as Orlans has said (1967, p. 20). Secondly, it is assumed that both researcher and bureaucrat see social research as a worthwhile enterprise. While the belief that societies could be reformed by political intervention and the application of social knowledge may have given way to a new scepticism (Nowotny, 1985), the continued involvement of governments and other agencies in research sponsorship speaks for itself in most countries. Since only 5 per cent of research results in any direct use in a policy context, the contribution of most research is indirect or through permeation into the public sphere (Nowotny, 1985). In fact, several authors have commented on the lack of proof that research has any direct impact on policy at all (Payne *et al.*, 1980; Kallen *et al.*, 1982; Wittrock, 1985), implying that effects result not from direct application but through influencing attitudes and accepted public knowledge. In this context, the continued support of social research may be interpreted as expressive of the intrinsic value of research.

As others have suggested (Lambiri-Dimaki, 1985; Nowotny, 1985; Wittrock, 1985), researchers and policy-makers appear to work with different internal models of the relationship between research and policy. Wittrock (1985) has argued that one determining factor of the model is whether the actor places primacy on research or policy. In other words, the researcher and the policy-maker have potentially different conceptions of the research enterprise. These fundamental differences, I contend, are at the source of the problems which develop. As Houghton (1985) summarizes it, the basic question for the committed social scientist is what *ought* to be done, while the question for the policy-maker is what *can* be done and what *must* be done. These questions apply to the research process as well as to the policy process.

Understanding the Research Process

While different models of the understanding of the relationship between social science research and social policy have been suggested, it is also possible to posit a model which draws attention to the different conceptions of the research process itself that are held by social scientists on the one hand and by policy-makers on the other. These models are influenced by the relative positions of researcher and policy-maker in the social structure. Table 12.1 summarizes what these two models might look like. It is based on theoretical ideal types designed as a foundation for discussion. In the real world, it is likely that conceptions will follow a continuum demonstrating more convergence than the table suggests, but social scientists will tend to cluster towards the conceptualizations listed in the centre column, and policy-makers towards those in the right.

Table 12.1. *Model of different understandings of the social research process*

	Social scientist	*Policy-maker/administrator*
Basic value orientations	Universalistic, humanistic	Nationalistic, pragmatic, politically expedient
Overt major objectives	Extension of knowledge Understanding of problem	Strategic Solving problem
Motivations	Academic credibility Commitment to policy arena Concern *re* specific social problem	Part of job description To inform policy To aid decision-making
Definition of problem	Based on expert knowledge in specific area, informed Analytical model May be new theory	Based on perception of social problem, conventional wisdom Folk model Accepted theory
Expectations	Avoid prejudging data Theoretical objectives Policy action	Often well defined, specific 'Useful' data Policy guidance/justification
Methodology	Chosen to suit problem Probably more than one source of data; quantitative and/or qualitative Risk-taking	Chosen to convince, e.g. quantitative, statistical Safe
Sampling	Sample from general population, stratified sample, control groups Study up and down In social context	Sample from problem population, input-output models Study down Not in context
Time scale	Defined by demands of research problem	Defined by political expediency
Findings	Maximum interpretation/analysis; may be critical, unfavourable, ambiguous, contradictory	Precise answers to specific questions; uncritical, numerical
Dissemination and publication	Seeks widest dissemination Academic audience Freedom of publication	Report to sponsors Policy audience May seek to limit publication

In terms of the theoretical categories, it can be seen that the internal models held by social scientists and policy-makers show very little overlap, thus exhibiting an inherent tension in the relative understandings of the parties to research agreements. In reality, these tensions are mediated through negotiation and similarity of academic background on the part of researchers and administrators and willingness on either side to compromise towards a convergence of the two views, illustrated by the differences between basic and applied research described by Nas *et al.* on page 25. From the point of view of the social scientist, colleagues can be seen at one extreme as purists who eschew policy research altogether, and at the other as 'poodles' who are prepared to make whatever compromises are necessary to maintain agency acceptability. There are, of course, many degrees of compromise between these two extremes where the majority of policy research falls. Most social policy researchers are neither purists nor poodles. Policy bodies and their administrators, likewise, vary in their degree of adherence to the bureaucratic model, from an extremely controlling instrumental approach to an enlightened understanding of the need for theoretically based research and academic freedom. It is when the divergence between the two views is or becomes accentuated that problems arise. When this results in conflict the potential for polarization is exacerbated.

Differences between the social scientific model and the policy model range from the abstract fundamentals of basic value orientations to the pragmatics of the form of the publication of findings. At the most abstract level, the social scientist's values are likely to be universalistic and humanistic, seeking general understandings of society and/or human behaviour, while those of the policy-maker are more likely to be nationalistic, pragmatic and politically expedient. These contrasting perspectives are reflected in the perception of major (overt) objectives of research. On the social science side, the researcher seeks primarily to extend knowledge, although those committed in the policy field are unlikely to perceive this as a single objective and are likely also to seek to understand some specific social problem. While sharing a concern with social problems, the policy-maker's objective will be problem *solving* rather than *understanding* and may also be strategic where research is used as a delaying or defusing tactic (Cox, Hausfeld and Wills, 1978). In the latter case, the frustration of researchers who make concrete and easily implemented recommendations for policy that are never acted upon, despite 'implications for policy' being a stated part of their original remit, may stem from some hidden strategic agenda. The publication of findings in this context can embarrass the policy body and may have unforeseen repercussions. Diagnosis of such hidden agendas is not easy. It is highly possible that Broadshire's research into gender discrimination (Jaeger and Wenger) was strategic, at least in part, to delay or avoid decision-making or to seek status and outside funding for the local authority.

Related to the objectives of research are the motivations for undertaking research. Social scientist and policy-maker appear to share the conviction that research is 'a good thing to do' but for different reasons. For the social scientist to be seen to conduct research is an essential and integral part of maintaining academic credibility. Most of those active in the policy arena are motivated by at least a desire to improve the human condition (Mair, 1985) even if indirectly, and some seek active involvement in social change, as the chapters by de Treville, McNamara, Hadley and Gupta demonstrate. Often their choice of research topic reflects a personal interest in a specific problem area. The motivations of the administrator are equally poly-stranded. Where sponsorship is involved, a mundane motivation is likely to be that the job description involves the commissioning of research. In this respect complementarity exists with the position of the social scientist; one is expected to do research, the other to see that research is done.

Obviously, research is also sought to inform policy, particularly in controversial areas. Motivations may also reflect bureaucratic or political expediency, such as equity between disadvantaged groups or postponement of the implementation of costly interventions. In this respect, there is some overlap with strategic objectives. It is possibly at the level of major objectives and motivations for initiating the research process that the social scientist and the policy-maker have most in common or at least share largely complementary interests.

One of the most contentious areas in the research relationship, on the other hand, concerns the definition of the problem. Perhaps the reason there is not more conflict in this area is that social scientists whose definition of the problem diverges too much from that of the sponsor do not get funded – for instance, research based on hypotheses which challenge existing structures (Kallen *et al.*, 1982), or which approaches a problem in an innovative way using unconventional methodology (Fineman, 1981). Hanmer and Leonard (1984) have described the failure of feminist researchers to acquire funds to study marital violence. They attribute this failure to an approach which sees such violence as a reflection of women's subordinate role in society, a view in conflict with the conventional view which suggests that violent marriages are somehow different from non-violent marriages and that the solution lies in discovering and minimizing the differences, i.e. identifying faults in the marriage and 'curing' them.

In his chapter, Jenkins makes a distinction between folk models of social process and analytical models held by social scientists. Research based on analytical models which diverge too extremely from commonly held folk models is unlikely to get funded (Fineman, 1981; Wittrock, 1985). Thus the necessary sponsorship of innovative research is withheld, leading to a conservatism which can stifle creativity. This can have the effect of delaying conceptual leaps forward that could lead to the development of new paradigms and more effective policy (see Reason and Rowan, 1981).

This caution on the part of policy-makers grows out of the basic differences which affect the shaping of problem definition. The social scientist's definition of the problem is based on expert knowledge in a specific field, building on existing theory; in other words, the analytical model described by Jenkins. The model is likely to be the product of academic discussion with colleagues in the same and allied disciplines. It may reflect a new departure from traditional theory but it is informed and considered. Ideally, it is a theoretical problem related to the understanding of a social problem. The policy-maker's emphasis in defining the problem will be on the solution to the *social* rather than the *theoretical* problem. While not naïve, the problem is likely to reflect folk models and accepted traditional theory (Reason and Rowan, 1981). It is likely to focus narrowly on a problem category of society rather than a problem category in its societal context. The communication problem between researcher and policy-maker is confounded because both sides may use the same categories and linguistic codes but with different semantic content (Wenger, 1982). The types of problem which arise are illustrated in the chapters of McDermott, McNamara and Jenkins. In McDermott's case, the policy body defined the problem as some deficit in unemployed youth, whereas the research team wanted to consider also the structural factors involved. In McNamara's case conflict was interpreted as tribal rather than related to management decisions; and Jenkins refers to research into the underachievement of blacks, which was studied without taking the possibility of racism into account.

It can be seen that different definitions of the problem can lead to different expectations of outcomes. For example, in McDermott's case the MSC expected to find out what needed correction in the young people themselves rather than in the society around them. Coming from a policy-making perspective the administrator has expectations of findings which will be 'useful' either to inform, guide, or justify policy decisions. Often their expectations of outcomes are well defined and specific. Researchers are frequently bemused or disconcerted by early requests to say what the findings are likely to be and what the implications will therefore be for policy. Such discomfiture on the part of the social scientist stems at least in part from their contrasting understanding of the research process which is hedged around with exhortations not to prejudge the data. While researchers may indeed have some ideas about likely outcomes and may hope for specific findings, their training leads them to be aware of their preconceptions and to bend over backwards to be as objective as possible, to consider the validity of counter-hypotheses and to relate outcomes to existing theory. Researchers with a commitment to the policy field also carry expectations of some action in the policy arena based on their findings.

Discontinuities of expectation can lead to the type of tension which resulted between Jenkins and those firms for whom he acted as consultant, and Jaeger ran into difficulties when unexpected findings cast doubts on the equity of the agency's dealings with teachers. In McNamara's case, as an in-house researcher he was constrained to move further towards the expectations of his employers to maintain his job and his role as intermediary. In de Treville's experience the expectations of policy bodies caused problems in local power relations which in one case had disastrous effects on the action research involved. The chapters by Hadley and Gupta, on the other hand, reflect the type of tension that results from unfulfilled expectations of the social scientist rather than the policy-maker.

So far I have discussed the more abstract aspects underlying the research process. Basic value orientations, objectives, motivations, problem definition and expectations, however, all have an impact on the more practical aspects of conducting the research. The interrelationship between these aspects and questions relating to methodology, sampling, time scale and the nature and form of findings can cause other conflicts.

Decisions about methodology are made by the social scientist to suit the particular scientific problem and to generate the type of data necessary to answer the questions that the research seeks to answer. While the social survey may be an appropriate tool in the methodological arsenal, other modes of data collection may be more appropriate particularly where questions involve process or observable behaviour, or where small-sample (of individuals or institutions) research is indicated, for example, in action research. Jenkins's data on racism could probably not have been elicited by the survey method. The social scientist is therefore likely to consider a range of possible methods of data collection and to gather data in more than one way by using triangulated methodology. Data may, for example, be collected from open-ended interviews, with secondary data from published sources and from observed behaviour, and will also take into account the policy context in which the study is conducted. An important aspect of the research process is the refinement of methodological tools; and while acknowledging the importance of replication for comparability, the professional social scientist may in addition wish to test new approaches or new methods of measurement, thus introducing innovation and risk-taking into the process.

The policy-maker, usually working within a structured bureaucracy (discussed in detail below), seeks methodologies which are well established, non-controversial and statistically based with which to convince superiors by weight of numbers. Their preference is for 'safe', quantitative, large-sample methodology which is unlikely to be easily dismissed on the basis of lack of statistical rigour. The fact that such data may be misleading when used to measure or explain certain phenomena is less important. One social scientist has suggested that the positivism of the survey is condemned to produce invalid results (Cicourel, 1964). In Britain, the Social Science Research Council (now the Economic and Social Research Council) has been characterized as conservative and orthodox 'with a preference for ritualism and a denial of innovation' (Bell, 1984, p. 18). Thus the same conservatism which affects the definition of problems leads towards a preference on the policy-maker's side for safe, large-scale, quantitative research. As a result qualitative method has remained underdeveloped in Britain due to lack of support (Fletcher, 1974). The more pluralist approach of the social scientist, in contrast, is more likely to involve the selection of qualitative types of data either as an alternative to or in addition to quantitative data. Put simply, the tendency of the social scientist is to select methodology on the basis of the research problem, while the acceptability of methodology to the sponsor is based on its likely acceptability to seniors in the bureaucracy. The policy-maker is uneasy with data based on qualitative findings because he or she is unable to assess its validity with tests of statistical significance. It is probably only fair to say that a wide range of attitude towards data collection exists amongst policy agencies, but the extreme model presented here can and does occur.

Disagreements stemming from these different attitudes towards methodologies can result in greater weight being given to quantitative data than to qualitative data from the same study, or in attempts to limit data collection to quantitative methods especially when levels of funding are discussed. In Wenger's study the development board questioned the validity of data which came from interviews with firms in the region regarding their experiences while accepting survey data about individual employment experience from a large sample; yet it was only by following the fortunes of the region's small businesses that the effects of policy could be monitored. McDermott experienced similar resistance to interviews with small numbers of employers despite the fact that their attitudes were an important intervening variable in the youth employment market.

This leads the discussion into the whole question of sampling, which is another area where the perceptions of social scientist and policy-maker may diverge. Growing out of the considerations discussed above, the researcher is more likely to seek to sample in terms of general populations, while the policy-maker frequently perceives a sample of the problem population to be appropriate. This perspective too is affected by questions of problem definition. The policy-maker wants to know the who, why and where of the problem. The social scientist on the other hand wants to understand the problem in context, wants to know which characteristics are shared with the general population and which are common only to the problem population, etc. in order to make comparisons. The researcher is therefore likely to want to use general population samples, stratified samples, or control groups, thus studying a wider sector of the society and probably a larger overall sample, which is likely to be more costly, while the policy administrator may push for a smaller overall non-stratified sample of client, patient, recipient, or target populations. In some instances, it seems likely that sampling procedures are not well understood. In at least one instance, to sample at all was seen as threatening, and in that case the administrator involved, albeit an academic institution, insisted on a survey of an entire sub-population (Blackstone and Hadley, 1979).

Because of the social science perspective of studying problems in context, the researcher is more likely to want to study up as well as down (Nader, 1974), looking at power relationships in the social environment – employers in McDermott's and Jenkins's chapters, officials of population agencies in Warwick's chapter, teachers in Jaeger and Wenger's chapter, small firms and the development board in Wenger's chapter. The policy perspective, by contrast, tends to study down, looking at subject groups in a policy context. The academic need of the researcher to understand contextual power relationships appears to be countered by the reluctance on the part of policy-makers to throw existing power relationships, of which they are part, into question. The chapters by de Treville, Jaeger and Wenger, and Warwick illustrate some of the problems which bureaucrats may anticipate. The scope of the project as conceptualized by the scientist is therefore likely to be much broader that that of the policy-maker. Broadening the scope of investigation entered into the negotiations reported in McDermott's, Warwick's, Jaeger and Wenger's, and Wenger's chapters.

The choice of methodology and the sampling technique are characterized by suitability to the research problem in its social context on the part of the researcher, and by the perception of the social problem in its bureaucratic context by the policy-maker. The same is true for time scales, which seem to be a major area for dissatisfaction. Here again, the researcher sets the time scale in terms of the research problem, which may involve, besides practical considerations of getting the work done competently, added considerations of sufficient passage of time to allow for the study of process, together with sufficient time for the considered analysis and interpretation of data. For the policy-maker, if data are needed, they are needed immediately. One United States sociologist has observed that 'the time required for the initiation, conduct and reporting of grant-supported research very nearly guarantees that the results will not be available in time to be useful in policy formulation and implementation' (Cowhig, 1972, p. 67). The longer the time-lapse between the commissioning of research and the presentation of findings the more likely it is that events will have overtaken the policy process and the less likely that the research will be used. As a result, researchers may be under recurrent pressure to report interim findings or, as they see it, to prejudge the outcome of the research. McDermott and Hadley describe some of the problems which this can cause. Again, conflict tends to arise from the mismatch between the needs of the research process and political expediency.

Problems can also arise in terms of the analysis and interpretation of data. The social scientist will seek to analyse data as fully as possible, to consider a range of possible interpretations and to relate findings to existing theory. One of the hidden agendas of the research relationship may be the existence of 'preferred' findings or outcomes in the minds of the policy-makers, as Cox, Hausfeld and Wills found (1978). Findings, however, may be critical of existing policy, unfavourable in terms of preferred interventions, ambiguous, contradictory, or inconclusive. Yet the policy-maker seeks answers to specific, well-defined questions and usually expects black-and-white judgements backed up by statistical significance. There is a tendency for policy-makers to accept findings which support agency perspectives less critically than findings which reflect unfavourably or raise questions about agencies or existing policy. The findings of Jaeger, Jenkins, Gupta, McDermott and Wenger, all of which criticized existing policies and by implication the policy bodies involved, all proved unacceptable to the agencies involved. Frequently, attempts are made to discredit unfavourable findings by criticizing sampling and data-collection methods.

Problems of the reliability of survey data on attitudes have been discussed at length elsewhere. The likelihood is that reliability is greater where no stigma attaches to possible responses and the respondent can answer freely, without fear of offending the interviewer. However, where attitudes are stigmatized as immoral, illegal, or unethical, such as the expression of racial prejudice, the observation of behaviour gives more accurate results. The reaction of policy bodies to attitude research is thus contradictory. Survey questions have been vetoed (e.g. Blackstone and Hadley, 1979) in some cases and preferred to observed behaviour in others. Recently, British research demonstrating racist attitudes towards black pupils by white teachers ran into trouble because the data which showed this was based on qualitative data from observed classroom behaviour (Eggleston, 1985).

It is not uncommon for agencies to try to suppress critical findings (see Moore, 1977; Eggleston, 1985). As Payne *et al.* (1980) have suggested, it is difficult for administrators to accept unfavourable findings as an important and essential part of the policy process. The more common response is for such findings to be perceived as a personal attack and for policy-makers to react defensively. As Blackstone and Hadley (1979) point out, 'well-meaning and intelligent people do not react in the same way when they feel they are under attack' (p. 483).

Policy-makers can make decisions about whether or not to take findings into account. In most cases, they have less control over the dissemination of findings, although in many instances conflicts find expression through attempts to limit or control publication. For the social scientist publication is an important, if not the most important, aspect of conducting research (Roberts, 1984), and for the sponsor the final report is the tangible end-product that they have paid for. In this respect, the preparation of a written report of findings fulfils complementary needs on the part of both social scientist and administrator. On other aspects of publication – audience, function, ownership and control – there is considerable divergence. In this area, the demands of the administrator are usually fairly modest. As Sharpe (1978a) has observed, policy-makers dislike too much information. The requirement is for a concise, factual, preferably quantitative report of the findings with a full discussion of policy implications. There is little interest in the theoretical background or the contribution of the research to the researcher's discipline, in inconclusive or ambiguous findings, in findings which are interesting or even important but peripheral to the main policy issues of the problem, or in significant contributions to the development of methodology. The policy audience for which such final reports are intended seeks a clear presentation of the major findings, free of social scientific jargon with a minimum of qualifications and complexity. Such reports are read by busy civil servants or other policy-makers seeking evidence to support policy decisions or, as Sharpe (1978b) has suggested, to close off as many options as possible by establishing criteria of rejection. Where the policy area is controversial or politically sensitive, or where findings may embarrass officials of the policy-making body, reports may be kept confidential or their circulation may be limited. However, many reports which eventually make an impact may be initially confidential (Orlans, 1967). In all instances, dissemination will be emphasized within the policy field – employment, education, development, etc.

For the social scientist, on the other hand, publication is the lifeblood of an academic reputation. The primary audience sought for reports, books, or papers is the academic social science community through the channels of the academic publisher and referred journals. The researcher seeks to analyse the data as fully as possible, paying attention to inconclusive or ambiguous findings as well as to reliable and convincing ones. In contrast to the policy audience, the academic audience demands attention to theoretical antecedents and to detail and complexity. The researcher is also concerned to write up the wider implications for theory and methodology. Dissemination will be sought within the broad academic discipline of sociology, anthropology, social psychology, etc.

Some social scientists may also seek to disseminate findings to the subjects of the research or the general public. Roberts (1984) has suggested that the responsibility of reciprocity exists to those who co-operated with the research and urges publication as widely as possible, although she acknowledges some of the dangers of popularization by journalists who may sensationalize or distort sensitive findings. Houghton (1985) has noted that social scientists are more frequently listening to popular movements as alternative voices in society either as the sponsors of research or users of research findings. As Hadley comments in his chapter, the social scientist may also find new constituencies which seek to challenge the *status quo*.

In short, social scientists have to write for their own audience as well as for the policy audience. They need, therefore, to address themselves to the different audiences, using different conventions, vocabularies and channels of dissemination. In most instances, the researcher accomplishes this with greater or lesser success. But where conflict over the nature or interpretation of findings develops between social scientist and policy-maker, publication frequently becomes the battleground (e.g. Eggleston, 1985). Jaeger and Wenger's chapter describes how parts of the report were edited, printing was held up, dissemination was limited and authorship was not acknowledged. In Warwick's case the publication of extensive reports was successfully blocked. In Wenger's experience, despite the fact that the policy body had not sponsored the research, demands were made for sight of the final manuscript before publication, and after publication the body refused all comment. It is perhaps only in the sphere of publication that the social scientist's power emerges. While the sponsors of research hold the purse-strings and thus are in a dominant power relationship to the researcher, through the publication of research findings and analysis and interpretation in the public domain the researcher has access to a wider audience, and thus the potential power, at worst, to expose the policy-maker's inadequacies and at least to stimulate demand for change, albeit at the expense of forfeiting future funding from the same source.

In comparing the social scientist's understanding of the social research process with that of the policy-maker or administrator, I have consciously overdrawn the distinction. This model as all models is an oversimplification of the real world. Most research relationships will converge completely on some points, come to some compromise on others and diverge slightly on others. The degree of tension will depend on the ease with which compromise is reached and the number and breadth of divergences. But the inherent tensions in the models are the source of the conflicts which do develop.

Different researchers find themselves in different types of relationship with the policy bodies active in the area of their research. The nature of the research relationship will at least in part be affected by the nature of the personal relationships developed between researcher and representatives of policy bodies. Tensions can develop between researchers and policy agencies which have no financial involvement in the research (see Wenger's chapter), but in these situations the policy body's power is limited. At the other end of the scale is the researcher who is employed by the policy-maker. In this case the power of the employer is maximized and pressures for convergence with the views of the sponsor are greatest. Conflict in these situations can be most damaging for the researcher. Between these extremes lies research funded by grants or on a contract or consultancy basis. Grant-aided research, where support is granted for research in a given area, is perhaps more likely to run into difficulties over problem definition and methodology, while consultancy research may find the nature and interpretation of findings to be the most likely area of quicksand. Contract research, because of the more detailed nature of pre-research proposals and negotiations, although not exempt from tension, is less likely to experience intense conflict (Orlans, 1967), and where this does occur it is likely to concern the publication of findings embarrassing to the funding agency. On the other hand, contract researchers are more likely to be without tenure or job security and may therefore be more susceptible to or threatened by pressures from funding agencies. Their ability to resist such pressures is likely to be related to their professional self-confidence and record of success (see Orlans, 1967).

In addition to the inherent tensions between the two models of the research process, the social scientist and the administrator or bureaucrat come from contrasting professional contexts which are distinct from but impinge upon their perceptions of the research process. It is perhaps important to understand the different personal–professional pressures under which the two sets of professionals operate.

Understanding the Professional Context

For both social scientist and administrator research is conducted within the wider context of a professional career. More important than the successful conduct and completion of any one research project is the presentation of self as a competent professional whose abilities and integrity can be relied upon. The professional worlds of the academic and the administrator, however, are based on different rationales and provide contrasting institutional cultures within which the research relationship is acted out, or, as Sharpe (1978a) suggests, different predispositions. Table 12.2 summarizes the differences in ethos and structure. On the one hand, at the level of basic value orientation, the academic ethos is one which places a high value on independence, intellectual autonomy and creativity, while on the other, the administrative ethos is one of agency loyalty, formal procedures and respect for authority. Related to the basic ethos are the hierarchical structures of the two institutional backgrounds. The academic is part of a collegiate structure, with few hierarchical strata, loosely defined in terms of administrative responsibility rather than authority. As an academic, her or his professional responsibilities are comparable irrespective of her or his administrative responsibilities. Within the academic community the researcher may have high or low status. The administrator, on the other hand, is part of a bureaucracy, with (many) hierarchical strata which are precisely defined in terms of administrative and professional (i.e. work-related) responsibilities. Those in charge of the administration of sponsored research are unlikely to have high status within the bureaucracy. The academic and the administrator are therefore unlikely to share similar professional perspectives, and status differences between them may lead to further tension in the relationship, where a low-status administrator is in a relatively powerful position *vis-à-vis* an established academic. Inexperienced administrators are often expected to evaluate research proposals or reports by experienced, well-established social scientists in whose discipline they may have little competence. Orlans (1967) goes as far as to perceive grant administrators as the 'underdogs' before an academic audience.

Table 12.2 *Model of different professional contexts*

	Academic	*Administrator*
Basic value orientations	Independence, creativity	Agency loyalty, respect for authority
Hierarchical structures	Collegiate Loosely defined May be high status	Bureaucratic Clearly defined May be low status
Reference groups	Academia (national/ international) Academic discipline Department colleagues	Fellow administrators, planners, etc.
Source of evaluation	Peer review	Superior review
Measures of success	Publications	Completion of projects
	Contribution to knowledge	Usefulness of research
	Academic reputation	Following procedures
Criteria for career advancement	Publication record Originality, innovation Academic reputation	Advice/reports of superiors Conformity
Climate of communication	Open debate, criticism and feedback	Closed evaluation/secrecy Confidentiality
	Freedom	*Control*

The professional experience of academic and administrator is contrastive also in terms of reference groups, sources of professional evaluation, measures of success, criteria for career advancement and patterns of professional communication. Reference groups for both academic and administrator share the same basic value orientations and work within the same institutional structures as the researcher and administrator. For the academic, reference groups are the academic community at large, nationally and internationally, other members of the same discipline and departmental colleagues, while those of the administrator (depending on the type of institution) are civil servants, planners, policy-makers and/or administrative colleagues. For each institutional setting mechanisms of hierarchical structure and reference groups reinforce the basic ethos.

Performance is monitored within both types of institution, but while the academic is subject to peer review, the administrator is evaluated by superiors, and different measures of success are appropriate. While the social scientist is evaluated on the basis of publications, contributions to knowledge and wider national and international academic reputation, the administrator is evaluated in more narrowly defined terms, such as the competent management of research programmes and funding, the completion of projects, getting reports in on time and the usefulness of the findings to superiors. Career advancement is related to these measures of success, based on the one hand on the academic's publication record, academic reputation and originality, and, on the other, on the reports from the administrator's senior, maintenance of a low profile and conformity to institutional norms. In the academic milieu, there exists a climate of communication about research work based on the open debate of scientific problems, criticism and feedback, while within the bureaucracy communication patterns based on closed evaluation, confidentiality and even secrecy (Bell, 1984) are common. Overall the academic professional milieu is characterized by professional (academic) freedom and that of the administrator by control.

The control of the administrative context carries over into the academic sphere when we come to look at the power relationship between the two. Ultimately, the administrator controls the funds and thus is in a dominant relationship to the researcher. The degree of power experienced by the social scientist is limited and is dependent on the relative status of the academic and whether or not they have tenure. Hadley's research findings attracted attention only when he achieved the status of a full professor. Warwick's conflict with the funding agency did not threaten his academic standing because his institute was behind him, but Jaeger as an employee lost her job. Publication of the facts may represent a limited power but it is a two-edged sword since the publication of controversial or critical findings can affect the researcher's future prospects for funding.

Establishing a Dialogue

Analysis of these two models – of the conceptualization of the research process and of the professional ethos – has shown that the potential differences between social scientist and policy-maker are extreme. It is hoped that by spelling out the differences in detail those who have faced mounting frustration, misunderstanding, or even incomprehension verging on cognitive dissonance may be able to see some of the reasons why communication problems occur. In short, the different sides of the relationship operate with different ground rules, different understandings of the situation and, perhaps most telling of all, different value orientations. Other analysts may not agree with all of the distinctions I have made, but by making a start towards a recognition of the divide, overt admission and discussion of the problems may begin on a less abstract basis than in the past. Awareness of these differences will not solve all the problems but it may stimulate open debate and a move towards informed solutions and compromises, moving discussion away from anecdote and horror story towards analytical understanding.

Payne *et al*. (1980) see a need for the mastery of two sociologies, the sociology of the academic and the more applied sociology of the administrator. They also perceive a need for greater understanding of how policy is made and implemented. Similarly, Lambiri-Dimaki (1985) has suggested a need for a 'sociology of policy research', and it is hoped that this book can make a contribution in that direction by analysis of the sources of conflict between researchers and sponsors/ users. From analyses of differences in the conceptualization of the research process and in the professional context of researchers and policy-makers the sources of tension and potential conflict can perhaps be better understood. To suggest that tensions can be resolved would be naïve. However, it is to be hoped that through greater understanding of the sources of differences on both sides, the resultant tensions can be creatively channelled into improved co-operation.

Urging a more collaborative approach is not new. Twenty years ago Orlans (1967) called for greater efforts in keeping open communication channels between researchers and sponsors as the research progressed, negotiating adjustments and discussing problems. In the present uncertain climate for social research, Houghton (1985), as a civil servant, has suggested that social scientists and policy-makers need to join efforts and visualizes a new hybrid breed of social policy researcher whose major allegiance would be to applied research rather than to an academic discipline. She is not clear how much she sees the researcher moving towards the policy-maker's conception of the research process but she does admit the need for such research to be rooted in theory, which indicates an understanding of the academic perspective. Lambiri-Dimaki (1985), as an academic, appears to go further and sees the social scientist making contributions to the public debate about policy goals and policy programmes, urging the assumption of the role of examining values and alternatives in public policy. She too urges closer contact. In promoting what he calls the 'dispositional model' of the relationship between the users and producers of social research, Wittrock (1985) sees a coalition of 'the wise men, the wizards and the clerks' – scholars, policy advisers and bureaucrats – implementing policy.

All of these views indicate a changing role for the social scientist, agreeing with Payne *et al.* (1980), who suggested greater involvement in the policy field by attempting to have greater influence on policy formation. They admit that this involves the social scientist in taking a political stance but claim that this is unavoidable. C. Wright Mills would applaud this development. All of this seems to move the discussion some way from Bulmer's (1978) assessment of such involvement as steering 'perilously close to the preserves of politicians and administrators' (p. 42).

Nowotny (1985) moves beyond the demand for closer partnership within the confines of the established predominant relationship between government agency and social scientist. While also urging *teamwork*, she suggests that the whole political agenda has changed, boundaries have become blurred, users of social research have multiplied and new types of societally relevant knowledge have appeared. In the face of the new problems of the degradation of the environment, widespread unemployment and the impact of science and technology on social relations, she identifies the emergence of new interdependencies and a new pluralism in social research, as a result of the demands of a participatory public for research, asking different kinds of questions in problem areas. In this she is supported by Hadley's recognition of new constituencies as users of research. She claims that an interdependence exists between social developments and the form research takes and suggests that new forms of organizing research are called for with firm institutionalized bases in order to support more long-term studies which take account of societal developments. If such changes are forthcoming, they represent shifts in the power relationship between policy-makers and researchers. In this Nowotny (1985) appears to agree with Kallen *et al.* (1982) who make a distinction between research which operates within the constraints of the existing system and research which challenges or criticizes it. The former is seen as helpful by policy-makers, the latter as a threat. There has to be room for both, they claim. If Nowotny is right about the growing pluralism in social research we may expect greater public debate of social research findings. In this context, Nowotny's recognition of a 'need for a more realistic assessment of the role of conflict surrounding or following research' (p. 13), and her suggestion that an arena for negotiation should be set up, makes the need for greater understanding of the differences between researchers and policy-makers more important.

In the current political and economic climate, Nowotny's optimism seems misplaced. However, if realignments are to occur it is unlikely that a more supportive environment for social research will develop equally in all countries. It has been noted, for instance, that the use of social research has been more intensive and productive in the USA than in Europe (Sharpe, 1978b; Lambiri-Dimaki, 1985), and it would be useful to explore what structural and institutional or other factors contribute to this better relationship. Wittrock (1985) has observed that within Europe differences exist in the relationship between the policy and research domains. The UK, for instance, appears to function with an engineering model which is antithetical to independent social research, whereas Sweden adopts an enlightenment model which assumes the percolation of research findings through the system, thus having an uncertain impact on policy.

If a creative atmosphere for social policy research is to emerge it will be necessary for the power relationship between researcher and policy-maker to become more equitable. As analysis of the different conceptualizations of the research process has shown, there are pressures on the policy-research social scientist towards conformity with the bureaucratic model. Pressures are exacerbated where researchers are employees of policy-makers or are working on short-term contracts. These pressures are towards narrowly defined research problems and conservative methodology. In other words, scientific risk-taking, innovation and creativity are, in most cases, severely limited. As growing proportions of social research are funded from policy-related sources, opportunities for the type of breakthrough in the creation of knowledge that results from the development of new paradigms and surges forward in the growth of understanding are restricted.

The fact that little research makes an immediate and direct impact on policy and that much research which is controversial at the time of publication subsequently becomes part of accepted public knowledge has already been discussed. The constraining influence of government-sponsored policy research, however, means that the development of social knowledge will be retarded. The creative research necessary to throw light on the kind of societal problem envisaged by Nowotny is less likely to find sources of funding because it does not fall neatly into the policy domain of any particular agency or government department. Such research would involve broad, far-reaching questions, and funded policy research has inherent pressures towards narrowly defined, specific questions. Current practice may not be the best way to develop insightful policy to solve the problems of the future.

The current situation, which is more extreme in some countries than others, indicates a need for partnership between the producers and users of research (Nowotny and Lambiri-Dimaki, 1985). At present the relationship is characterized by mutual mistrust growing out of the unequal power relationship between them (Houghton, 1985). True partnership rests on equality between partners. But as more and more research is funded by policy bodies, social scientists find themselves increasingly in the position of supplicant with all of the insidious pressures towards conformity which that implies. Some policy bodies have built up good relationships with researchers, through improved understanding of the academic model. In some countries, notably the USA and Sweden, the relationship between researcher and policy is less restrictive than in others. For a creative, experimental and dynamic social scientific research community to exist, researchers will need security of employment and freedom to pursue research problems and to develop research methodology which questions old paradigms. In an atmosphere where social research is seen as a national resource to be developed, enlightened policy development follows naturally. The first step towards such an atmosphere is for both sides of the problematic relationship to become more aware of the working research model and the professional ethos of the other. If this book can provide an impetus for greater understanding and better collaboration between social scientists and policy-makers it will have achieved its primary objective.

References

Bell, Colin (1984), 'The SSRC: restructured and defended', in Colin Bell and Helen Roberts (eds.), *Social Researching: Politics, Problems, Practice* (London: Routledge & Kegan Paul), pp. 14–31.

Blackstone, Tessa, and Hadley, Roger (1979), 'A battlefield revisited – problems of social science research in universities', *National University Quarterly*, Autumn 1979, pp. 472–86.

Bulmer, Martin (1978), 'Social science research and policy-making in Britain', in Martin Bulmer (ed.), *Social Policy Research* (London: Macmillan), pp. 3–43.

Cicourel, A. V. (1964), *Method and Measurement in Sociology* (New York: Free Press).

Cowhig, J. D. (1972), 'Federal grant supported research and "relevance": some reservations', *American Sociologist*, vol. 6, pp. 60–72.

Cox, Eva; Hausfeld, Fran; and Wills, Sue (1978), 'Taking the queen's shilling: accepting social research consultancies in the 1970s', in C. Bell and S. Encel, *Inside the Whale* (Sydney: Pergamon), pp. 121–41.

Eggleston, John (1985), 'Low achievement of the young black pupils is often a consequence of the system', *Guardian*, 29 October.

Fineman, S. (1981), 'Funding research: practice and politics', in Peter Reason and John Rowe (eds.), *Human Inquiry: A Sourcebook of New Paradigms Research* (Chichester: Wiley), pp. 473–84.

Fletcher, Colin (1974), *Beneath the Surface: An Account of Three Styles of Sociological Research* (London: Routledge & Kegan Paul).

Hanmer, Jalna, and Leonard, Diana (1984), 'Negotiating the problem: the DHSS and research on violence in marriage', in Colin Bell and Helen Roberts (eds.), *Social Researching: Politics, Problems, Practice* (London: Routledge & Kegan Paul), pp. 32–53.

Houghton, Hazel (1985), 'Summary and conclusions', in Nowotny and Lambiri-Dimaki, op. cit., pp. 111–34.

Kallen, D. B. P., Kosse, G. B., Wagenaar, H. C., Kloprogge, J. J. J., and Vorbeck, M. (eds.) (1982), *Social Science Research and Public Policy-Making: A Reappraisal* (Slough: NFER/Nelson).

Lambiri-Dimaki, Jane (1985), 'The difficult dialogue between producers and users of social science research: some comments on the theme', in Nowotny and Lambiri-Dimaki, op. cit., pp. 15–25.

Mair, Lucy (1985), 'Development anthropology: some new views', *Anthropology Today*, vol. 1, no. 1, pp. 19–21.

Moore, Robert (1977), 'Becoming a sociologist in Sparkbrook', in Colin Bell and Howard Newby (eds.), *Doing Sociological Research* (London: Allen & Unwin), pp. 87–107.

Nader, L. (1974), 'Up the anthropologist – perspectives gained from studying up', in D. Hymes (ed.), *Reinventing Anthropology* (New York: Vantage Books), pp. 284–311.

Nowotny, Helga (1985), 'Social science research in a changing policy context', in Nowotny and Lambiri-Dimaki, op. cit., pp. 7–14.

Nowotny, H., and Lambiri-Dimaki, J. (eds.) (1985), *The Difficult Dialogue between Producers and Users of Social Science Research* (Vienna: European Centre for Social Welfare Training and Research).

Orlans, Harold (1967), 'Ethical problems in the relations of research sponsors and investigators', in Gideon Sjoberg (ed.), *Ethics, Politics and Social Research* (London: Routledge & Kegan Paul), pp. 3–24.

Payne, G., Dingwall, R., Payne, J., and Carter, M. (1980), 'Sociology and research', in G. Payne *et al.*, *Sociology and Social Research* (London: Routledge & Kegan Paul), pp. 142–59.

Reason, Peter, and Rowan, John (1981), *Human Inquiry: A Sourcebook of New Paradigm Research* (Chichester: Wiley).

Roberts, Helen (1984), 'Putting the show on the road: the dissemination of research findings', in Colin Bell and Helen Roberts (eds.), *Social Researching: Politics, Problems, Practice* (London: Routledge & Kegan Paul), pp. 199–212.

Sharpe, L. J. (1978a), 'Government as clients for social science research', in Martin Bulmer (ed.), *Social Policy Research* (London: Macmillan), pp. 67–82 (reprinted from *Zeitschrift fir Soziologie*, 5, 1, 1976, pp. 70–9).

Sharpe, L. J. (1978b), 'The social scientist and policy-making in Britain and America', in Martin Bulmer (ed.), *Social Policy Research* (London: Macmillan), pp. 302–12 (reprinted from *Policy and Politics*, 4. 1975, pp. 10–18).

Wenger, G. Clare (1982), 'The problem of perspective in development policy', *Sociologia Ruralis*, vol. XXII, no. 1, pp. 5–16.

Wittrock, Bjorn (1985), 'Knowledge and policy: eight models of interaction', in Nowotny and Lambiri-Dimaki, op. cit., pp. 89–109.

Index